Masks, Transformation, and Paradox

Masks,
Transformation,
and Paradox

·A. DAVID NAPIER

University of California Press

Berkeley   Los Angeles   London

The publication of these volumes has been made
possible in part by a grant from the Division of
Research Programs of the National Endowment
of the Humanities, an independent federal
agency.

Frontispiece. Medusa. Tazza Farnese. Hellenistic
sardonyx cameo, 3rd–2nd c. B.C. Naples, Museo
Nazionale, no. 27611.

University of California Press
Berkeley and Los Angeles, California
University of California Press, Ltd.
London, England
© 1986 by
The Regents of the University of California
Printed in the United States of America

2   3   4   5   6   7   8   9

Library of Congress Cataloging in Publication Data
Napier, A. David.
  Masks, transformation, and paradox.

  Bibliography:
  Includes index.
1. Masks.
2. Mythology—Comparative studies.
3. Mythology, Hindu.
4. Mythology, Greek.
5. Paradox.   I. Title.
GN419.5.N36   1984   391′.8   83-17980
ISBN 0-520-04532-7
ISBN 0-520-04533-5 (pbk.)

To E.

Contents

List of Illustrations

Foreword

Śrī-Gaṇeśāya namaḥ

I

There is an auspicious formula with which Indian books tradition-ally begin: "Obeisance to the Illustrious Gaṇeśa." This reverent (and prudent) phrase invokes the favor of the god who is patron of scholars: Gaṇeśa, "destroyer of obstacles," "bestower of success."

In eastern Java there has been found a statue of Gaṇeśa, since asso-ciated with the town of Bara; it dates from 1239 A.D., in the early Sin-gasāri period. From the front, the image is conventional enough: it shows the elephant-headed god with a pot belly; the eyes are downcast and the trunk curves indolently to a bowl in the left hand; the deity appears solid, composed, benign. It is a fine and impressive work of art, but what makes it remarkable is the carving of the back. This displays a "fearsome mask"[1] known in Sanskrit as *kīrttimukha*, the face of glory, and in Java-nese as *kāla*, a word denoting a class of evil spirits and also express-ing the notion of time (cf. Skt. *kāla*, time; one of the names of Śiva and also of the god of death). In popular Javanese lore it is called Banaspati, lord of the woods, and to an historian of Asian art it is a "Śivaite Indian demon."[2] It has huge bulbous eyes; "the large canines and the long tongue recall modern Balinese masks";[3] its claws are menacingly raised,

---

1. Heinrich Zimmer, *The Art of Indian Asia* (New York: Pantheon Books, 1955), vol. 1, p. 315. The statue is shown, front and back, in text plate B12a, reproduced in the accom-panying illustration.
2. Zimmer, loc. cit.
3. A. J. Bernet Kempers, *Ancient Indonesian Art* (Cambridge, Mass.: Harvard Univer-sity Press, 1959), p. 73.

Plate 1. Gaṇeśa of Bara. *a,* Front view. *b,* Back view with *kīrttimukha.* Java, 13th c. A.D. Bara Museum, Java.

and below its bared fangs there is, voraciously, no lower jaw. The demonic appearance of this mask is arresting and terrifying.

There is no doubt as to the identification of the *kīrttimukha,* or about the legend that explains its character and presence. It represents a creature of Śiva, in his form as Rudra, "the Roarer,"[4] when the god was asked to give up to Jalandhara his exquisitely beautiful wife Pārvatī. At this insolent demand, Śiva produced from the region of his spiritual third eye a being "resonant like thunder," with the appearance of a man-lion. The creature immediately rushed at the messenger, Rāhu, who desperately begged the protection of Śiva. The demon, foiled of his prey, pleaded piteously for something to eat; the god commanded him to consume his own body, which he did until all that remained was the head. Śiva was greatly pleased by this demonstration of obedience; he gave the demon the title Kīrttimukha and appointed him as his door-keeper, "very heroic and terrible to all wicked persons."[5] Hence the *kīrttimukha*

4. Heinrich Zimmer, *Myths and Symbols in Indian Art and Civilization* (New York: Harper, 1962; first ed., New York: Pantheon Books, 1946), p. 181.

5. *The Śiva-Purāṇa* (Delhi: Motilal Banarsidass, 1969), pt. 2, pp. 886–90.

device "serves primarily as an apotropaic demon-mask, a gruesome, awe-inspiring guardian of the threshold."[6] Originally a special emblem of Śiva himself, and a characteristic element on the lintels of Śivaite temples, the face became used indiscriminately on various parts of Hindu shrines as an auspicious device to ward off evil, though its typical location remained at the threshold.

When we return, however, to the particular significance of the *kīrttimukha* on the back of the statue of Gaṇeśa, we do find uncertainty about its interpretation. Zimmer writes: "We see here a Javanese development of the idea that when Vighneśvara, 'The Lord of Obstacles,' turns his back, disaster befalls . . ."; "blessed is he who faces this . . . son of the Goddess from before, but woe to him on whom the divinity turns its back."[7] In other words, the worshiper or suppliant can be denied the favor of the god and will in that event suffer terrible consequences. Yet Bernet Kempers proposes an opposite view: "Gaṇeça is the god who removes all kinds of difficulties and dangers. In this case he is himself protected by a large *kāla*-head against dangerous influences threatening him from the rear."[8] By this interpretation the face is not punitive but defensive, and the object of its power is not he who seeks protection but the protector himself. These two interpretations, contrasted though they are, do not contradict each other and they are not mutually exclusive; each is plausible in its own terms and may on certain premises be correct. The explanatory legend makes a steady background, and the terrible power of the mask is central to its significance; but all the same the function of the *kīrttimukha* in this place is far from certain, and its intended efficacy can be read in opposite senses. It is this ambiguity of the mask that calls for attention. The curiosity of this example is stressed, moreover, by a number of discrepancies. The *kīrttimukha* is described as a mask, though in the legend it is only a head, and this is what is represented. It does not conceal a face; instead, it covers or even constitutes the back of Gaṇeśa. Whether it is on this statue or, as usually, over a gateway, it is not mobile as a mask typically is; rather than moving with its wearer, it statically symbolizes a point of transition, either the beginning of an undertaking or the passage of a threshold. Nevertheless, the intrinsic ambivalence of this figure of Gaṇeśa is displayed by its conjunction of a benign front with a terrifying back. The god masks the demon.

---

6. Zimmer, *Myths and Symbols*, p. 182.
7. Zimmer, *The Art of Indian Asia*, vol. 1, p. 315; idem, *Myths and Symbols*, p. 184.
8. *Ancient Indonesian Art*, p. 73.

II

Throughout the above relation there runs a sequence of distinctive features which can be isolated as follows: mask—roaring—lion—eye—arrest—threshold—ambivalence. These happen to be crucial and recurrent topics in Dr. Napier's argument.

Masks are almost invariably related to transition, and the author proposes that the mask is a means of transgressing boundaries because it provides an avenue for selective personification in manipulating certain recognized paradoxes. A major part of Dr. Napier's study is devoted to the question of what relationship may exist between "leonine iconographical forms" and "daimonic ambivalence," and also to the question of what the recurrence of such faces might tell us about the role of sensation in coming to terms with "the metaphysics of ambivalence." The leonine apotropaic face is, he argues, the natural symbolic manifestation of the most intense sensory experience; it commands attention but thwarts the assessment of what its precise meaning may be. Eyes and the superciliary protuberances of leonine features are arresting precisely because of the ambivalence between the expression of fear through withdrawal and the opposite expression of aggression and attack. In the end, Dr. Napier suggests that a simple metaphysical supposition such as that of an ambivalent underworld daimon may result in attitudes that greatly affect "the interpretation of the visible world and the human body, of perception and mimesis, of transformation and masks."

These lines, abstracted from the course of a lengthy exposition, give hardly a cryptic intimation of the density and consequence of Dr. Napier's engrossing work, though they should provide a glimpse of the fundamental themes with which it is concerned. The substantive focus seems plain enough: it is the apotropaic facial iconography epitomized in the Gorgon head of classical Greece, set against the mythical and religious imagery of the Asiatic mainland, and its possible connection with the ideology and plastic arts of India and Bali. A central hypothesis advanced by Dr. Napier is that the Gorgon of preclassical Greece "is figured, at least in part, by superimposing Indo-Iranian and even purely Indian ideas on an earlier Great Goddess figure, or a Perseus legend, already known to the Greeks." Zimmer has already assimilated the Gorgon head to the Kīrttimukha,[9] and Coomaraswamy has asserted that "the Kīrttimukha as the terrible Face of God [sic], who as the Sun and Death both generates and devours his children, is analogous to the Greek Gorgoneion."[10] Moreover, it does not call for special perception or learn-

9. *Myths and Symbols*, p. 182.
10. A. K. Coomaraswamy, supplementary note in: Zimmer, *Myths and Symbols*, p. 175.

ing in order to see that there are striking similarities between them. Where Dr. Napier makes admirable progress is in the scope, historical detail, and scholarly pertinacity with which he traces the connection. On this score, incidentally, it may be well to recommend his mode of exposition in more particular respects. His style is accretive and his contentions are delineated by way of slow divagations; not Samuel Beckett but Henry James is the aesthetic parallel here—and it is not insignificant, either, that Dr. Napier should have selected his epigraph, lengthy as it is, from Herman Melville's *The Confidence-Man*. His argumentation has an insistent character, and it advances by means of a deep and seemingly inexorable impulsion. If at first it can seem obscure in parts, this is because the author is often groping for subliminal determinants which call exceptionally for the articulation of hard thought. The work is quite long, yet there is scarcely any portion that could obviously be removed without impairing the total organization; carefully, it is a construction, and only by taking account of all its components in due order can its sustaining forces and its proper form be well appreciated.

One reason for the gravity of its presentation is that Dr. Napier is not working simply in the history of ideas; direct evidence is often lacking, and the case must at outlying points depend on speculation. A degree of inference is called for which makes a resemblance with another discipline, so that Dr. Napier can be said to be contributing to what Dumézil has called an "archaeology of representations."[11] In this regard one naturally seeks to compare *Masks, Transformation, and Paradox* with like works of scholarship. To an Indonesianist a ready comparison is with the magisterial monograph on Indian symbolism, *The Golden Germ*,[12] by F. D. K. Bosch. More directly within the European tradition, another kind of resemblance can be seen in *The Origins of European Thought* by R. B. Onians.[13] There are of course numerous differences, also, both in subject and in treatment, but one that marks out Dr. Napier's book is the ultimate, and fundamental, concentration on the factor of sensation. The crucial problem of his entire study, he tells us, is "the relationship of the senses to the phenomenon of mask wearing." Eventually, the horrific leonine face comes to be seen as "a natural image grounded in the senses." At this point, it can be maintained, Dr. Napier is dealing with primary factors in the determination of human experience.

This is not to say that *Masks* is in any particular respect either complete or definitive. One untreated matter, to which the author himself alludes, is the place of China in his historical scheme. Coomaraswamy

11. Georges Dumézil, *L'Héritage indo-européen à Rome* (Paris: Gallimard, 1949), p. 43.
12. The Hague: Mouton, 1960.
13. Cambridge: At the University Press, 1951.

has explicitly connected the Kīrttimukha not only with the Gorgoneion but also with the *t'ao t'ieh* of China,[14] and much work doubtless remains to be done on the importance of the Silk Route in the dissemination of the image of the leonine mask. Another promising matter is a possible connection between the iconography of Mithraism and that of Hinduism; there is an image of Durgā Mahiṣamardinī in which the goddess is in the same attitude, flanking the buffalo while she hooks her left fingers into the beast's nostrils and stabs with her right hand, as is Mithra in the canonical depiction of him sacrificing the bull. Also, in a work of such a range, there must remain numerous further points to explore and connections to establish. It is a measure of the radical nature of Dr. Napier's investigation that it indicates how much more has yet to be done.

Doubtless, also, *Masks* will attract some corrective comments, for although Dr. Napier has turned constantly to experts and specialists in one or another field, no single scholar can be master of all that this ambitious book treats of, and there must be slips and gaps and uncertainties in the argument. Nevertheless, the author's synthetic approach raises a methodological issue that is of general interest. Although *Masks* is the product of what can well be called comparativism, it was in its earlier form a thesis in social anthropology presented at Oxford, and in his preparation for that academic enterprise the author was introduced methodically to a range of topics that have proved pertinent, and sometimes even crucial, to his present study. These topics included the body image, symbolic classification, myth, modes of thought, structural analysis, primitive art, rites of transition, the localization of danger. This purview (to mention only what is relevant to the present undertaking) expresses an eclectic conception of the scope of a comparative study of social facts, and if it is conceded that Dr. Napier's inquiry eventuates in a success of method, then this outcome will tend to validate the comprehension and the analytical resources of that approach. No method, however, could have taken the place of the imaginative intelligence that Dr. Napier has deployed in his work, and it is this quality above all that will be needed if the enigma of the mask, the paradoxical transmutation of appearance and reality, is to be still further resolved.

All Souls College, Oxford   Rodney Needham
Trinity Term 1982

14. In: Zimmer, *Myths and Symbols*, p. 175 n.

That fiction, where every character can, by reason of its consistency, be comprehended at a glance, either exhibits but sections of character, making them appear for wholes, or else is very untrue to reality; while, on the other hand, that author who draws a character, even though to common view incongruous in its parts, as the flying-squirrel, and, at different periods, as much at variance with itself as the butterfly is from the caterpillar from which it changes, may yet, in so doing, be not false but faithful to facts.

If reason be judge, no writer has produced such inconsistent characters as nature herself has. It must call for no small sagacity in a reader unerringly to discriminate in a novel between the inconsistencies of conception and those of life as elsewhere. Experience is the only guide here; but as no one man can be coextensive with what is, it may be unwise in every case to rest upon it. When the duck-billed beaver of Australia was first brought stuffed to England, the naturalists, appealing to their classifications, maintained that there was, in reality, no such creature; the bill in the specimen must needs be, in some way, artificially stuck on.

HERMAN MELVILLE
The Confidence-Man: His Masquerade

Preface

Throughout the anthropological literature, masks appear in conjunction with categorical change. They occur in connection with rites of passage and curative ceremonies such as exorcisms. They are, as well, frequently associated with funerary rites and death. Though they occur in a multitude of instances, their predominance during transitional periods attests to their appropriateness in the context of formal change. The special efficacy of masks in transformation results, perhaps, not only from their ability to address the ambiguities of point of view, but also from their capacity to elaborate what is paradoxical about appearances and perceptions in the context of a changing viewpoint. Masks, that is, testify to an awareness of the ambiguities of appearance and to a tendency toward paradox characteristic of transitional states. They provide a medium for exploring formal boundaries and a means of investigating the problems that appearances pose in the experience of change.

"'Tis certain," wrote Hume, "that there is no question in philosophy more abstruse than that concerning identity, and the nature of the uniting principle, which constitutes a person" ([1739–40] 1888, 189). The following study especially concerns the role of masks in impersonation and the anthropological problem of interpreting masked performances where ritual and entertainment are—as they are in so many cultures—indivisible. In the West, the word "mask" has come to connote something disingenuous, something false, but in many other cultures, such connotations do not pertain, or at least are secondary to the development of personae that the masks incarnate. For Westerners, persona tends to be distinguished from personality rather than accepted as part of it. Imitators are doomed to mediocrity, and impersonating is a phenomenon we relegate to the theater. There, the antithesis of belief is not disbelief, but the suspension of disbelief; we are licensed, that is, to accept disguises as legitimate manifestations of personality while tacitly maintaining their fictitious character. In the theater, appearances are no longer simply obstacles to an inner reality, to an essence or continuity of self.

Clearly, these are in large measure psychological issues, a realization that to a great extent places them in a separate field of study. It is also clear, however, that cultural attitudes concerning the interpretation of appearances and of apparent evidence bear considerably upon individuals as representatives of social groups and as purveyors of social categories of thought. In this regard, personae and the rules governing their manifestations in masks are very much a part of the anthropological discipline. I am, therefore, more concerned with the methodology involved in the use and interpretation of masks than with arguing for a plurality of modes of thought or for the incommensurability of certain notions of the person. I cannot, in other words, suggest a manner of investigating masks that can completely obviate the notions of superficiality plaguing our vocabulary for appearances and visual phenomena in general. Because of these limitations, anthropologists are often incapable of adequately describing the roles masks play in other cultures. Our researches on the significance of masks often lead us into conflicting views that result, at least in part, from a need to see mask wearers exclusively as either true incarnators or mere dramatists. Neither our critical faculties nor our modes of description allow us to envision a context in which both of these dispositions might function at one and the same time. It would, however, be a mistake to expect as anthropologists that this dilemma might be resolved only by maintaining that ritual and theatrical attitudes are essentially the same, since our vocabulary and our categories have at best placed them apart, if not in direct opposition to each other. For us, this segregation of roles is indispensable to our critical framework.

What, then, can we make of this conflation in other cultures? How can we approach masked performances whose presuppositions about the role of appearances seem so remote from our own? In addressing these questions, I have focused on two main areas. My first concern, after a consideration of what I take to be the main problems of mask interpretation, is to summarize some issues relevant to the study of the origins of drama in the West. Through a brief survey of the mask iconography of preclassical Greece, it becomes clear that two types of faces are so well defined as to be archetypal. These are the figures of the Satyr and the apotropaic Gorgon. These images not only embody the fundamental characteristics of the daimons they incarnate; they also reveal the extent to which ambivalence is basic to masks in the broadest sense. What may be called the metaphysics of ambivalence—what may or may not be expected of an ambivalent daimon—is central to masking. And if we posit a pantheon of such ambivalent figures, as is the case in Greek antiquity, we make an initial step toward recognizing the significance of masks for cultures in which ambivalence is a primary cosmological factor. A study of such a metaphysical framework may, therefore, be heuristically useful not only in examining our frequent inability to come to terms with the use of masks in other cultures; it may also help us to understand more fully the nature of what we call the theater.

My second major concern is with the apotropaic iconography of South and Southeast Asia and with the plastic arts of India and Bali in particular. By comparing the Gorgon with Indian images that are superficially similar, I attempt to isolate some features of iconography and mythology that are the property of each of the traditions considered. Such associations lead, by definition, to the question of the real historical relationships of these traditions. The nature of my project, however, prohibits extensive consideration of such questions and rightly prevents my entering too deeply into the domain of historians and archaeologists. The investigation, indeed, neither argues for the independent invention nor posits the intercultural diffusion of the icons considered. As Tylor first pointed out, the idea of diffusion presupposes some fundamental level of agreement, some foundation for useful comparison; an iconographic influence, in other words, cannot be of consequence unless it corresponds to metaphysical ideas already at work in the culture in question. My goal in the present study is, rather, to illustrate how mythological similarities that occur cross-culturally relate to equatable attitudes toward experience and appearance. I also argue that certain mask iconographies constitute autonomous images "to which the human mind is naturally disposed" (Needham 1978, 45) and, crediting these predispositions, that an intercultural awareness among ancients ought not to be discounted only because historical evidence of actual contact is lacking. My final concern, however, is to show how a particular epistemological viewpoint can inspire the manifestation of these autonomous images through masks and explain, at least in part, why autonomous expressions have a mondial distribution, yet do not have kindred significance for every culture.

In my research I have received much assistance for which I am most grateful. I would like to thank the American Philosophical Society, the National Endowment for the Humanities, and the Social Science Research Council for generously supporting my study, and the Rockefeller

Foundation for providing me with a month at the Bellagio Study and Conference Center, during which time I made final revisions to the manuscript for this book. I should also like to thank the Philip Bagby Bequest for research funds received while a student at Oxford University, and Middlebury College for a grant to help defray typing expenses.

Of the individuals who most influenced my work, I would first like to thank Francis Huxley, who encouraged me to pursue further the issues of masking after examining an earlier thesis, "The Interpretation of Masks." Mr. Huxley throughout the course of my research provided engaging ideas and useful references. For reading earlier drafts of all or part of this study, I am indebted to R. H. Barnes, Mary Boyce, Alessandro Falassi, Hugh Flick, John Hamilton, S. J., James Littlejohn, Gregory Nagy, Wendy Doniger O'Flaherty, Nicholas Richardson, Frank Ryder, Huston Smith, and S. J. Tambiah. I would also like to thank the following people for answering specific questions and offering recommendations: John Boardman, I Gusti Ngurah Bagus, I Madé Bandem, Peter Collett, P. K. Feyerabend, Anthony Forge, J. C. Harle, John Irwin, B. K. Matilal, and P. J. Zoetmulder, S.J. For drawings, I owe thanks to Mary Ryder, and, for photographic assistance, to Megan Battey. Three other individuals deserve special recognition. For his many interesting thoughts on the topic of masks, including, on a lighter note, the suggestion that I grow the beard I wore in the initial stages of this study, I am indebted to the late Gregory Bateson. I would most of all like to express my gratitude to Rodney Needham. To him I owe not only the initial encouragement to undertake a thesis on masks, but particularly my appreciation for his thoughtful guidance over the past years. For his continued encouragement, diligence, and rigor I remain ever grateful. Finally, my greatest appreciation and thanks go to my wife, Elizabeth, whose ideas, support, and faithful assistance made this book possible.

· 1 ·

Masks, Transformation, and Paradox

Paradox

A paradox is something that appears self-contradictory, a thing that at some time, or from a particular point of view, appears to be what it is not. Logically, paradoxes appear to infringe upon the law of contradiction, upon the logical prohibition against a thing being and not being at the same time. While there are several commonly recognized types of paradox, what remains much argued is whether paradoxes are by nature antinomous or whether they demand a reconciliation of two things that only seem incompatible (see, e.g., Quine 1960 and 1976). Though reconciliation is part of one common perception of what a paradox is, paradox also refers to those contradictions that we accept as genuinely irreconcilable, with the proviso that an explanation may be possible at a future date or with new information. Vexing as this problem may be, we can say with certainty that a paradox must by definition lead us at some time to perceive a contradiction, and in so doing necessitate an acceptance that things may look like what they are not. Our ability to accept this ambiguity is also fundamental to our recognition and signification of change. We know what things look like and recognize specific change because we are aware that something no longer is what it was. Our awareness of change is, thus, essential for resolving the ambiguity that is basic to paradox.

Because change by definition demands an alteration in some idea or thing, our recognition of change depends upon the way we identify— that is, upon the way we ascertain what identity is. By identity, we may admit not only the "absolute likeness of two or more things," but also a "sameness with self; selfsameness; oneness."[1] In the first case, the term

Plate 2. The Dream. Chalk drawing by Michelangelo, ca. 1533. The virtuous mind, awakened from slumber by the trumpet of fame, is called back from the six vices in the background and from the masked dreams below. London, Courtauld Institute Galleries (Princes Gate Collection), Inv. no. 424.

refers to things that are equatable, referential, and class-oriented. In the second, it suggests something innate, indivisible, and unique—an entity that is called the self. A comparison of these two notions of identity is, as it has been from the days of Parmenides and Zeno,[2] fundamental to our understanding of change; for, most simply, the recognition of change hinges both on the apprehension of identity and on the awareness of a potential for paradox. It is primarily by these perceptions that we determine whether an authentic change has taken place.

Our ability to recognize illusion depends upon the extent to which we accept some method of apprehending it. Such a statement sounds self-evident, yet what is called for is basically paradoxical: the acceptance of what empirically is not. This is the skill of make-believe; in science, it is in the very nature of hypothesizing. Pretending, whether it be something about ourselves or about the outside world, is basic to our apprehension of change. Thus, the recognition of illusion is the single prerequisite for understanding something that seems self-contradictory—in other words, for recognizing paradox—and the recognition of change is possible only with this understanding: that something may appear to be something else.

Now disguise is, in the study of humankind, the foremost example of how we articulate the problems of appearance in the context of change. Why should this be the case—why disguise and not true change? The answer, again, rests in our recognition of the possibility for illusion—in the awareness of an ambiguity informing the simplest transitions. This awareness aids us in establishing a point of view and in evaluating phenomena that we may later view quite differently. The *potential* for ambiguity, therefore, remains fundamental to change despite any claims we might make about an inferred, innate, or even empirically perceived identity, and disguise is, in our ontological experience, the primary way of expressing this ambiguity. The use of disguise is thus conducive both to make-believe and to changes of state that are imputed to be real.

Because the human face is the primary means of our recognizing, and thus identifying, one another, it deserves special attention in a study of appearances and their ambiguities. And because a mask is itself not merely the most direct but the most widespread form of disguise, the function of illusion in change may be most directly explored through an analysis of masks and masking conventions. Masks exhibit this function more directly than other facial embellishments such as make-up or tattooing because masks themselves are not only illusory, but are as well most uncompromising and simple devices for analyzing the relationship between illusion on the one hand and the recognition and integrity of a human face on the other. Masks are hypothetical and make-believe. They are paradoxical.

I thus wish here to consider masking in a more general sense as an emphatic expression of ambiguity in the study of appearance. In keeping with this perspective, it will be useful to note not only some details in the history of the convention, but also some matters of epistemology that are of especial significance for an anthropological analysis of such practices. These observations, lastly, will be related in a paradigmatic way to some transformational problems in the general and classificatory study of representations.

Christianity and Polytheism: The Problem of *Prima Facie* Evidence

Probably nowhere in the history of Western civilizations do we find more pervasive attention to masks than in the classical theatrical traditions of Greece and Rome. Though from these cultures the West inherits much of its philosophy and art, what it categorically does not inherit in its Judaeo-Christian tradition are their polytheistic preferences. This metaphysical difference is fundamental to a study of masks and perceptual paradox, since polytheism is arguably not merely a religious preference but a distinct mode of thought and of universal organization. It is not only a fundamentally different way of understanding the mechanics of the cosmos but—and this is a special interest of this investigation—a unique way of assessing appearance. What leads to this contention? And how strong a case can be made for its relevance to the anthropological study of masking, to the empirical and phenomenological problems we associate with masks and their interpretation? Evidence supporting this contention and its significance in the examination of masks may be derived from a wealth of historical data. The present chapter will be concerned only with facts lending specific focus to selected problems in the representation of appearances and their relationship to what we know about masks.

A primary consequence of a world generated by a single omniscient force is that all change can be made accountable to that one ideation. Thus, the purposive and unified nature of all events is as old as the first reflections on the idea of omniscience. Like reason, omniscience is guaranteed by first principles predisposing our apprehensions about the visible world. The same emphasis on singularity of purpose holds true for the more hierarchical forms of polytheism as well as for monotheism, and it has even been argued that polytheism cannot exist in the presence of hierarchy. But, by degrees, the validity with which a religion may be called polytheistic is directly related to its ultimate division of power and its lack of a single, omniscient figure of authority. In the cases where one finds a genuine pantheon, there is, in the advent of unusual phenomena or events, a natural tendency toward uncertainty and divination that at least in part results from not knowing which member is to be held responsible. In a monotheistic tradition the converse results. In this case, any unaccountable transition or inexplicable manifestation may be attributed in the end either to God or to Satan; traffic between supernatural forces and multiple conflicts among them become highly improbable. In short, people were meant to concern themselves not so much with the supernatural interrelations of spirits as with their own status in the eyes of an all-seeing god. For the mortal's part, the understanding arose that beneath the guise of appearance, beneath *prima facie* evidence, was an innate reality that was not diverse, but devoid of unaccountable diversities—a reality in which all people were equal in their potential for salvation provided they were faithful to the deity. The Christian idea, which we now accept as the more sophisticated, was that "the differences are superficial appearances which have to be explained (away)" (Jarvie 1964, 8).

Admittedly, the hierarchical nature of Roman society, with its excesses and inequalities, provided Christians with myriad practices against which to strengthen their beliefs. But the problem of appearance with respect to *prima facie* evidence has, of course, a timeless and direct relationship with the interpretation of any experience. It is a problem essential to masks and crucial to anthropology insofar as groups of people are identified by recognizing similarities, whereas individuals are identified by isolating differences. It is not surprising, therefore, that during patristic times, when Christianity was formulating a way of accounting for the representation of the Trinity, the problems of appearance, of paradox, and of the mask were frequently debated. The variety of opinions at that time concerning God's most suitable representation was quite diverse and metaphysically complex. Among the more interesting theological speculations that were eventually denounced were the notion, attributed to Marcellus, of "one *hypostasis triprosopos* (one object with three faces)" (Prestige [1936] 1964, 161) and the Sabellian idea that "the three forms of divine presentation were mere forms and nothing more, that behind each mask there stood individually the same actor, portray-

ing in succession the roles of creation, redemption, and sanctification"
(ibid., 113).

The denunciation of the theater—from Tertullian to Jerome, Augustine, and a legion of others—was in large measure a criticism of cor-
ruption and ribaldry. But even in the worst of times the shrines continued to be an integral part of the pagan theaters, and it was perhaps
more than convenient that the condemnation of one practice could put a
stop to both. In short, the stage was seen by Christians as not only im-
moral but as completely antithetical to the Christian world view:

> the continuing intent to glorify the god, the fundamentally religious
> character of theatrical events—that is, in Christian eyes, their funda-
> mentally pagan character—is emphasized and reemphasized in pa-
> tristic writings down to the end of antiquity. . . . A man cannot be a
> Christian and remain an actor, because he is serving pagan gods, and
> the audience are his abettors. (Garton 1972, 37)

It is helpful in this context to recall just how popular the theaters
were. Chambers, for example (1903, 1: 19), remarks the case of the citi-
zens of Trèves, who, though their city was destroyed three times, "still
called upon their rulers for races and a theatre." In Rome, a similar popularity prevailed; between 13 and 11 B.C., as Garton notes, two new theaters opened, increasing the permanent seating capacity from an esti-
mated 17,580 to over 38,000 people (1972, 267).[3] Moreover, as late as the
second century A.D., and not long before the appearance of Tertullian's
De spectaculis (ca. A.D. 200), Julius Pollux assembled his famous and detailed description of more than forty (mostly classical) masks and the
conditions for identifying the various personae. To be sure, the theaters
increasingly came to be detested by those who considered themselves
more discriminating, but despite their protests the stage flourished by
force of popular sentiment. And while historians may argue that the theater began its literary decline long before the first century A.D., the evidence attests incontrovertibly to a continuing demand for it beyond that
date. People attended the theater well into early Christian times because
they enjoyed it; this is surely a social fact of the most persuasive sort.

The decline of the pagan stage was the consequence of several religious, political, and economic factors, and its demise was in no way arrested by any Christian interest. The Romans, importantly, had at first
expressed willingness to accommodate the Christian god within their
growing pantheon[4] and only later saw in the radical Christian denial of
that pantheon a provocation of those gods upon whom the political stability of Rome itself depended. We therefore have confirmation on several levels that the classical theater—and especially the persona—was in

principle incompatible with a Christian world view. Such deep-seated mistrust on the part of Christians demands that we consider this incommensurability in more detail.

Though the mask survived in several forms into the Middle Ages, interestingly what did not survive beyond the classical period was a sophisticated theater of personae, an extensive pantheon of mask types. Theatrical masking of the postclassical and early medieval eras was in fact far less organized and complex than in earlier times, so that when personae did appear, they did so in the standard plots common to the mystery plays and folk performances that may be witnessed in some European villages to the present day. In the absence of complex personae—and particularly when personae hinted, as in polytheism, at idolatry—masks naturally lost some of the easy familiarity given to them on stage and came more frequently to be associated solely with the sinister and the evil. That the Church Councils inveighed against the demonic nature of ambiguous modes of transformation and of all forms of appearance indicated the extent of this persuasion, as did the Church's intolerance for any elements in its own doctrine that might be construed as pagan. New evidence concerning the role of folk religion in the Christian Church, however, continues to be discovered, despite what was for a long time the Church's aggravated campaign to satanize even the most harmless spirits of the pagan world. Moreover, it should be clear to anthropologists that many present-day debates over the problems of translation—and of assimilation especially—have been argued with eloquence not only in reformational and schismatic controversies throughout the Church's history, but originally in the first formulations of a doctrine that would gather the pagan flocks into the Christian fold. Thus, despite arguments—by the Church Fathers as well as by modern theologians—professing the aberrant nature of much patristic speculation, the question posed to Sabellius about the characterization of the Christian god is as cogent for a modern catechism as it was in his day:

> "What shall we say," urge his followers in Epiphanius (ch. 2), "have we one God or three Gods?" . . . and Epiphanius (ch. 3) replies: "we do not propound polytheism." (Harnack 1958, 3: 84–85)

The challenge of providing an acceptable rendition of the Trinity—that is, of its paradoxical nature—was, as it is now, an ambitious undertaking, and the solution of Sabellius, expounded in the so-called Prosopon Doctrine, was considerably more subtle than many commentators will admit.[5] The contention that "the three forms of divine presentation were mere forms and nothing more" (Prestige [1936] 1964, 113) should be contrasted with the descriptions of Epiphanius and Athanasius, who maintained that, according to Sabellius, "God had put forth his activity in three successive 'energies'" (Harnack 1958, 3: 85). The difference in these two interpretations rests in what was classically understood by the words *hypostasis triprosōpos* and, more specifically, by the term *prosōpon* itself.

The Greek word *prosōpon* was, as was the Latin *persona*, used to designate a mask. To suggest, however, that *prosōpon* and "mask" are entirely equatable would be inaccurate; *prosōpon* is a much more complex term. *Prosōpon* properly referred to a manifestation, a figure;[6] such a primary meaning implies that masks were conceived of as belonging to a much broader class of phenomena than the mere object (mask) *prosōpon* is usually taken to mean. The word *prosōpon* could mean the mask, the dramatic part, the person, and the face; likewise, *persona*, being not only (and some suggest even secondarily) a mask used by a player, could also refer to one who plays a part or to characters acted, e.g., as in *dramatis personae* (Onions 1966, 671; Partridge 1966, 487; Skeat [1879–82] 1974, 444). We derive, of course, our word "person" from this origin, but it is more to the present point to note that the connection between person and face in this case is quite explicitly etymological. *Prosōpon* derives from the Greek *pros*, meaning "to," "toward," or "at," and *ōpa*, "the face," "the eye."

By the beginning of the Middle Ages, the ever more sparing use of *persona* in referring to anything intangible is seen not only in the turning away from the basically monotheistic view of Sabellius; it may also be observed in the early Church's increasing drive toward objectification—as, for example, when Augustine condemns the holy men of the Donatists, favoring the inherent holiness of the Church as an institution and, consequently, the fundamental objectification of the Sacraments necessitated by his position.[7] Such objectification is evidenced not only in the term *persona*'s increasingly concrete meaning; it is demonstrated even today in our crediting Augustine, who viewed theater and its personae as antithetical to true identity, with arriving at a Christian notion of the person. By medieval times the effects of this objectifying can be clearly seen when the Scholastics adopt Boethius's definition of *persona* while at the same time discounting his knowledge of the persona's theatrical complexities (M. Marshall 1950, 471–82). Through such examples we may observe a major transformation in the compass of the term *persona*, and we may also recognize in such change a disdain for the type of persona that John Jones has called the "ultimate dramatic entity"[8] of the pagan world (1971, 275).

The problems of dramatic entities and of theatrical interpretation in general were well known to the Greeks; and it is, therefore, remarkable that the mask was, according to Jones, "known to have no inside":

> Its being is exhausted in its features. To think of the mask as an appendage to the human actor is to destroy the basis of the ancient masking convention by inviting the audience to peer behind the mask and demand of the actor that he shall cease merely to support the action, and shall begin instead to exploit the action in the service of inwardness. (Jones 1971, 44–45)

The issue here is not the denial of the individual actor's role; rather, in this case, Jones is, after Aristotle, addressing a philosophical question concerning human perfectibility through aesthetic convention. Tragedy for Aristotle incorporated a theory of perception wherein art was addressed to "the sensibility and image-making faculty" (Butcher 1951, 127), and where the stage thus would make possible the perfection of impressive acts. Tragedy was not, in other words, a mere imitation of human activity. Aristotle understood theater as a convention for elaborating classificatory changes through the contemplation of *praxis*, as a correspondence between tragic art and action, and action and plot (Jones 1971, 24)—a correspondence sufficiently overt that Jones concludes, "mutability is Aristotle's tragic focus, not misfortune" (ibid., 47).

At first it seems curious that such a theater should use the mask as a formal device; to employ an artificial and unchanging visage to address mutability seems odd in the extreme. It may not be so, however, if we consider the didactic effect of contemplating something discrete or archetypal in action. Within the visual framework made possible by masked drama, perfecting a definition, or establishing a *prosōpon*, is accomplished through the repeated exposure of the viewer to a concrete image displayed in a variety of contexts. Here, the character of the event gives additional strength and dimension to an image with known eidetic powers. This event—and the way it relates to other events in which the mask has already appeared—becomes the focus for the learning experience. The mask object, being conventional, remains unremarkable, despite what may seem to us its far wider implications. Such an interpretation explains not only Aristotle's emphasis on *praxis,* on the capacity of a repeated event to induce in one's memory "the effect of a single experience" (Clark 1975, 22);[9] it also explains the relative lateness of any literary information concerning masks as objects and the failure of Aristotle ever to discuss them specifically:

> [Aristotle] assumes that any mature drama is bound to be masked; like the open-air theatre and the sacred character of Attic Tragedy, the mask

is accepted, very much taken into account, but not discussed; for Aristotle it is simply there, a permanent feature of his dramatic universe. (Jones 1971, 43)

Some years ago, F. B. Jevons made much the same point:

> there was no acting without masks, and there were no masks without acting. To wear a mask was to act a part; and the idea that it was ever possible to act a part or to perform in a play without wearing a mask was one which never occurred to the mind of those responsible for the Greek stage. (Jevons 1916b, 173–74)

What, then, is the connection between the classical theatrical convention of wearing masks and the commonly observed masking practices of so-called archaic societies? To compare the mimetic art of acting as it occurred in ancient times with the role of masks in other cultures, we must come to terms with the cross-cultural differences in what it is to personify and what personification implies categorically. For T. B. L. Webster, the Greek stage was part of a struggle between two radical tendencies: "between the tendency to personify and the tendency to schematize" (1954, 20). The tension he wished to describe by such a distinction was that existing between personification—"the natural feeling that something deeply moving is in some sense a person" (ibid., 21)—and an Aristotelian conception of schematization whereby things are understood by delineation and definition of their parts.[10] For Aristotle, for the classical tradition as a whole, and for much of the ethnographical literature on masks, this paradox of identity and observation finds its resolution in a theatrical context—in a theatrical pantheon, that is, where the powers of personification are attributed to and exercised by a variety of mimetic characterizations.

Interpreting Transformations

The process of personification is, as is any system of classification or mode of thought, affected by culture. Understanding perceptual paradoxes, such as those made possible by masks, is likewise connected with knowing something about the process of personification in its cultural context. In developmental psychology, the significance of processes of personification and their consequences for both individual and social systems of classification are well known. Vygotsky's famous study of concept formation in children demonstrates not only how the category of the person in use at a given time becomes the basis for the individual's entire system of classifying and understanding, but also how the child, in establishing this category, often admits of and manipulates apparent contradictions and perceptual paradoxes.[11] Insofar as language and culture establish the parameters of learning experiences, the development of individual perceptual systems cannot be separated from social categories; the notion of how personae function on a metaphysical level—how changes in state or status are effected—is thus in the final analysis a cultural phenomenon.

Though it is necessary to consider at least briefly the role played by masks in the development of Christian categories of thought, this is not the place to debate whether that development was a reaction to either the complex or the debased dramatic practices of late antiquity. Clearly, the social function of the classical Greek stage in large measure gave way in Roman times to a preference for mime and the excitement of games. But the patristic writers' condemnation of the stage and the overall slowness of Christianity in adopting any theater of its own[12] show both a theological objection to and a general distaste for pagan practice. While the latter aversion may have incited Christians to be openly hostile toward the Roman theater—a hostility exacerbated by the fact that Christian rites were themselves the frequent source of parody in the mime—only a direct epistemological incompatibility can account for the Church's persistent criticism of the stage. Without committing ourselves to the evolutionary principles or historical methods attributed to Chambers or to Young in his *Drama of the Medieval Church*, it is still clear that by the Middle Ages both the mask object and the terms relating to it had taken on an almost entirely non-classical significance. This is not to say that many medieval ideas about masks did not persist from ancient times, or that they could not be related to pagan folk beliefs; but the Christian emphasis was undeniably different. From medieval times onward, the prevalent interpretation of the mask focuses on its role as an evil disguise. Such an association is perhaps nowhere more obvious than in its connection with the word *larva*, a word meaning, according to Skeat ([1879–82] 1974, 330), "a ghost, spectre, or mask; the insect's first stage being the mask (disguise) of its last one." That *larva* came to have truly sinister overtones is, in the view of André Chastel, explicit and incontrovertible:

> Comme le latin *larva*, qui désigne le spectre en même temps que l'instrument du déguisement, le mot *masque*, et l'italien *maschera*—dont il procède—, a dû désigner anciennement une strige, une création fantomatique de caractère démoniaque. La notion a été longtemps associée aux manifestations diaboliques: *larvas daemonum*, dont se préoccupent les sinodes et les conciles. (Chastel 1959, 88)

For the Christian Middle Ages, the mask clearly implied something suspicious and dangerous, while at the same time it insured the survival of all manner of pagan beliefs within Christian civilization.[13] The result was incontestible: the association between a diabolical nature and a mask that disfigures and conceals came to exclude nearly all other interpretations,[14] despite what might in other times have been the representation of merely mischievous, if not altogether harmless, pagan spirits.

Though the Janus, tricephalic, and other multi-visaged heads may be universal embodiments of evil, what distinguished medieval visual representations was the conviction that all ambiguous personifications save the Trinity were both morally unacceptable and categorically harmful. While, therefore, it could be argued that the association between *larva* and mask was, on an epistemological level, not new to the Middle Ages,[15] what definitely was new was that mutability ceased to be a function of the persona.[16] Melville's Aristotelian metaphor for character—that of a caterpillar becoming a butterfly—would have been especially unacceptable in the Middle Ages, when the word *larva* stood for all that was insidious and deceitful. For Christians, an all-knowing god cannot be moved by mimesis; transformation through visual performance and supernatural omniscience must remain antithetical. For the Middle Ages, the body itself became a persona—a mask that its wearer only escaped at death.

The idea that an internal integrity of essence should stand out beyond the impermanent nature of appearance is fundamental to Augustine and the more objective attitude of Christians; it is also part of an ancient predilection for viewing the knowable world in familial terms. Kinship relations are among those most readily understood as transformational. They are the contexts wherein we can most easily test how applicable to an understanding of others our apprehensions about ourselves are. Through family resemblances, that is, we take our first step into the purely external world, our first step away from the unique combination of subjective and objective understanding that we can have only of ourselves.[17] Family resemblances are, therefore, a major means of extending the ontological realm of the personal; they enable us to establish a personal prerogative for understanding change within the schematic and objective world of other things. As Vygotsky remarks,

> Like a Biblical tribe that longed to multiply until it became countless like the stars in the sky or the sands of the sea, a diffuse complex in the child's mind is a kind of family that has limitless powers to expand by adding more and more individuals to the original group. (Vygotsky [1934] 1964, 65)

Family resemblances, therefore, are intellectually advantageous; they provide us with a context for complex thought. For Christians, however, and arguably for all monotheists, attempting to understand the supernatural through mimesis, to make it part of a system of thought by establishing visual resemblances, is sacrilege. By contrast, the failure of polytheistic forces to be omniscient means that they may be approached, understood, and controlled through mimesis; they may be made part of our intellectual family through impersonation.

Vygotsky's analogy (relating the tribal family to complex thought) is, however, relevant not only to the expanding and transformational concepts of adolescents; surprisingly, it may also be applied to the uniformitarian modes of examining appearance and change characteristic of certain types of scientific investigation.[18] In science, such an analogy would suggest that the need for a uniformitarian idea of evolution—such as Darwin's "assumption that 'evolution' and 'descent' necessarily imply a very slow and gradual development" (R. Hooykaas 1959, 127)—corresponds to our faith in the reliability of inference. The family resemblance is the fundamental connection between two things that makes change possible at all in the enclosed systems of scientific inference. This topic is mentioned here merely to draw attention to the pervasive significance of family resemblances and to the fact that changes, in both metaphysics and science, rely on culture-specific assumptions about the hypostatized persona.

If, in the Christian view, an essential existence must be inferred from non-visual, non-mimetic modes of perception and categories of thought (since to impersonate or materialize the supernatural is idolatrous), how do we know whether apparent changes are real changes? If there is no probable connection between appearance and essence, we must conclude that the reality of all change—that is, the question of whether the change we see is in essence or appearance—is known only in retrospect and, better yet, over a long period. Such knowledge can never be part of our present experience, of the actual experiencing of change. Eidetic reality can never be known as such at its moment of visualization. We live necessarily and literally on blind faith to the extent that we arrive at our first principles through inference. Thus, the Donatist debate over the indelibility of the Holy Orders and of the Sacraments and the consequent problem of determining the character of officiating priests[19] are echoed in the remarkable role of inference in the major epistemological revolutions in Western thought. From Descartes's "mental" truths to the character of Newton's attractive forces, even to the problem of what Niels Bohr meant by the "complementarity" of things apparently incommensurable, we are continually beset with major teleological dilemmas that are complicated by the often harsh manner in which science resists and later embraces major change. Given that visualization becomes most problematic in these significant changes,[20] and given the many epistemological problems posed by ambiguities thus created,[21] it becomes less and less surprising that an Aristotelian focus on the utility of superficial impressions should prove helpful even in scientific approaches with a markedly uniformitarian character.[22]

What Christians gave up to Augustine's sense of spiritual ecstasy was not merely an indulgence in the physical world, but a more tolerant disposition toward the possible significance of appearances. The nearly unanimous agreement among theologians and historians of science and of philosophy that Augustine was responsible for an unequivocal alteration in human ontological apprehension shows better than any specific argument how much the Church altered the interpreted nature of appearance.[23] What Catholics thereby gained in morals and egalitarianism[24] they may have lost to an outright disdain for appearance and to an inability to take account of it—except in its apocalyptic formulation and, of course, through the institutions of the Church: *Sacramenta per se esse sancta, non per homines.*[25]

From the perceptual point of view, it does not matter in the end whether science, in undergoing change, becomes something totally incommensurate with what is currently accepted as true. What matters is that, in attempting change, it exhibits a consistent apprehension, shared with the Christian tradition as a whole, about appearances in the relativistic context of a changing viewpoint. In this regard, science's future is both imminently anthropological[26] and analogous to a thesis on masks—whether the question be Russell's mathematical antinomy, the visualization of a quantum-mechanical reality, or a rite of passage in an exotic culture. Similarly, because a flexible point of view is so characteristic of the theater and its personae, the structural distinctions between the classical and the Christian view of masks have implications far beyond the theater proper.

Examples of how, in the Middle Ages, this difference manifests itself are not hard to find. The transformation of the *homme sauvage* into a symbol of the demonic is a case in point. Here the semi- or half-human wild man of pagan folklore provides the image both for the diabolical and sinister *larvae* of which the councils and synods made so much, as well as for much of the demonic iconography adorning medieval churches.[27] From the perspective of modern science, this medieval sense of the diabolical transmutation, no doubt, is relevant to problems raised by nineteenth-century evolutionary theory. Was it not inevitable that the new evolutionary class of primates would come to evoke thoughts of yet one more horrific *larva* in the eyes of Christians, who now found themselves "strange bedfellows" to these "damned in the demon-wood"?[28]

As, therefore, *persona* increasingly became a primarily corporeal term, so, equally, the need to distinguish between natural and supernatural ways became a mark of medieval science and religion.[29] Historiographically, we not only find an intellectual campaign wherein even the innocuous pagan spirits came to be viewed as malevolent;[30] in their associating the mask with the disguised and ghoulish *larvae*, we observe, in addition, how medieval thinkers cemented, at least until the Renaissance, the idea that appearance had more to do with the dangers of "concrete persons transubstantiated" than with "abstract personifications."[31] Their attributing such associations to *larvae* confirms our observations about the Christian attitude toward masks: as humans are equal in essence, we cannot, as Christians, rely on human appearance; but since the Church and the Sacraments are holy *per se*, their outward objective character becomes crucial. Hence, by tampering with human appearances, as in instances of masking, we either (1) invite idolatry, (2) act disingenuously, or (3) risk identification with the devil, for whom apparent changes are real ones. This view of appearances is reiterated again and again in the debates throughout medieval times over whether *larvae* were kindred with other, more obscure, though no less ubiquitous, manifestations. An especially telling case is the *lemures*, who were popularly taken to be spirits of the dead, and as such would visit during the night to cause disorder and mischief. This nocturnal and invisible association accounts for our word "lemur"—an animal so noted for "its habit of going about at night that it has been nicknamed 'ghost' by naturalists" (Skeat [1879–82] 1974, 336).

Ambiguity and Saltation

If change and the apprehension of illusion are interrelated in such a way that masking exemplifies perceptual paradox, then a study of mask wearing will lead implicitly to an understanding of how appearances are manipulated in the context of a changing viewpoint. Whether a paradox involves a change in view as the result of recognizing an illusion, or whether it is understood as the recognition of an incommensurable antinomy, the convention of masking offers a prospect for reconciling the ambiguities of change. Moreover, the metaphor of the mask, as a device for dealing with categorical difference, can also provide a model for elucidating problems in interpretation that exist between radically different modes of thought.

The presence of masks in situations relating to transition is so commonly the rule that exceptions to it are hard to find. Whether the change is from one social status to another or in the conscious states of the mask wearers or their audiences, again and again mask users or their observers or both attest to some change in conjunction with a mask's presence. These transitions from one state to the next may occur in any number of easily recognizable categories, the most common being rites of passage, curative ceremonies and exorcisms, and religious and secular dramas. In such cases, social rules and laws are nearly always altered, either by inversion, by opposition, or by complete suspension of normal rules and prohibitions. Characteristic of such alterations are the important role of point of view and the special dual status of those who mediate between the natural and supernatural realms and are charged with the knowledge and control of formal change. Whether the controlling power is centralized in a shaman or exorcist, or whether the power rests in controlling the formalities of make-believe, or even when that power is entirely distributed in the approval of a discriminating audience (as, for example, through what we commonly call the suspension of disbelief), these various transitions are recognized through alterations in point of view and through the ambiguities—the illusions and appearances—to which those alterations give rise.

It would be exceptional were we to discover any instances where masks were used to state empirically that no transformation had occurred in the mask wearer, because a mask does, in fact, cover the face, and therefore explicitly subverts the credibility of apparent evidence. This subversion is especially marked in the anthropological problem of accounting for the supposed special states of mask wearers, and in the predominance in the anthropological literature of statements about such states in conjunction with the act of wearing masks. However, the most extreme sign that mask wearers are attempting to undermine the credibility of our empirical faculties is not their saying that they have undergone a transformation (into another being, ancestor, or demon) but rather their insisting, as the New Caledonians reportedly did, that the person disappears, becomes invisible, or temporarily ceases to exist when wearing a certain mask (Leenhardt 1970, 29). This explicit denial of personality is accomplished by manipulating, as in Russell's paradox, the incompatibilities of inference and of personification—i.e., in those cases where self-membership cannot be predicated without contradicting an outstanding empirical premise. Here the tendency to personify is, in the empirical sense, not merely an attempt at monopolizing appearances, but a fundamental way of shifting judgment away from an empirical account. Again, the New Caledonians come to our aid with an interesting example of such a shift, this time in a myth in which a woman's infidelity is discovered when the tell-tale black paint, used in myth as well as reality to decorate a type of sacred mask, is noticed on her face by her husband. She has fallen in love with a deity who is known in the myth by the mask used in reality to designate his presence, to *re-present* him (Guiart 1966, 61–62). One is unsure in this myth whether the god is behind the mask or whether the mask itself incorporates the god's personage. By definition, the god's persona and the mask's persona become united. Thus, not only does the myth make the mask a more convincing personification; the mask in turn helps to illustrate a transgression of the boundary between the object-person and a supposed experience of the supernatural—if, that is, such boundaries can be said in this case legitimately to exist.

However, if such a translation of metaphysical categories is epistemologically feasible—that is, if such a distinction in body-image boundaries is discernible—we might wish to suggest that the mask is a means of transgressing boundaries *because it provides an avenue for selective personification in manipulating certain recognized paradoxes.* In this light, masking seems hardly primitive or alogical, or, worse yet, in league only with children and psychotics. One cannot, it is true, easily personify if an objective description contains no ambiguities; but, conversely, one cannot selectively personify if all the world is a personification. That we uncover in apparent mutability the basis of a theory of personality and not the destruction of all such theories is evidenced by the following interchange recorded by Maurice Leenhardt:

> Un jour que, sous ces impressions, je voulais mesurer cependant le progrès accompli chez ceux que j'avais instruits de longues années, je dis à l'un d'eux:
> —En somme, c'est la notion d'esprit que nous avons porté dans votre pensée.
> —Pas du tout, objecta-t-il brusquement, nous avons toujours connu l'esprit. Ce que vous nous avez apporté, c'est le corps.
> —???? (Leenhardt 1970, 195)

Clearly, for the New Caledonians, the category of the person required no opposition of appearance to essence, as their emphasis on the *personnage* (person + role) elsewhere attests (Leenhardt 1970, 104). In fact, the response to Leenhardt's inquiry indicates that indeed it was the Christian sense of the body—the Christian notion of the person—that they found unique. It is worth remembering, moreover, that a New Caledonian, rather than a Westerner, was the source of this corporeal distinction, for this fact suggests that personification does not tend necessarily toward either overtly subjective discriminations—as, for example, we somewhat erroneously tend to denominate the play of children—or objective chaos, such as occurs in what we designate as mental disease. Rather, we must conclude that the act of personifying is intimately connected with and dependent upon stating in a selective, discriminatory way that a thing that is emotionally moving is in some sense personal. Personification, in other words, is a means of imputing an ontological status not only to oneself as an individual thinker, but to the substance of one's thoughts as well.[32]

As, therefore, personificatory thought is inseparable from the fact of experience, the transforming role of masks is developmentally most dramatic in their association with the greatest paradoxes of all—that is, with creation and destruction, birth and death. In these most moving and difficult of all transitions, the use of masks illustrates the continued attempt to confront paradox by recourse to personification, to state that mutability is a precondition of personality rather than an aberration. Jevons, in attempting to discover the specific origins of Greek drama, labored at some length to establish both the connection of tragic drama with funerary rites and the persistent association of mummer's plays from antiquity to the present day with rites of revivification. It seems that as death undermines the supposition that important and lasting change occurs on a very gradual, apprehensible time table, so too, funerary rites and revivifications formalize sudden changes of state—such as what evolutionists at one time very appropriately labeled saltations. Saltations were, literally, leaps or jumps that, in evolutionary theory, might be attributed to nature in light of the gaps, as T. H. Huxley said, "which appear to exist in the series of known forms" (1874, 312).[33] It would, of course, seem perfectly natural that such unprecedented changes would appear from time to time as a part of being, especially when there is a tendency toward diversity, according to Aristotle, "in animals capable of living well" (*De partibus animalium*, 656ª3f.; see Clark 1975, 4).

The suddenness of saltatory change, however, and as well its developmental peculiarities,[34] presented obvious evidential problems for Darwin, as indeed they do, though in different terminologies, for scientific thinkers today. The argument here is not whether such cases occur naturally, but rather, in view of the imaginative capacities of human thought, whether we could account for them if they did. That the idea of saltation, in other words, might, like a mask, play havoc with an empirical account of things, is analogous, for example, to a chess game, in which many individually complex problems interfere with our comprehension of a much simpler, yet all-encompassing, difficulty of a higher order.[35] The problem of apparent ambiguity and the consequent apprehension of paradox need not, as so many cases of masking attest, be methodologically different from this problem of chess; for here too we have followed certain rules and repetitive gestures through an otherwise existential chaos to some often profoundly simple conclusion.

In a similar manner, the inductive utility of the real and false hidden lemmas of scientific thought become, on a formal level, analogous to Jevons's conclusions about the persistence of masks in conjunction with funerary rites and/or rites of revivification:

> What holds together each and every one of the mummer's plays is that, in each and all of them, one of the characters is killed and brought to life again. (Jevons 1916b, 184)

Revivification, thus, replaces a real awareness of the paradox of life and death with an apparent ambiguity—that is, with another paradox that makes a developmental rule out of saltatory change.

Plate 3. Mummers with beasts' heads. Marginal illustration from the *Romance of Alexander*, ca. 1340. Oxford, Bodleian Library, Ms. Bodley 264, folio 181 verso.

Revivification and Reincarnation;
Supernatural and Social Order

Though it is easy to see how masks might accompany a metaphorical death and rebirth—such as the transition in rites of passage from one social category to another—it is remarkable that masking persists even in the physical absence, the apparent saltation, caused by human death.[36] The common occurrence of death masks throughout the world and, in particular, in Aegean cultures attests to this persistence, but most remarkable are the revivificational, the re-presentational, features of the funerary rites themselves. "In ancient Italy," for example,

> one mask was buried with the deceased whilst another was carefully preserved, and the masks or *imagines* they preserved were . . . worn on the occasion of the funeral of a member of the household by persons who in the funeral procession represented the deceased ancestors whose *imagines* they wore. (Jevons 1916b, 179)

J. H. Croon, in a study of the myths and rituals connected with hot springs in ancient Greece, is similarly convinced about the importance of masks in funerary rites. In the presentation of much evidence for the possible relationship between the Perseus-Gorgon story and the use of masks in death rituals, he recalls an arresting episode portrayed on a certain Etruscan tomb-fresco (Pl. 4):

> It is a picture of a sort of gladiatorial games, no doubt performed at the funeral of the man buried here. One of the captives used in the games is held on a rope by a masked figure, above and beside whom is written the word "φersu." We owe the interpretation of the scene to F. Altheim [1929], who . . . examining the tomb picture more closely . . . points out that the figure called φersu is a sort of manager of funeral performances.[37] (Croon 1955, 15–16)

This interpretation is in part based on the now more widely accepted etymology of the term *persona* that relates it to the Etruscan *phersu* and on the structural correspondence between the underworld and names with the same prefix (the Greek *perse-* or Etruscan *pherse-*). Croon, moreover, corroborates the argument that the mask cannot be understood as exclusive of the character manifested by pointing out that the word in this fresco referred to the complete figure and not to the mask alone.

The mask's role in managing perceived oppositions is emphasized by the radical categories to which masks call attention. The repeated presence of masks in conjunction with shamanistic practices—they are often used in exorcisms and even recovered from shamans' graves—indicates their indispensibility in making special contact with an unapprehen-

Plate 4. Rendering of detail of the Tomba degli Auguri (Tomb of the Augurs) at Tarquinia showing masked funerary personage or *phersu* engaging in funeral games. Archaic period. The *phersu*, with his dog, combats a condemned (?) man who, wearing a sack over his head, attempts to turn the fight in his favor by striking the dog with his cudgel. At left, the Etruscan word *phersu*, a word etymologically related to the English "person", designates the "manager" of this performance. Pallottino 1968, Pl. 69.

sible, often radically dissimilar world. Among the many cultures deploying masks expressly to contact another world, the New Caledonians stated explicitly that people who reside in the land under the sea go about everything in an inverted fashion: they walk backwards, women carry their babies upside down, people eat their own feces, and for the most part do everything exactly as it should not be done in the land above the sea. The special nature of this other world and the mask's mediatory role in the sacred and natural opposition is reflected in the very construction of the mask object: it uses a sacred and otherwise unused wood, the feathers of a sacred bird, and human hair cut from the heads of mourners after a lengthy ritual observance. Among the Kwakiutl Indians of the Pacific Northwest, masks likewise call attention to the radical nature of categories whose differences the mask transcends. The use of masks in their performing societies and in their individual initiation ceremonies corresponds specifically to the contrast between the summer and winter seasons. Men acquire their supernatural masks in initiations held only in winter, only at night, and concerned exclusively with those supernaturals who are the inverse of what people recognize themselves naturally to be: each man possesses his own mask; myth people may borrow freely. Masks demonstrate among the Kwakiutl that the vitality of this opposition depends upon the strength of the masking paradox that is its transformer. The changing nature of things visible and invisible, the ambiguous and illusionary status of appearance, is nowhere more directly stated than in their beautifully crafted transformation masks: manipulated by ingenious devices, these open to reveal a second and sometimes a third animal or human visage (Pl. 5).

Lastly, it is necessary to remark the importance of iconography in evaluating the mask's perceptual mandate. While formal variation in the decoration of masks has been profitably considered in recent structural studies of natural and supernatural organization,[38] it is essential to recognize how fundamentally our perceptual categories are predisposed and governed by established iconographic tradition. Merely by contrasting the dogmatically strict rendition of Christian icons with the more experimental iconographic systems often characteristic of mask pantheons, we easily sense that the great efficacy of the more complex groups of masks derives at least in part from certain epistemological advantages that characterize—and are perhaps even peculiar to—a pantheon. Among these advantages are the educational and semiotic devices that become functional when people find themselves in close proximity to supernatural forces, as well as a formal set of mimetic relationships in which roles can be attributed to spirits or personae who independently address each other and an audience at large. Because of this special way that a mask pantheon combines religious belief with the cathartic value of mimesis, it embodies a type of order and a means of accommodating religious and perceptual paradoxes that legitimize appearance in a potentially constructive and educational manner. In doing so, the mask pantheon does not function so to oppose appearance and essence that masking *per se* becomes a wholly disingenuous or evil activity.[39] The creation and use of personae and the act of personification in general thus involve both performers and audience in a catharsis both supernatural and natural, both religious and educational in a specific way. Masks are, in this sense, a means of describing transitions in substance and in idea, a way of expressing selected modes of both natural and supernatural classification.

Plate 5. Kwakiutl transformation mask (bullhead-raven-human). A bullhead opens to reveal a raven, which in turn opens to disclose a human face. New York, American Museum of Natural History. Courtesy American Museum of Natural History, neg. no. 31198. (Photo: R. Weber.)

Numen Inest: Pantheons and Presuppositions

Gilbert Ryle once remarked that "we have to learn to give verdicts before we can learn to operate with suspended judgements" ([1949] 1963, 249). In saying this, Ryle wished to dispel the common misconception that supposition is more elementary than affirmation. According to Ryle, "the concept of make-believe is of a higher order than that of belief" (ibid., 250); it is "compatible with all degrees of scepticism and credulity" (ibid., 244). Talking about pretending, Ryle maintained, involves talking obliquely about ingenuousness:

> One cannot know how to play a part without knowing what it is like to
> be or do ingenuously that which one is staging; nor can one find a
> mock-performance convincing or unconvincing, or dub it skillful or in-
> efficient, without knowing how the ingenuous performance itself is
> conducted. (Ryle [1949] 1963, 245)

Ryle's attempt at a formal outline of perceptual apprehensions, moreover, provides us with some indication that a hierarchy of perceptions
that is empirically ascertained may be subsumed by an understanding
that is not; this is especially so if one recognizes that a mock form may be
of a higher order, at least on a functional plane, than its genuine counterpart that we call real.[40] Recognizing the possible disjunction between
two forms that are apparently identical is evident today in the continued
and specific attention of contemporary thinkers to the problem of apparent paradox in the apprehension of change.[41] Yet the inseparability of
mock forms, such as masks, and sacred practices has been demonstrated by the coexistence of worship and drama from the earliest of
times—a coexistence that makes possible the manipulation of those paradoxes that are essential to the psychology of transformation. Although,
as Huxley remarks, the use of theatrical devices in sacred contexts en-
courages charlatans,

> they are at bottom devices necessary for the staging of the transforma-
> tion scene, at which time the inner and outer stages are experienced as
> one. (F. Huxley 1976, 284)

The shift, therefore, from belief to a suspension of disbelief or to a
state of make-believe is a skill that we associate with an altered sense of
credulity. A circumstance once unquestionably immediate and overwhelming is in that event subjected to a more discriminating sensibility.
And it is because the best theater is still cathartic that it naturally exists,
not only in Greece and Rome but elsewhere around the world, in conjunction with religious shrines. That efficacy can coexist with make-believe
suggests how readily ritual may be transformed or even parodied; it also
suggests that the sacred and the profane may be less segregated than we
generally think. This mysterious capacity to bring together categories that
are often assumed to be radically opposite at least in part explains Waley's
remark that in truth "there is no 'real reason' for ritual acts" (1938, 57) and
likewise clarifies what Hocart meant when he said:

> The trouble is that we talk of ritual very much as if it were a thing in
> itself, an unchanging entity which can be defined like mass or ele-
> ments. In reality, the word merely describes chains of action which can
> vary infinitely. They are in a perpetual state of flux, so that, as we have
> seen, ritual may become the negation of ritual. (Hocart [1950] 1969,
> 63–64)

Radical categories merge perhaps most startlingly where successful exorcistic practices are accompanied, in a highly unsolemn manner, by a simultaneous and overt theatrical display. The healing rites common to the Sinhalese of Sri Lanka are one example of this remarkable coexistence (see especially Wirz 1954). There, various demons appear throughout the night of an exorcism to entertain an audience with scenes appropriate to each spirit's shortcomings and vices as well as to its efficacious powers (Pl. 6). The religious incorporates the theatrical and the theatrical the religious; supernatural efficacy and theatrical device are no longer opposing conditions.

Given how unamenable polytheism is to probably all known notions of science, it might seem that a confirmation of a pantheon's conflicting powers would give rise to an equally unamenable experiential view.[42] A polytheistic relationship, however, is of a disjunctive rather than an incommensurable nature; that is, it gives rise to a unique experience because it originates in a different hypothesis, not because it cannot be compared to anything currently known.[43] Because the pantheon has institutionalized uncertainty itself in recognizing more than one possible standard, it has as major functional drawbacks the less than unanimous character of any justification for human action and the melancholic tendencies that result from the individual's inability to know what force can be held accountable for a specific event. Huston Smith has adequately paraphrased this dilemma:

> If man's life is not to be scattered, if he is not to spend his days darting from one cosmic bureaucrat to another to discover who is setting the standards today, if, in short, there is a consistent way in which life is to live if it is to move toward fulfillment, a way that can be searched out and approximated, there must be a singleness to the Other that supports this way.[44] (H. Smith 1958, 228)

If such chaos is indeed the natural consequence of polytheism, why then study it, much less endorse it intellectually? First, it must be studied because an understanding of disjunction and of mutability is, undeniably, a precondition to the understanding of unity. Second, polytheism may account for the complexities of appearance without resorting to what Huxley has called Christianity's peculiar morbidity,[45] to the obsessive sense of personal guilt and the self-destructiveness that often characterize the monotheist's reaction to uncertainty. Third, a polytheist may theorize about transformations, paradoxes, and perhaps even contradictions without conjuring up what is by definition empirically unascertainable on cosmological grounds. And last, polytheism presents special problems for describing the unique psychological states often reported in conjunction with wearing masks. The ethnographic lit-

Plate 6. Sri Lankan exorcistic mask. This mask represents Mahā-kolā Sanni Yakā and the eighteen demons who are responsible for specific diseases. Each demon is represented by a different face, and each must be exorcised in a manner appropriate to his special capacity for inflicting illness. Basel, Museum für Völkerkunde und Schweizerisches Museum für Volkskunde.

erature is filled with instances—usually described in the past tense, as if they occurred in a distant past—of people "actually becoming" the spirits, the dead, or whatever the mask was meant to give life to. It is misguided, and maybe naive, to expect that we could ever verify such mental conditions as distinct psychological states, except by recourse to preexisting psychological classifications that ignore indigenous categories and that are, therefore, unacceptable on teleological grounds. Moreover, such an endeavor would merely reiterate the major structural difficulty described by Clark: "if new forms are produced only by isolating existing tendencies the end result would be a dead level of nonvarying, enclosed types" (1975, 39).

All of these arguments combine to show how culturally disposed is the category of the person and how fundamentally different is the understanding of that category in situations where the world may be motivated by more than one force. In contrast to the vocabulary of monotheism that radically opposes the religious to the theatrical as, respectively, sacred and profane, the polytheistic and polythetic nature of a pantheon frequently illustrates how the appearance of spirits in the form of mask wearers is not so unamenable to human perceptions and so psychologically special if we assume from the beginning a less rigid bifurcation of metaphysical categories. Often in polytheistic contexts, people and spirits are both necessary participants in the process of change. Greeks not only thought that they could have personal contact with the supernatural but that they could even, at least in principle, have offspring with them. How do we apply the categories of modern psychology here or, as in New Caledonia, where the dimension of personhood is defined by the personage (i.e., physical person + social role) rather than by the physical person only, and where in the normal course of events one's personage requires contact with spiritual personifications? How can we, in such cases, even begin to construe spirit possession as a radical or special state wherein we might remark some loss of self?

Masks are, without a doubt, heresy to any sort of positivistic psychology, because they suggest a sensibility for multiplicity and for saltatory change. They also challenge our perceptions of what is ethical. How do we attribute intentions and responsibility to personages whose images of themselves literally shift from plane to plane, in and out of focus? Indeed, as Clark maintains of Aristotle, "structural change is dependent, in the broadest sense, on ethical change" (1975, 43),[46] and it is ultimately on ethical grounds that the character of masks and the role of humankind in the artistic manifestation of the divine must be judged. Here, I hope to indicate what helps make certain kinds of masked practices efficacious and to show how their transformational success depends upon the exploitation of diffuse, polythetic classes (see Needham 1975), whether they be classes of human psychological states (as in the transformational cases of mask wearing) or classes of spiritual forces (such as might be outlined by the genealogy of a pantheon).

There is already much evidence in the sciences to suggest that a polythetic view of personality and the classificatory conditions for personhood need not always be, as many psychoanalysts would suggest, either destructive or deconstructive. Vygotsky has pointed to the far-reaching effects of the unnucleated chain complex, the character of which extends the child's sensibility for transformation through "the fluidity of the very attribute that unites its single elements" ([1934] 1964, 65). As an example, Vygotsky offers us the case of the child who in matching a yellow triangle would "pick out trapezoids as well as triangles, because they made him think of triangles with their tops cut off. Trapezoids would lead to squares, squares to hexagons, hexagons to semicircles, and finally to circles." He found that color as the basis of selection is "equally floating and changeable. Yellow objects are apt to be followed by green ones; then green may change to blue, and blue to black." Most important, however, is the realization that the exploitation of such family relations is not limited to the thoughts of children:

> Apart from the primitive thought processes of dreams, the adult constantly shifts from conceptual to concrete, complexlike thinking. The transitional, pseudo-concept form of thought is not confined to child thinking; we too resort to it very often in our daily life. (Vygotsky [1934] 1964, 75)

Indeed, we may recognize the role of a complex, polythetic understanding not only in the way we outline certain processes of learning or the efficacy of certain cathartic cures, but in the very way we construe phenomena, such as diseases, that may be either internal or external to our understanding of ourselves.[47] In this respect, Huxley has called attention to the relationship between classification and catharsis, pointing out that catharsis can have no meaning except with reference to an audience. Here, his discussion of miming in hypnotic cures[48] suggests how special mental states can alter the human body-image so as to make changes possible, much as polytheism and complex thought facilitate similar transformations.

Finally, in considering the inherently explanatory features of a polythetic understanding we need to study further the educational possibilities presented by a pantheon. Vygotsky's description of concept formation in children is supported by early learning practices in a variety of cultures[49] as well as by what we may come to understand in general about the paradoxical problems of apprehending change. The remarkable diversity of institutions that have been devised to take account of transition is mirrored not only in the many uses to which masks are put, but in the diverse ways that structural change affects ethical change. The study of masks, therefore, results in an awareness of both how the analysis of history and science is, in part, a moral exercise, as well as how, in an Aristotelian sense (*De incessu animalium* 713ᵇ31ff.), the crab's side can indeed function as a back when the crab moves obliquely.

· 2 ·

Masks and the Beginnings of
Greek Drama

Ritual as Entertainment; Entertainment as Ritual

Because performative art, like any other type of art, is amenable to
intellectual discrimination and criticism, we conventionally compare it
with ritual behavior governed by something other than rational thought.
Every religious dogma, wrote Jane Harrison, is first

> a confident statement about something unknown and therefore prac-
> tically always untrustworthy; secondly, if it were right and based on real
> knowledge, then its subject-matter would no longer belong to the realm
> of religion; it would belong to science or philosophy. (Harrison [1912]
> 1977, xxiii)

Religious understanding and ritual awareness (so far as it is emotive)
are, by this view, antithetical to critical knowledge; for, strictly speaking,
knowledge without reason is not knowledge at all.[1] In the broadest
terms, a discussion of the relationship between ritual and drama proper
thus encompasses the entire field of ritual theory, if only because inquir-
ies into the origins of drama require (or so it has been assumed) a critical
vocabulary for differentiating religious actions from modes of entertainment[2]—for distinguishing, that is, between a sacred activity and a secular one, between unknowable categories and those that we may intellectually apprehend.[3]

Because classical stagecraft has been thought to lie at the foundation
of all Western dramatic practice, its rich religious character has been of
special interest to scholars who have rejected the predominant literary-
critical approach to the classical stage. Among these scholars, Ridgeway,

Plate 7. Menander relief. The poet Menander contemplates the masks of a young man, a girl, and an old man. Marble relief, ca. 1st c. A.D. Vatican Museum.

Murray, Harrison, Farnell, and Cornford in particular focused on two major problems: the failure of previous investigators adequately to address the sociological character of the many ritual elements of Greek drama—which contemporary drama does not inherit—and the all-consuming importance of identifying what each believed to be the ritual origins of the Greek stage. Though considerable effort was spent on both of these issues, it is the second, unfortunately, that any mention of their works most often calls to mind. And it is their attention to the second of these concerns that has tended to disqualify them as serious commentators for students of the classical stage. This disqualification has arisen, in part, because some of their ideas have been eclipsed by archaeological discoveries, while others were excessively evolutionary or complicated by neologisms.[4] But perhaps such a dismissal may also be attributed to their openly discussing what we now find to be an ethnocentric belief—namely, that both modern philosophy and the Greek literary mind are fundamentally incomparable with something called "primitive thought." On such grounds their studies might be, and have been, expeditiously dismissed. Nonetheless, their search for dramatic origins in various forms of ritual evokes many central and difficult issues with which we still struggle. To some modern anthropologists, questioning what may be reasonably known about art is seen as a Western ethnocentric statement of distrust about exotic modes of perception. However, it may also be a statement about the sanctity of what we may apprehend but do not know in any empirical sense. What most disturbs the intellectual, in other words, is not the subjective nature of artistic sensibility or of religious experience, but dogmas—that is, in Jane Harrison's terms, religious ideas presented as facts in a culture where facts and religion form distinctly different, if not radically divergent, categories of thought. Those who sought the origins of drama did so with zeal because they believed it was crucial to distinguish intellectually between dramatic convention and ritual practice and to describe—as Lévy-Bruhl later would—the conflation of entertainment and ritual in cathartic states that they did not know in any strict sense but suspected to exist in ancient Greece and in many exotic cultures around the world.

Tragedy and the Evolution of Drama

The mask, Albin Lesky has said, "is the device used to effect that transformation which is the first requirement of any genuinely dramatic practice" (Lesky 1966, 223). Though in itself Lesky's statement about the prehistory of Greek drama seems unproblematic, the connection it makes between transformation on the one hand and "genuinely dramatic practice" on the other reveals a major contradiction in our critical dramatic vocabulary. By suggesting that a kinship exists between transformation (such as we attribute to ritual) and drama, Lesky not only brings into question the scholarly view that there is "no evidence for the controlling influence of ritual on Greek tragedy" but leads us to doubt the equally popular persuasion that "the two 'forms' are almost antithetically opposed" (Vickers 1979, 41).[5] The truth of the former assertion ultimately depends on the accumulation and interpretation of facts and on what, on an epistemological level, constitutes a "controlling influence." The veracity of the latter, more generally, hinges upon what is understood by the term "ritual"—a concept freely used in contradistinction to drama, but one whose misuse, as we shall see, makes that distinction almost meaningless. First, therefore, we must ask just what is known about how much preclassical performances may have influenced the dramatic forms of the sixth century B.C., when the classical stage began to assume its characteristic shape.

A close reading of the evidence, such as that given by Pickard-Cambridge (1927; 1953; see also Else 1965), demonstrates that there exists no real foundation for positing a direct evolution from Dionysian worship to Greek drama. Such a non-evolutionary view is based specifically on the content of early plays and on the diminished role of Dionysus in the performances as a whole, despite the fact that he was central to the festivals and that they continued to be given in his name. Moreover, the recurrence of the popular proverb "nothing to do with Dionysus" suggests that the ancients themselves were anxious to point out the difference between Dionysian abandon and the deliberate, intellectual tone of their new theatrical invention. A phrase such as "nothing to do with Dionysus," however, is, like any other disclaimer, usually raised by way of objection to another equally popular or at least equally verbalized opinion, and we have, therefore, some reason for suspecting that the Greeks were themselves involved in a disagreement resembling our current debate over the nature of ritual and the paradox of acting. The phrase might very well have been a way of putting an end to an opinion easily resorted to, and the connection with Dionysus a very common one to make. To these problems I will turn shortly, but before doing so I must suggest some reasons for the continuing scholarly tendency to connect prehistoric ritual and Greek drama despite the absence in the plays themselves of textual evidence allowing such a link.

It is necessary in this regard first to distinguish a structural study of the relationship between ritual and drama from the Frazerian search for evolutionary origins. True, the latter no longer presents an acceptable analytic perspective, but it is all too easy to view the methodological persuasions of such past theorizing as a reason for disavowing any substantive preclassical influence on the classical stage. We should, that is, strive not to confuse contemporary anthropological concerns with the earlier view that dramatic evolution was part of a natural hierarchical order. To say that ritual and drama are related is not to say that one evolved out of the other; to argue that all drama originates in ritual is clearly quite a separate proposition, one for which there exists little support. Nor can an anthropological inquiry assent to the perspective of those critics who maintain that relationships cannot be postulated where actual testimonies are absent. One of the primary concerns for anthropologists in the field is the fact that collective representations may be so obvious to the members of a given society as not to merit comment or so problematic as to remain tacit or unconscious. Anthropologists often discover that first principles have in the absence of inquiry remained unstated, and they frequently conclude that not only is a studied critical distance often unwise in enumerating categories of thought, but that, indeed, it may even disguise a simple ethnocentric bias.[6] To say that there is no evidence that drama arose out of ritual may in point of fact be true enough, but that statement, of course, does not prove that masked practices before the sixth century B.C. are unrelated to those occurring during and after that time.

Likewise, if we approach the Greek stage from a contemporary dramatic viewpoint, we see that there are some critical differences not accounted for simply by striking the ritualistic elements from the classical practices and then equating what is left to a more modern view. A comparison, in other words, of modern, classical, and preclassical practices is not finally reducible to a comparison of a non-ritualistic modern mode with a ritualistic preclassical one. There is, in fact, a great deal of evidence, however peripheral to a literary study of the texts, that reminds us of how the classical stage in certain particulars differed markedly from our own. Foremost, of course, is the overwhelming presence of masks, whose iconography made possible political and social allegory on a level perhaps unknown to and unmanageable on our contemporary stage. We can only imagine how the use of *dramatis personae* could be manipulated through masks into a sophisticated commentary on real events, as when social tensions could be played out for the initiated directly under the eyes of those who were being satirized.

Though one can never be entirely certain how masks created humor for an audience with an informed understanding of specific *dramatis personae*, the unlikelihood of a stylized mask resembling exactly the face of a known individual must have made recognizing a lampoon all the more delightful. That a mask might be an abstract enough imitation of a character to be lost to part of an audience or so grotesque an exaggeration that the person satirized refuses to perceive the connection must all be part of what makes for humor in the eyes of those initiated into the mask's complexities. It is possible, moreover, that the less representational character of certain masks arose at times for practical reasons—that is, because of the real political threat posed by the unsympathetic reactions of some powerful victims. In a discussion of this possibility, Pickard-Cambridge points out that portrait masks were probably no longer used by the end of the fifth century:

> Platonios makes it characteristic of the Middle and New Comedy that they deliberately avoided such resemblances and made use of masks

with features so exaggerated that they could not possibly be like any real human being. (He ascribes the change to the fear lest any mask should even by accident resemble some Macedonian ruler.) (Pickard-Cambridge 1953, 197)

But how far must a caricature be transformed before it ceases to resemble some known individual? While such ambiguities are freely exploited by any good cartoonist,[7] the risks were naturally quite high from the classical author's perspective—as is exampled by Cleon's attempted impeachment of Aristophanes for libel.[8] Moreover, we know from such theatrical genres as the *commedia dell'arte* that a good dialogue with plenty of pointed remarks, combined with a number of archetypal masked personae, does little to disguise the aims of the satire, regardless of how exaggerated the portraits themselves may appear. Satire, of course, becomes more sophisticated as the education of its audience increases, and the complex roles that personae help produce might even be turned, in the hands of skilled actors, against the authors themselves.

The connection between the supposed states of belief and make-believe is, therefore, not only a matter of relating ritual to or diverting it away from drama or of determining the real or fictitious nature of the character acted. Indeed, a closer look at the way performances are manipulated reveals a *dramatis persona*'s very special role in commenting on real events. We are, in this respect, in no position to argue with those who maintain that the Greek plays as works of art are self-explanatory; discussing the preclassical use of masks in this context seems almost meaningless. Moreover, it is not within the feasible bounds of a study of masks to consider whether preclassical practices can be uncovered in the theatrical inventions of Aeschylus or Sophocles. Surely, such discoveries of origins are of great importance and interest, but the mask was by this time a secular convention in its own right and clearly functional for innovative artistic ends. We would, moreover, be very unlikely to be able to connect directly any examples of ritual activities in the plays with the actual masking trends of a fully developed stagecraft. Or at least, if we could do so, it would be quite difficult to argue that this formal relationship was essential to the content of the overall performance. Nonetheless, though it is only sensible to approach the plays as directly as possible, we should not be deterred from pointing out various instances where ritual elements are imbedded in either the form or the content of the specific texts and of the specific performances of the various plays.[9] Modern literary approaches do, with some exceptions, try to incorporate the wider criteria of iconologists, philologists, and historians; and, in any case, the pervasive role of masks cannot be properly studied in the context of an evolutionary debate when, as anthropologists have elsewhere noted, important categories of thought need not themselves become the focus of a given myth or a particular text.

Aristotle's Testimony

Without doubt, the most problematic evidence in any attempt to sort out the complex relationship between the dramatic festivals and the numerous other forms of masked behavior is the difficult testimony of Aristotle concerning the origins of tragedy and comedy. The question as to Aristotle's accuracy is not answered simply by checking what he said against the available facts; the difficulty is complicated by our lack of a clear idea as to how we should interpret the testimony itself. The following famous passage provides the substance of Aristotle's view:

> It certainly began in improvisations—as did also Comedy; the one originating with the authors of the Dithyramb, the other with those of the phallic songs, which still survive as institutions in many of our cities. And its advance after that was little by little, through their improving on whatever they had before them at each stage. It was in fact only after a long series of changes that the movement of Tragedy stopped on its attaining to its natural form. (1) The number of actors was first increased to two by Aeschylus, who curtailed the business of the Chorus, and made the dialogue, or spoken portion, take the leading part in the play. (2) A third actor and scenery were due to Sophocles. (3) Tragedy acquired also its magnitude. Discarding short stories and a ludicrous diction, through its passing out of its satyric stage, it assumed, though only at a late point in its progress, a tone of dignity; and its metre changed then from trochaic to iambic. The reason for their original use of the trochaic tetrameter was that their poetry was satyric and more connected with dancing than it now is. As soon, however, as a spoken part came in, nature herself found the appropriate metre. The iambic, we know, is the most speakable of metres, as is shown by the fact that we very often fall into it in conversation, whereas we rarely talk hexameters, and only when we depart from the speaking tone of voice. (4) Another change was a plurality of episodes or acts. As for the remaining matters, the superadded embellishments and the account of their introduction, these must be taken as said, as it would probably be a long piece of work to go through the details.[10] (*Poetics* 4.1449ª9ff., trans. W. D. Ross)

This passage, from a contemporary standpoint, is replete with ambiguity. We do not know what sort of dithyramb Aristotle is speaking of here; indeed, we are not even clear about the meaning of the word "dithyramb."

Opinions as to how this passage ought to be interpreted are, thus, predictably, quite varied. At one extreme, Wilamowitz suggests that we should do no more than accept the passage at face value; at the other, Vickers at one point suggests that we discard entirely this part of Aristotle's testimony and instead study the plays directly. Pickard-Cambridge's very cautious close reading leads him to doubt that Aristotle's description agrees very closely with known facts; he emphasizes that we simply do not know what qualifies for Aristotle as a true dramatic change:

> From what kind or stage of dithyramb did Aristotle think that tragedy was derived? And with this is bound up the further question, what did he think of the relation of dithyramb and tragedy to satyric drama? It is at this point that the task of discovering his meaning becomes almost hopeless. For "because it changed from *satyric*" may mean either "through it ceasing to be satyric drama" or "through it passing out of a shape in which it was grotesque"; and *satyric* in the next sentence can similarly be taken either literally or metaphysically. Accordingly we cannot tell whether Aristotle means that tragedy developed out of a dithyramb danced by persons made up as satyrs, or only that it developed out of a dithyramb which had an *exarchon* [i.e., a leader], and that in its early stages its language was grotesque. (Pickard-Cambridge 1962, 91)

Though Pickard-Cambridge goes on to doubt Aristotle's rendition, he is careful never to rule it out completely. Lesky, on the other hand ([1964] 1978, 32ff.), is quite convinced that new evidence tends to justify what Aristotle says, especially when we take into account the possibility that the *Poetics* was compiled as a notebook rather than as a coherent written argument. Moreover, Pickard-Cambridge's caution must be understood in the context of his concern over the often incautious speculations of his anthropologically minded contemporaries. Webster, in his revisions to Pickard-Cambridge's *Dithyramb, Tragedy and Comedy*, speaks directly to this point when he justifies deleting Pickard-Cambridge's lengthy rebuttals of his contemporaries' views about the ritual focus of early drama. Webster himself was of the opinion that a ritual origin, while perhaps exaggerated by some, still required consideration. Drawing on different and frequently new historical and iconographical evidence, he maintained that the study of preclassical Greek ritual was viable and necessary in describing the preconditions of Greek drama (Webster 1958).

Thus, we see a great variety of opinions concerning not only the relevance of this cryptic though important piece of Aristotelian evidence for the prehistory of the Greek stage, but concerning, as well, the entire question of the relationship between theater and religion. Indeed, for many authorities it is difficult to determine to what extent they restrict their comments to ancient Greece, and the tenor of some arguments indicates that much more is at stake in this debate than its ostensible terms. Even one so analytically inclined as Pickard-Cambridge resorts to an *ad hominem* argument when he says that "above all, it is extraordinarily difficult to suppose that the noble seriousness of tragedy can have grown so rapidly, or even at all, out of the ribald satiric drama" (Pickard-Cambridge 1962, 92–93). On this point in particular, I think, comparative anthropological evidence may be most useful.

A great part of the problem of understanding Aristotle's theory of the origins of drama, as Pickard-Cambridge shows, is a simple one of translation: we just do not know the best way to render Aristotle's terms. Some writers, such as Lesky, insist that the best way—and, in fact, the only way—to reconcile Aristotle's opinion with what seems natural is to refrain from strictly defining his ambiguous terms. In discussing some problematic cases, Lesky argues that we must be aware of the way slightly different renditions of words entail drastically different conclusions about the *Poetics*. A case in point is Pickard-Cambridge's insight into the difference between Aristotle's saying that one dramatic form changed in light of an earlier form and saying merely that one form ceased to be and another took its place. While, as Pickard-Cambridge argues, most scholars are inclined toward the evolutionary sense of connectedness, such a point of view is doubly problematic. First, it can be suspect because, in seeking to give meaning to history, it can easily mistake what is contingent for a universal principle. Second, and more specifically, it is an inescapable fact that the changes that culminated in the classical stage came from more than one dramatic tradition, so that even in the sixth century B.C. we find little agreement as to what individuals, and frequently as to what cultures, were responsible for what. Was Thespis or was Arion the inventor of tragedy? Hellenistic consensus credited Thespis with the introduction of speeches, of an actor distinct from the chorus, and of masks or at least some form of facial disguise. But here we may suspect a popular conclusion following the considered position of Aristotle. Conversely, Herodotus informs us that Arion,

> so far as anyone knew, was the first man to write a dithyramb, to name it, and to present it in Corinth [Herodotus (1.23)]. . . . Now it is quite obvious that Arion did not invent the ancient ritual hymn to Dionysus. His contribution must then be that he raised the dithyramb to an artistic form of choral lyric. (Lesky 1966, 225)

This notion of an artistic form is so ambiguous, however, that it forces us to consider whether the Greeks themselves may have had no precise idea about the genesis of drama because similar changes could well have come from more than one tradition and at different moments in history. In other words, the supposedly evolutionary development of Greek drama may, in fact, have been a synthesis of separate but analogous practices.[11]

Lesky, in his thoughtful treatment of Aristotle, is careful to speak in terms of forerunners or precursors—notions enabling us to understand Aristotle's reasoning without recourse to an evolutionary and developmental explanation characterized by necessary connections. Lesky's analysis, in turn, leads us to consider more closely the idea of simple succession—a possibility that the complexity of ancient descriptions could easily support. Aristotle himself warns us that "it would probably be a long piece of work to go through the details" of this history. Is it not possible, therefore, that his account deliberately simplifies very complex relationships that may have been to his mind less than certain?

But where would an acceptance of Aristotle's testimony leave us? Pickard-Cambridge, like many other scholars, doubts that there is any relationship between tragedy and Satyr drama. He concludes that, "We are no longer obliged to derive tragedy from satyr drama," and that such a resolution of the uncertainties in Aristotle "robs his statements of all historical value" (1962, 95). On the other hand, we are certain that the dithyramb could be performed by men dressed as Satyrs; on this point all authorities agree. We must ask, therefore, if there is any sensible way to consider the connection of Satyrs with tragedy without arguing over what appears to be unclear, if not contradictory, information. Is there any way such seemingly dissimilar categories may be reconciled through a change in intellectual posture? Are we simply looking at the issue incorrectly?

Though Aristotle's theoretical focus is sometimes thought by historians to diminish his historical accuracy, it is this interest that, luckily, provides the synthesis we seek. We find this synthesis in his emphasis on both the importance of improvisation and the role of the grotesque. "We know," states Vickers,

> that the dithyramb was the original song of Dionysus, god of wine, that it was partly improvised and perhaps had a traditional refrain. We know that as early as the *Iliad* (the Chorus of mourners in Book 24) the dithyrambic singers were led by a Chorus leader, an *exarchon*, who was in effect an independent actor. In one of the fragments of Archilocus the poet claims 'I know how to lead off the fair song of the lord Dionysus, the dithyramb, when my wits are blasted with wine.' (Vickers 1979, 34)

So when Aristotle tells us that tragedy achieved its seriousness when it changed from the trochaic tetrameter of the Satyr performance to the iambic mode, we might speculate that the nature of improvisation changed as well. Thus, to posit a morphological connection between tragedy and the early forms of the Satyr play—as opposed to its fully developed form (see Lesky 1966, 224)—is to posit an analogy between two forms of improvisation, each with its own restraints on vocal performance, and each constituting a creative interlude in a specific structural sequence. This interpretation conforms at least with what little we do know of the worship of Dionysus: that his place in the hearts of the people (unlike that of the Homeric Olympians) was intense and immediate, and that worship of him surrounded the improvisational and individualistic aspects of the plays themselves. It is all too easy to forget while reading the plays or viewing them on a modern stage that they were restricted to the Dionysia (Haigh 1898, 7), that the shrine was an essential part of the theater and the priests occupied a special place at each performance, that the plays were often preceded by the parading of a statue of the god or a phallus along a specified route, that this procession took place only after appropriate sacrifice, and that the effigy was eventually carried to the theater, where it was installed for the performances. Thus, not only did "the god himself [watch] every play in the person of his statue," but the Athenian actors "were sacred officers of the cult of Dionysus," and "an altar to the same god commanded the dancing floor" (Garton 1972, 34).

Ritual Drama and Tragic Sentiment

Whether or not tragedy and comedy did, as Aristotle states, have a similar origin is an issue that undoubtedly will be argued for many years to come, and one that, perhaps, may never be resolved through fact. What is important, anthropologically, is to assess the merits of certain kinds of arguments and to evaluate on the structural level their applicability to the cross-cultural understanding of categories of thought. Though tragedy and comedy may not have derived from the same source, structurally speaking, they in principle could have done so; for even were we to have many more statements such as Aristotle's, their meaning could be likewise debated, and without a complete understanding of the structure of preclassical thought and an awareness of certain prejudices that predispose our critical vocabulary we could never explain the matter. Two such prejudices need to be dismissed straightaway. The first is that ritual activity is, insofar as it is ritualistic, unchanging. The second is that there is a necessary and exclusive connection between solemnity and the tragic. In fact, these two prejudices are, perhaps, most responsible for our misconceiving the character of preclassical metaphysics and, thus, cloud the prospect of ever understanding what Aristotle might have meant.

When Hocart says that ritual is ever changing, he does not mean to undermine our traditional understanding that ritual is a formal, customary repetition of some act or series of acts. What he means to suggest is, first, that a particular aspect of a given prescribed sequence may so alter over time as to bear little resemblance to its earlier form; second, that the content may so vary within that prescribed sequence that the affective meaning of a particular ritual may alter entirely; and third, that the form of the ritual itself may completely change if it is found to be no longer efficacious, or if those who decide such things in a culture are influenced by other, overriding concerns. All of these perceptions are based upon the understanding that while the ritual acts themselves may be efficacious, they occasionally allow, within that prescribed sequence, room for structural change and frequently provide some context for changes in meaning and interpretation. A ritual act, while usually consistent as to its structure, frequently varies in its contextual meaning, and two ritual events called by the same name may even, at times, vary in structure. What needs to be overcome by contemporary scholars is the idea that ritual activity in preclassical Greece might have anything at all to do with the misleading use of the word "ritual" in the sense in which it is, for example, used in the behavioral sciences to describe mindless repetitive actions. There is absolutely no evidence to endorse universally Kirkwood's claim that "a ritual formula is sacred and moving precisely because it is unchangeable" (1958, 14), or Dodds's that "it is only ritual that repeats itself *exactly*" (1960, xxvii), or Vickers's that "ritual patterns, once fixed never vary" (1979, 41). While all of these claims are in certain instances true, more often they are less than correct and none, certainly, is in principle acceptable. Ritual patterns vary no more nor less than do the meanings of words or the characters of social institutions, and, indeed, they do vary enough to make the standard juxtapositions of ritual and drama, dogma and freedom, mindless prescribed behavior and inspired creative thought completely inappropriate categories for the further analysis of the preclassical meaning of Greek masks, mask ritual, or mask drama. What elevates ritual from a pedestrian concern—what distinguishes it, to use Arthur Waley's contrast, from mere good manners— is how it can be relied upon to produce an effect, whether that effect be some change of category or simply the agreeable stimulation of the imag-

ination.[12] When traditional practices persistently fail (or bore), and especially when social instability reflects this insufficiency, the constraints of
a particular practice may be radically tested and redefined. Moreover,
even though in such instances the participants responsible for innova-
tion sometimes lay claim to an ancient precedent, the scope of ritual
flexibility may become enormous. Under the stress of obvious inade-
quacies, the structural variations of a given ritual may be explored and
exploited to a remarkable degree.

What must be understood about the potential character of preclassical metaphysics is not only that it was governed by a theism in which
individuals attempted to influence the cosmic cycle of events through
membership in a particular cult, but that the forces that moved the universe were not viewed, in themselves, as ethically good or bad. Under
such conditions, one's sense of what is required of ritual and how, psychologically, individuals approach ritual events, may be entirely different
from what Westerners often ethnocentrically assume to characterize ritual behavior. Responding to an ambivalent supernatural force may require a form of worship that is repetitive and solemn, but it may also
require a calculated manipulation of ritual—much as a lawyer attempts
to influence the members of a jury in conflict. It is this awareness—the
desire in another culture to make ritual effective—combined with the
ambivalence of supernatural forces, that helps us to overcome in the
Greek case the second prejudice: the belief that there is a relationship
between the tragic and the solemn that precludes any possible connection between tragedy and the ribald ways of Satyrs.

If we assume from the start a kind of demonology in preclassical
Greece whereby the grotesque Satyrs were taken for the uncivilized
powers of the wild that occasionally ventured into the civilized, human
world, we can readily understand how tragedy could have been connected to things far from solemn. Simply because Satyrs came to be associated with comic disrespect is no reason for assuming that there was not
a period in history when the Greeks were compelled to take them seriously, a reason they should be connected with performative activities of
a serious sort. From the time of Pratinas, the Satyr play—as a combination of the grotesque and the tragic—was always written by a tragedian,
and the sole specimen of early Satyr drama that survives intact, the
Cyclops of Euripides, has elements that are both demonic and truly ma-
cabre. Odysseus's blinding of Polyphemus is notably grotesque, but it is
no less monstrous than the behavior of the Cyclopes themselves who,
like the Satyrs and Centaurs, display a marked ambivalence toward all
human conventions.

"Sin," Endo has written,

is not what it is usually thought to be; it is not to steal and tell lies. Sin is for one man to walk brutally over the life of another and to be quite oblivious of the wounds he has left behind. (Endo 1969, 144)

By this definition, Satyrs ought to be considered sinners of the first order—at one moment stupidly pursuing some menial domestic task, at the next acting maliciously and irresponsibly (see, e.g., Kirk 1974, 152ff.). Aware of their ignorant ambivalence, we can easily imagine how the common Greek could at one moment treat them with fear and deference and at the next laugh heartily at their awkwardness—how the sort of respect we associate with solemnity could give way to the comic, how the earlier superstitions of Greek folk religion could be modeled into Attic comedy or into true farce. We need only exchange "tragedy" for "sin" in Endo's definition to recognize at once how valid Aristotle's aetiology of tragedy and comedy could be.

Not only is there little to suggest that tragedy could have nothing to do with the comic, but there is everything to suggest that the structure of early theater practice is a direct extension of the periodic inversion characteristic of rites of passage, even though, by the sixth century, theater stood independently as a fine art. As the Satyrs are themselves the creatures of the wild, so too, as attendants of Dionysus, they share in the intoxicated revelry that takes place when points of transformation are marked by the ritual inversion of what is normal. In mythology, Dionysus himself ascends from the underworld through the intoxication of Hephaestus, who had been thrown from heaven by Hera; Dionysus wins his way to deification by striking a clever bargain for Hephaestus's return. When Dionysus made his annual visit to the sacred enclosure of Eleuthereus on the southern Acropolis, he came from the underworld as a god of nature, fertility, and ecstasy—as an epiphanic symbol of the structural inversion of the everyday. While Heraclitus once remarked that "Hades and Dionysus, for whom they go mad and rage, are one and the same" (fr. 15), good structural evidence for the chthonian focus of the cult of Dionysus is found in his association with spirits of the underworld—e.g., Erinyes, Sphinx, Hades—and in the connection between Satyrs, Centaurs, and Silens as ferrymen or guardians of rivers and springs. Here we must imagine the Greek vision of the world as a disc afloat on the waters of Oceanus, a disc perforated by openings leading to the subterranean home of Hades and to the passages from which issue the rivers of the underworld, such as the Styx.[13] These oceanic and underworld associations were pervasive enough to be incorporated into the very structure of the dramatic festivals. Sifakis, for example, suggests that the boat-car carrying the phallus may have arrived at the Athenian festival in a real boat (1967, 10),[14] and Keuls points out that the Greek pictorial vision of the underworld could "reflect the physical appearance of the theatre" (1974, 6).

The standard academic objection—that noble tragedy could have nothing to do with ribaldry—is also ruled out by the ritual character of iambic invective, that is, by "a belief (forgotten by later ages) in the apotropaic power of obscenity" (Lesky 1966, 234). The magic power of obscenity is a concomitant, no doubt, of the potential for pollution and destruction that is identified with the raw and the grotesque forces of nature—the forces of inversion that can, if not supplicated by the proper rituals and sacrifices, brutally and quite obliviously walk over another's life. It is rather unfortunate that writers such as Murray, Harrison, and Cornford (the so-called Cambridge School) had to resort to neologisms and that, as a partial result, their work is no longer taken seriously; for they, though perhaps quite wrong about the ritual character of classical drama, were aware of the tragic aspects of ritual and that sacrifice is a kind of tragedy.

· 3 ·

Satyr, Centaur, Theriomorphic Healer

Types of Preclassical Greek Masks

In looking at the preclassical Greek masks of which we have archaeo-logical examples, we see that, while varying enormously, they may be or-ganized into distinct types. Dickins (1929, 163ff.; also Bosanquet 1905–6), in categorizing those seventh- and sixth-century B.C. masks found in Sparta at the temple of Artemis Orthia (pls. 9–12), divided the finds into seven types that for the present purposes will serve quite well. Of these divisions, four represent normal human faces: old women, youths, war-riors, and portraits. The remaining three types are abnormal or super-natural figures: on the one hand, the well-known Satyrs and Gorgons, and on the other, various caricatures—that is, grotesque exaggerations of an undetermined nature. These latter types of masks—especially the Satyrs and Gorgons—are, as personae, indicative of Greek supernatural expectations; as masks, they concretely manifest Greek iconographical preferences.

The study of masks that represent specific human types, and the study of portraits, cannot play an important part in this investigation, since these divisions are extremely general and since they derive from the need for organizing artifacts rather than from categories of Greek thought. However, the significance of portrait masks in the early history of representational art must be briefly noted; first, because portrait masks bear importantly upon a functional analysis of masks, and, second, be-cause mask iconography has so much to do with received ideas about personae and the social categories governing personification. Inevitably, portrait masks and all such conventions by which masks may be identi-fied with specific people become increasingly significant when individu-

Plate 8. Satyrs making wine. Attic black-figure belly amphora by the Amasis Painter, ca. 530 B.C. Above sits the god Dionysus, while Satyrs and Maenads dance. Würzburg, Martin v. Wagner-Museum der Universität, no. L265.

als attempt to have prayers granted through personal initiative, and in particular when fulfilling a social obligation does not in itself guarantee results (see Brilliant 1971). In such circumstances, establishing a relationship with a certain spirit through a votive surrogate can help to effect a binding correspondence based increasingly on the pictorial identification of individuals. The shift from generic type to individual portrait—a shift evident, for example, in the Etruscan canopic urns that held the ashes of the deceased and were covered with a clay head (Pl. 13)—can only reflect a change in the individual's conception of the self and of its relationship with the forces of nature (see, e.g., Brendel 1978, 106–9). This assertion does not, of course, imply that private initiatives and personal interests need be tangential to an individual's social role. But when individuality becomes the focus of a particular event, invariably portraits will predominate over generic types. That canopic urns and votive masks come to display portraits is, therefore, likely to be part of a shift in the notion of the person from *personnage*—that is, in Maurice Leenhardt's

terms, a state wherein a person cannot be separated from a social role—
to individuality, wherein the character of the votive object must not be
confused with a social persona or a generic type. Though portraiture as
such may or may not have made possible in preclassical times the nuances
it later does in, for example, the theater of Aristophanes, it is important
in any discussion of masks to bear in mind just how nebulous are the
visual categories that make caricature effective, as in comedy, where the
deliberate confusion of grotesque character types with known individuals is essential.[1] While at first deciding what ought to constitute a portrait seems, in other words, a simple matter, there are some cases in
which ambiguity is both desirable and quite intentional, so that it may be
a mistake to endeavor to uncover any clear precedents for portraiture in
art that does not immediately appear to be representational. Conversely,
and especially with masks, it is important to recognize that notions
about personification as a function of social role are always inherent
when personae are employed.[2] It is therefore especially meaningful to
identify the various uses to which masks were put in preclassical times
and to ascertain what generic types were primarily involved.

As with the designs of the various preclassical masks, their uses and
roles may be divided into a few major categories. There are those used
for sepulchral purposes. Among these sepulchral masks are the death
masks and, later, the roman *imagines*. Second, there are the votive and
honorific masks that tend to be natural in appearance. These are generally thought to have been commemorative, standing as a dedication to
some famous individual, and most often not worn. Third, there are the
apotropaic masks that put their ugliness to some purpose. They are, of
course, considerably exaggerated, though their forms may be stereo-
typical and controlled, depending on prevailing notions of iconography
and efficacy. Clearly these types are only generalized distinctions and in
no way exclusive categories: funerary masks may be votive, votive masks
apotropaic, and so on. Lastly, there are the dramatic masks. This is a
very ambiguous functional distinction. Though we know of several later
types of masks used only in the theater, in the preclassical era the problem is more confusing; for if we mean by dramatic any mask worn by a
person in a performance—many masks were not so worn—then any one
of the above types may well have been dramatic. There is very little evidence beyond such purely practical considerations as size, weight, or
whether there are holes for eyes that enables us to say categorically that a
mask was or was not ever worn. It has, in fact, often been suggested that
even some votive masks may have been worn in certain ceremonies.[3] The
anthropological literature from around the world is full of evidence that

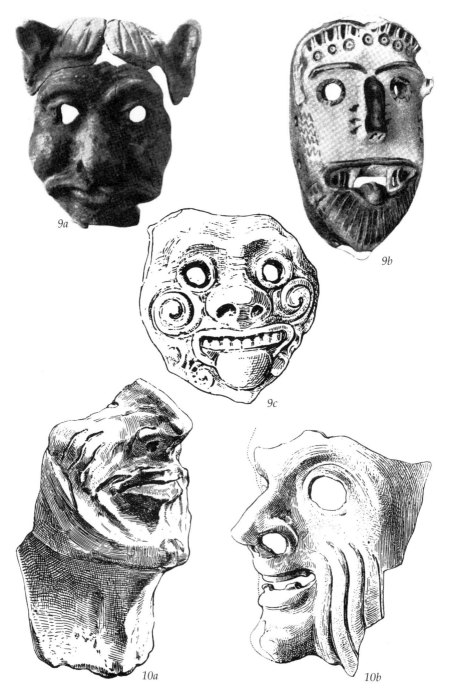

Plates 9–12. Terra-cotta votive masks from the Temple of Artemis Orthia, Sparta. 7th–6th c. B.C. These artifacts are significant in the categorizing of preclassical masks and important for comparative purposes, as they have frequently been associated with facial types found as far away as Carthage and Babylonia. Portrayed are probably either mask molds or votive copies of actual masks. Courtesy British School at Athens.

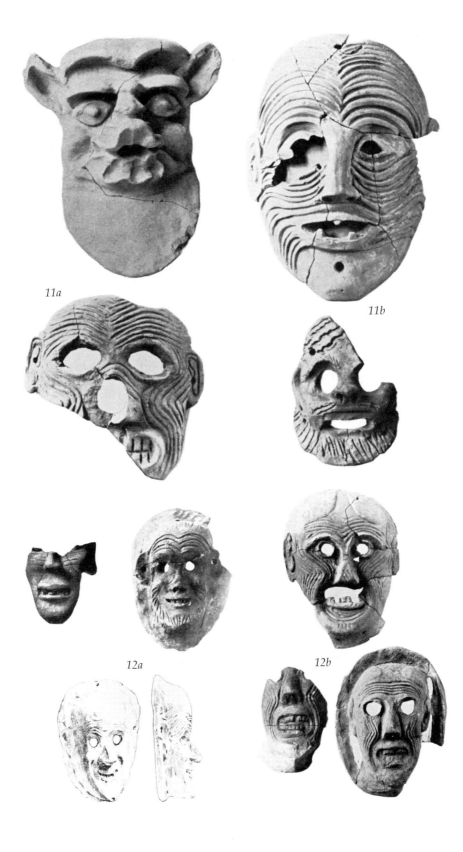

11a

11b

12a

12b

Plate 13. Head of an Etruscan canopic urn. After 600 B.C. The terra-cotta head represents the features of the deceased whose ashes are contained in the urn. For this reason, canopic urns are excellent indicators of a shift from generic types toward individual portraiture. Florence, Soprintendenza Alle Antichità, no. 4497.

the most elaborate devices may be contrived to enable an individual to support an extremely awkward or heavy mask, and there are also masks whose weight is so extreme, or whose visibility so poor, that the wearer cannot move without assistance. In this light, it becomes difficult to argue that a particular sanctuary mask could not have been worn because it impeded either sight or movement.

In Greece, masks placed on posts in the worship of Dionysus (see Pl. 14 and, e.g., Pickard-Cambridge 1968, 30; Burkert 1972, 260ff.) may at some point have been worn by a priest to invoke the god's presence. Similar changes in function have often been proffered as providing some clues about the origins of drama; however, functional transformations do not always result in a transference of iconographical meaning. Because, for example, Athenian dramatic masks may bear certain resemblances to earlier votive masks from Sparta (Pickard-Cambridge 1953, 195), one ought not to conclude that they are necessarily connected on the level of dramatic significance. Thus, the question of dramatic practice, in the sense of a theatrical performance, is not a suitable criterion for categorizing Greek preclassical masks, since they may or may not have been worn, and the fact that they were worn does not necessarily mean that they were worn in an active performance wherein vision and physical dexterity were required. Preclassical masks, moreover, may be sacred in themselves or may have no special supernatural status. They may be worn by one person, such as a priest; by several individuals, as, for example, by worshipers; by inanimate objects such as pillars or *hermai*; or by no one or nothing at all, as when they are used as votive objects in conjunction with a certain disease and its cure. The existence of such a range of uses of masks in ancient Greece is thoroughly supported by archaeological evidence. On an epistemological level, the question arises as to how much this great variation of uses may have been encouraged by the animistic notions possible in the context of a true pantheon of conflicting forces, forces capable of making conflicting demands upon the cults that grew up around them. To what extent, in other words, does a tendency to decentralize supernatural power become itself responsible for the plethora of valences attached to material manifestations of those forces? It remains to be seen whether this great variation in usage, as well as the recurrence of certain iconographical types, occurs in other cultures whose cosmologies may be seen as structurally comparable. One might, however, move in the direction of answering this question by asking others of more manageable proportions.

First, do the types of preclassical Greek masks point, on the level of the emotions, to any masks that might be considered archetypal within Greek culture? Do these representations, in other words, pertain to any special nature peculiar to certain iconographical manifestations? Second, on a comparative level, do the Greek mask types correspond to any other known types from cultures that might have shared their traditions with the Greeks? Are there, for example, any Indo-European traditions exhibiting mask types with iconographies and mythological roles similar to those of the Greeks? Last, if such comparative similarities are demonstrable, may the mask types then be said to be archetypal on a cross-

Plate 14. Dionysus represented by a mask mounted on a post. Attic red-figure cup by Macron and the potter Hieron, ca. 480 B.C. Bacchantes dance before the idol of Dionysus. Berlin, Antikenmuseum, Staatliche Museen Preussischer Kulturbesitz, no. F2290. (See Pl. 17.)

cultural as well as a psychological level? Are they, in other words, fundamental, not to say primordial?

In discussing how social, psychological, and cosmological ideas are reflected in the iconography of preclassical Greek masks, we see that those types most frequently found fall generally into three categories. Broadly speaking, the first category of masks encompasses those that were used in conjunction with the worship of such vegetation and fertility spirits as Dionysus, Artemis, or Demeter[4] and have been discovered by archaeologists in shrines dedicated to these figures. There is a problem, however, with utilizing this archaeological category as a critical one, in that we often have little knowledge of the masks' meaning; these objects, in other words, are known to us because they are made of durable materials, not because they represent any enduring categories of thought. Many masks were in all likelihood made of animal skin, cloth, or wood, and in view of this fact we must not make the mistake of assuming that their absence today is any indication of a secondary role. It is much safer to adopt as classificatory categories those types of mythological beings that we know from Greek art were impersonated and for whose relationship to masking we consequently have both mythological and artistic evidence. Using this criterion, we must certainly conclude that the two most coherent categories of masks not restricted to a specific cult or merely spared the effects of nature are, on the one hand, the Satyrs, Silens, and Centaurs, and, on the other, the apotropaic face—that is, the mask and aegis of the Gorgon head. These two categories not only present the most persistent cases of mythological creatures finding their way into mask iconography—indeed, many other forms of facial iconography hardly seem like types in comparison—but as well provide us with the richest material for addressing the question of what role the mask might have played in the manifestation and manipulation of supernatural forces. Thus, two classes encompass the most significant cases of facial iconography in preclassical Greece: the first class I will call simply the Satyr, for reasons that will shortly be clear; the second class includes all varieties of the Gorgon and Gorgoneion (i.e., the disembodied Gorgon head). Interestingly, they are also among the earliest masked representations of daimons in Greek mythology and art.

The Satyr: Its Character and Iconography

The major difficulty in determining the part the Satyrs might have played in the origins of both tragedy and comedy is complicated by their frequently ambivalent status as daimons. It cannot be said with any certainty that Satyrs are only to be connected with a single dramatic form. Their ambivalence, which can conflate solemnity and seriousness with humor and abandon, is fundamental to Satyrs and to the daimons Satyr masks represent. This ambivalence is evident not only in practices of an ecstatic and orgiastic nature, such as in the worship of Dionysus, but is also explicitly encountered in the epistemological problems posed by the supposed dual origins of tragedy and comedy in the impersonation of Satyrs. We have already discussed tragedy in these terms and with respect to the difficulties contemporary scholars have experienced in supposing that it could possibly have anything to do with performances lacking solemnity. But in comedy itself we see that the problem is really no less complex. Aristotle felt simply that the tragedians descended from the epic poets and the comedians from the lampooners who were more ancient still, putting comedy thereby in a class of performance as old as any other human institution and governed by a natural preference of some people for the ribald and ignoble over the noble and serious.

The so-called Old Comedy does not occur as an important Attic dramatic form much before the middle of the fifth century B.C. We should thus accept Aristotle's view that by the time there were any records of the comic poets or of a chorus, the basic forms (*schēmata*) of comedy had already been established. Choruses of men dressed in animal masks and dancing to the song of a flute appear on many early black-figure vases (Pl. 15),[5] so that even if we could say something meaningful about the origins of tragedy or of Old Comedy—or of the Satyr plays of Sophocles or of Euripides that were performed only after the middle of the fifth century (Pl. 16)—it would not take us very far beyond the end of the sixth century. It was only at this time that Pratinas introduced Satyr drama into Athens, thirty years or so after the institution of dramatic competitions—that is, after 534 B.C., the date, as recorded on the Parian Marble, of the victory in public competition of Thespis, the supposed inventor of the dramatic mask (Pickard-Cambridge 1927, 93). If it is true that Arion was, in Corinth in the mid-seventh century, the first to give performers a stage position around an altar rather than have them wander as revelers (ibid., 20), then we can assume that almost a century passed during which performers gathered at specific places for organized performances. The hundreds of vase paintings, however, that illustrate Satyric reveling and the unlikelihood that a tradition is adopted at its advent by all members of a culture suggest the conjectural nature of such a history. Likewise, it would be injudicious to derive comedy, as a style of performance, from phallic revelry simply because of common features of costume. The accusation of inventing just such developmental connections is frequently leveled against Aristotle, and his open theoretical concern with formal evolution has led many commentators to discredit his testimony.

Though Aristotle's desire to establish some scheme for the origins of drama has, as we have seen, led to the questioning of his historical accuracy, his opinion is nonetheless important because it draws attention to how various Greeks, and especially Dorians and Megarians, vied for the honor of having invented either tragedy or comedy. That Epicharmus—one of the earliest comedians, if not the originator of the dramatic form—was a Sicilian writer and that his language was Sicilian Doric indicates how diverse are the origins of what came to be Attic convention. Far more important, it seems, is the fact that the character of Greek drama—whatever were the conventions of fifth-century Athens—was recognized by Greeks to be an ancient one; that in addition to the various ethnocentric claims made by Greeks of different origin, and in addition to the modern focus on individual authors and the limited textual evidence (Else 1963, 90–220), what is equally important is that to the

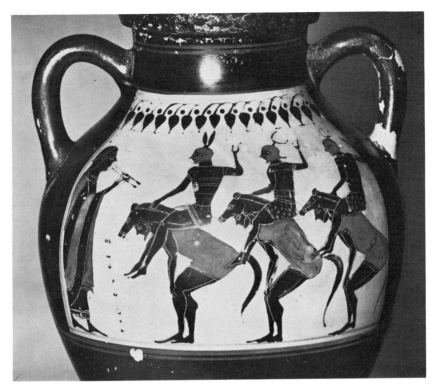

Plate 15. Chorus of horsemen ("Knights") dancing to the flute. Attic black-figure belly amphora by the Painter of Berlin 1686, 6th c. B.C. Berlin, Staatliche Museen, no. F1697.

Plate 16. Cast and chorus of Satyr play with Dionysus. Attic red-figure volute krater, late 5th c. B.C. Naples, Museo Nazionale, no. 3240.

Plate 17. Dionysus and Silen. Attic red-figure cup by Macron and the potter Hieron, ca. 480 B.C. This depiction appears on the inside of the cup illustrated in Plate 14. Berlin, Antikenmuseum, Staatliche Museen Preussischer Kulturbesitz, no. F2290.

Greek mind the origins of drama had any connection at all with epic poets or ancient lampooners. That the common character of Greek drama gave different ethnic groups cause to find its origin in their own social conventions points not to the influence of individuals but to the popular character of folk performances and pantomimes epitomized by ancient Satyr masks and modern-day Callicantzari as well (Lawson 1910, 190ff.). This common character, furthermore, points to an iconography that is not only Greek but Indo-European, to an iconography based upon the feral nature of the Satyrs and on their characteristic ambivalence.[6] The function of the Satyrs as wild men and the relationship between the periodic appearance of wild men and the periodic character of dramatic performances become increasingly important as we look more closely at the psychological dispositions of, and the specific legends relating to, Satyrs, Silens, and Centaurs—three types of creatures with similar attributes and backgrounds.

Of these mythological figures, the first two (the Satyrs and Silens [pls. 17 and 18]) are quite similar and, indeed, are often indistinguishable in art. The major difference between them seems to be one of age. (The Satyr chorus of Euripides' *Cyclops* and the Satyrs of Dionysus are led, for example, by the old Silenus.) Because of his age, Silenus is frequently represented as a fat little man, bald, and with a snub nose. Like Papposilenus, his mythological father, he is covered with hair and usually has a quite bestial face. Silenus is of special Indo-European interest because he is a very old deity from Asia Minor who has a particular significance in legends about Phrygia.[7] It is said that King Midas of Phrygia put Silenus under his power and forced him to disclose his secrets by polluting with wine the stream from which he drank.[8] Now Phrygian, as

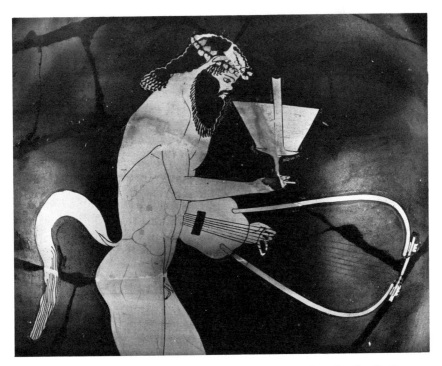

Plate 18. The Silen Orochares. Attic red-figure belly amphora by the Berlin Painter, ca. 500–490 B.C. Berlin, Antikenmuseum, Staatliche Museen Preussischer Kulturbesitz, no. F2160.

is well known, is, like Greek, an Indo-European language. The Phrygians were said to have come into Asia Minor from Europe in the second millennium B.C. by way of Thrace, bringing with them their wild music and the orgiastic rites for which they became famous. The cult of Dionysus, which may have had a Thracian origin,[9] adopted Silenus as a teacher of the young Satyr-initiates—Silenus being the foster father of Bacchus.[10]

While the short, fat figure of Silenus is important because it calls to mind the padded phallic dancers frequently illustrated in Greek art from the fifth century B.C. onward (Pl. 19), even more important is his position as a divinity of the woodlands who, when caught, may reveal his wisdom. In this he displays the true extent of his paradoxical and ambivalent nature—a being who, though as inventor of the vintner's art was continually drunk, could nonetheless be coerced to disclose secrets and offer wise counsel[11]—simultaneously wild and controlled, stupid and intelligent, thoughtless and thoughtful. As early as 1875–77, when Mannhardt published his Wald- und Feldkulte, the connection between this kind of being and the wild men of Germanic and Russian folklore (see Chap. 1) was addressed, and the curious ambivalence of these creatures discussed on a comparative level. Thus, the general connection with a larger class of ambivalent wild men may be seen in the fact that the Satyrs, Silens, and Centaurs are themselves all known for their hairiness, their outrageous sexual behavior, and the belief that they come out of their woodland habitats during certain transitional times of the year, often bringing with them profound truths and secret knowledge.

The problem with ascertaining a possible Indo-European element in the Satyr is that anthropomorphism frequently invites all manner of lending and borrowing in the name of exaggeration, as in the hybrid monsters of Mesopotamia or Egypt. More importantly, if we attempt to reduce the Satyr mask iconography to a list of essential features, they may be so general as to be of no analytical consequence; indeed, the success of this kind of mask is often achieved by only the subtlest indication of a bestial and not a human form. Iconographically, such features as pointed ears or horns are shared by a great many animals, and it is frequently impossible to establish relationships or derivations on these grounds alone.[12] After the fourth century B.C., Satyrs are often shown with goatlike horns, and the Centaurs, too, are sometimes shown with horns, or with ears so elongated as to appear hornlike (see Pl. 20), even though, as the Centaur is a combination of man and horse, no horns ought rightly to appear on it.[13]

It would be unwise, therefore, to make very much of iconographical similarities between certain representations of Satyrs and creatures from

Plate 19. Comic impersonators. Attic red-figure chous, ca. 410–400 B.C. Leningrad, Hermitage Museum.

beyond Greece that share only their bestial, and sometimes horned, attributes. When we consider the Satyrs in their mythological character, however, and as representations of specific animals, we are able to make more assured comparative generalizations. That the Satyrs can be connected, through the impersonation of goats and horses, with seasonal performances, and that they, like Centaurs, have a distinctly equine aspect, are two facts that together connect Satyrs intimately with European folk culture and Indo-European tradition. That the Greek Satyr and its mythology have specific Indo-European correlates seems most likely not only when we consider Indo-European equine symbolism, but also from the simple fact that the horse was not known in Mediterranean countries much before the second millennium B.C.

Though during classical times the Satyrs were said to be goat-men, as we move back into the sixth and seventh centuries B.C., we see that wild men were once conceived of as equine in nature—either as a complete man attached to a horse's front (pls. 21 and 25; see also plates in Dunbabin 1957), or as a man's upper body attached to the shoulders of an otherwise complete horse (Pl. 30). Often, in other words, these animals were depicted as men standing on horses' legs, sometimes without the elongated horse's body and hind legs; and though they are known from Mycenaean times, it is not until the sixth and, more commonly, the fifth

Plate 20. Chiron. Attic black-figure amphora, ca. 520 B.C. Drawing by
K. Reichhold. Furtwängler and Reichhold 1900–1932, 3: Fig. 112.

century B.C. that the full-horse type of Centaur, with which we are most
familiar, takes form. It is not difficult, therefore, to see how these horsemen (Centaurs) and goat-men (Satyrs and Silens) form a single class
of anthropomorphic beings. One of the earliest representations of the
Perseus-Gorgon story from Boeotia may be seen as part of this anthropomorphic group. Here, the Gorgon is also depicted as a Centaur (Pl. 22),
which can only mean either that the Centaur played a very significant
mythological role to which the Perseus-Gorgon story was adapted, or
else that there possibly existed some similar or related legend in which a
Centaur was decapitated. According to Boardman,

> The attachment of a horse's body recalls one of the basic features of the
> Greek Gorgon, and Medusa especially as mother of the winged horse
> Pegasos and consort of Poseidon. (Boardman 1968, 28)

Plate 21. Etruscan Centaur. Early Archaic period, ca. 590 B.C. The monstrous Centaur here clearly illustrates its hybrid form—half man, half horse. The *kouros*-like shape of the human figure resembles the earliest form of Greek figure sculpture. Rome, Museo di Villa Giulia.

Plate 22. Perseus slaying Medusa. Detail of a Boeotian relief-decorated amphora, early 7th c. B.C. The Medusa's depiction here as a Centaur indicates a significant variation from her legend as it is generally known. Paris, Louvre CA795. (Photo: Musées Nationaux.)

Burkert also notes the relation of horse and Gorgon in conjunction with the horse-headed, or "Black," Demeter, saying that the Gorgon mother of Pegasus is "just another variant" of the myth, which recurs in Vedic India, of an equine figure who mates with an "infuriated, wrathful mother" (Burkert 1979, 127). Moreover, other recent studies (O'Flaherty 1971; Puhvel 1970) have pointed to several mythological analogies between European and Vedic Indian equine themes. The likelihood, therefore, that this Gorgon-Centaur represents a lost myth that was at one time well known increases significantly in light of other similar icons wherein Gorgons and horses are conflated (Pl. 23).

Plate 23. Gorgon-horse with lion. Cornelian scarab, Greek, mid-6th c. B.C. Courtesy John Boardman. Oxford, Ashmolean Museum.

Indo-European Elements in the Satyrs and Centaurs of Ancient Greece

Though George Dumézil's effort to equate the name Κένταυρος with the Indian Gandharva (the name of a celestial attendant of Indra) and its Iranian equivalent (Dumézil 1929) has not met with unanimous approval, and though Dumézil himself later expressed reservations about the idea, his contribution to connecting the Satyrs and Centaurs and the seasonal festivals of central Europe cannot be overlooked (note Pl. 24). The simple fact that the complexity of the Greek material and of its development prevents us from making absolute correspondences between certain Indo-European figures does not mean that a general cultural and mythological connection is not feasible; one would expect that any important mythological creature would have a broad and richly diversified history. From Frazer and Tylor to the Cambridge anthropologists such as Cornford, Harrison, and Murray, and from recent classical folklorists such as Meuli to Indo-Europeanists such as Dumézil, scholars have repeatedly affirmed the similarities between Centaurs and the wild men of European folk tradition. The analogy has been based upon four or five major points and focuses primarily on the interaction of and differences between natural and cultural proclivities during transitional states.

The first and one of the most important of these points of comparison concerns the role played by the masked impersonators of Centaurs and wild men in calendric transitions. Throughout the Greek and European world, the belief is held even to the present day that wild half-human beings (see Chap. 1) appear during the Twelve Days of Christmas, the Carnival preceding Lent, or in general at festivals marking the change of seasons. Like the modern-day wild men of European folklore, the Centaurs were portrayed as sub-human hairy beasts who used a branch or other such primitive truncheon as a weapon (Pl. 25); like the Dionysian Satyrs, they tended especially to be imagined as present during rituals and celebrations marking the change of seasons (Lawson 1910, 223ff.), when, it was supposed, they endeavored to fulfill their lascivious desires. The fertility of the land thus came to be equated with human fertility in the context of a seasonal interlude when rules and prohibitions were reversed or done away with completely.

Anyone who has attended a *Fasnacht* or Shrovetide carnival can easily imagine how it has come to pass that wild men, Satyrs, and Centaurs are associated with legends of drunken abandon. They dance from dusk until dawn. In some cases, they may require the humans whom they capture at crossroads, or under other inauspicious circumstances,

Plate 24. Yugoslavian carnival figures. Such personages suggest the survival of equine imagery of a distinctly Indo-European character and of padded goatmen who call to mind the Satyrs of ancient Greece. Courtesy Ethnographic Museum, Zagreb.

Plate 25. Centaurs bearing branches. Corinthian skyphos, ca. 580 B.C. Centaurs are depicted running from Heracles, who is portrayed on the reverse side. The bodies of the hairy figures appear almost independent of the horses to which they are attached. Paris, Louvre L173.

to dance continuously until exhausted or, in some legends, until dead. But the wild dancing also plays a clearly structural role in its own right, for in dancing the idea is repeatedly emphasized that transition and change are based upon some ecstatic, frenzied, and unusual movement (see Chap. 1 on saltation) in which appearances are undermined by disguise and sudden shifts, and in which loud, percussive sounds mark literally every step of the process.[14] Thus, as Dumézil has pointed out, change is emphasized by the role reversals the human participants engage in while wearing the disguises of half-human creatures. Even today, throughout Germanic Europe and Greece, people put on masks made of goatskin or the hide of a wild animal, act unruly, and beat the percussive instruments that, as Needham has shown, are a hallmark of transitional and revivificatory states (Pl. 26). That this cycle of revivification is of foremost importance to the structure of culture is emphasized repeatedly when seasonal plays are performed in which someone or something— often a horse—dies and is brought to life again. Even the visual impression of half-human beings can epitomize, especially in the case of Centaurs, something in the midst of change—transfixed, as it were, in the act of a human becoming an animal or an animal a human.

Though the etymologies of terms such as "Satyr" and "Centaur" are unknown or in any case very obscure, there are other good comparative grounds for seeing in the concepts an archetypal Indo-European character. That such an anomalous combination of human and animal may be connected with other well-known and important Indo-European ideas becomes apparent as we look further into the background of this peculiar equine form that the Greeks themselves believed to have come from Thessaly in the north. To the extent that the horse is known to have been the most important of sacrificial animals among the Indo-Europeans, it is pertinent to ask to what extent the Centaurs' and Satyrs' origin might be construed as ritual and sacrificial.

In this regard, one thinks of the long-popular idea that animals, and especially goats, were offered to Dionysus in the place of the actually more appropriate human offering (cf. Ridgeway's excursus on the goat sacrifice [1910, 79ff.]).[15] The followers of Dionysus in their ritual frenzy were said to rend apart living animals, and while the Centaurs may not always be described as carnivores—though Apollodorus, for example, does speak of the Centaur Pholus as eating raw meat (*The Library* 2.5.4)— or even as cannibals, they at least are said to be violently aggressive—giving, as all wild men do, a good thrashing to any poor humans who happen upon them. Thus, on the surface at least, the popular notion of these creatures is based upon the destruction that they usually engage in during some ritual or transitional period; here, sacrifice and savagery are structurally equatable.

This ritual and sacrificial element becomes especially obvious when we examine myths of how Centaurs were created and compare these legends with Indo-European themes involving sacrificial horses. Greek legend explains the Centaur's origin primarily by two stories. According to one version, Ixion, king of the Lapithae, purified by Zeus after he had murdered his own father-in-law, was not only absolved but was even invited to dine with the gods; at the feast he took a liking for Hera, Zeus's wife. Ixion's intention to seduce Hera was perceived by Zeus, who formed a cloud-phantom (Nephele) in Hera's image. It was from Ixion's union with this cloud that the Centaurs were created.[16] Later, the Centaurs attended the wedding of another Lapith king, Pirithous of Thessaly; their attempt to rape the women present is one of the few examples of their playing a major role in a specific legend. According to the other popular origin myth—both of these myths are generally thought to be accretions—Centaurus, the son of Ixion and Nephele, sired the Centaurs upon the mares of Thessaly, so that in this second case they result directly from the unnatural union with beasts.

While this unbridled passion (as it were) between human and beast readily explains why the Centaur assumed its unusual shape, the transformation of Kronos into a stallion and his fathering of the Centaur Chiron offers an additional mythological explanation. It is well known that the basic idea of a union between humans and horses also forms the substance of a very important Indo-European rite, the Indic *aśvamedha* (see P. Dumont 1927). Puhvel, in an article on Indo-European equine mythology, describes a Celtic tradition that involved the ritual mating of mares and kings (1970, 167) and compares it specifically to the aforementioned Indic sacrificial rite. Puhvel explains (ibid., 160ff.) the most salient features of the rite as a sequence of quite involved rituals beginning with the springtime purification of the king and of a sacrificial stallion one year before the sacrifice. During the intervening months the stallion ran free but was kept from contact with mares and from immersion in water. He was accompanied by geldings or aged horses and by several attendants. After a year of preparation by various rituals, a fire-altar was erected, the king underwent another purificatory rite, and then the three-day ritual began. On the second day of this ritual, which involved the replenishing of the sacred *soma*, the drink of immortality, the king rode in a war chariot pulled by the sacrificial stallion. The stallion was anointed by the king's main wives and was sacrificed by smothering; the two other principal victims were a hornless ram and a he-goat. The king's

Plate 26. a, Carnival figure, Skyros.
Ridgeway 1910, Figure 8.

Plates 26b–d. Carnival figures, Yugoslavia. Courtesy Ethnographic Museum, Zagreb. These illustrations provide excellent examples of the typical costume of transformation: a mask or headdress of a goat or of another domestic animal, a padded costume, and a garland of bells that provide the percussive sounds so essential to the change from one temporal category to the next.

main wife was then confined with the sacrifice, which in this case represented the king himself, while the entourage engaged in raillery. Their cohabitation symbolically marked the fertile revivificatory nature of the rite. According to the Vedic hymns, the equine cohabitation, the role of goats, and the obscene banter were all necessary aspects of the *aśvamedha;* these activities, of course, parallel those in which the Satyrs and Centaurs were, in legend or in ritual, meant to participate.[17] Moreover, that the *aśvamedha* was no minor ritual is clear not only from its elaborate preparations, but also from what we know of the horse sacrifice in general in Indo-European cultures[18]—from the Celtic tradition, to the elaborate Scythian burials (where, almost as a reversal of the *aśvamedha*, the dead king was carried out on a cart pulled by sacrificial horses and slaves), to the ancient Indic *aśvamedha* itself. That the Satyr-like conflation of human and animal played, in addition, an important part in Indian myth and art from the earliest times may be seen in the uncanny, not to say stunning, similarity between the archetypal Satyr-masks from ancient Greece and one of the most memorable small clay masks (Pl. 27) found in excavations of the Indus Valley civilization (ca. 2500–1500 B.C.). Here we have not only a very carefully modeled human head with horns, but the goatlike beard as well, which is the standard of the Greek Satyr mask and the half-human creature to which it is meant to give life.

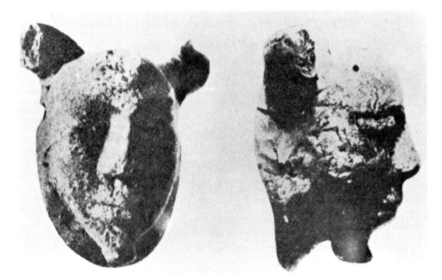

Plate 27. Pottery mask with horns. Though less than three inches long, this mask from Mohenjodaro, Indus Valley civilization (ca. 2500–1500 B.C.), presents a very convincing representation of a human face with a goat's beard and horns. Mackay 1937, Pl. 74, nos. 25–26.

These anthropomorphic similarities—between humans and goats, and humans and horses—are notable because they provide evidence for correspondences that seem particularly Indo-European. As a generalization, this conclusion would appear especially plausible if we add to what has already been said about these ambivalent half-humans our knowledge that metempsychosis, as West points out (1971, 61), is a doctrine shared by Indians and certain Greeks. Metempsychosis, though perhaps not a widespread notion among Greeks, was certainly an Orphic and Pythagorean tenet; its emphasis on the genuine transformation of humans into animals in natural and supernatural life cycles underlies both the ritual sense of bestial cohabitation and the sacred nature of cyclical revivification. Thus, the nature of each person's transmigration, the character of one's future identity, is inseparable from ritual identity, since every individual embodies an ambivalence overcome only by appropriate ritual acts. The success or failure of ritual, finally, provides every reason for one's present state.

Centaurs and Heracles

The early date at which the Satyrs and Centaurs appear in Greek mythology and art and the fact that they are common background figures in various legends suggest that by the eighth and seventh centuries B.C. they already enjoyed an old and broad-based popularity in Indo-European folk traditions.[19] By now, their appearance as an important iconographic form has been shown to have corresponded also with their continued occurrence in conjunction with transitional rituals. The question that remains to be answered is how, and to what degree, notions of transformation and change are emphasized in the myths in which Centaurs play a notable role.

An examination of these myths reveals that such notions appear repeatedly. One of the myths—the assault on the Lapith women at the wedding of Pirithous—has already been mentioned. Eurytion, the Centaur who was said to have been the chief offender at the feast, was later killed by Heracles for trying to rape the daughter of another king. This incident, though a minor one in the travels of Heracles, again repeats the typical themes for which the Centaurs were well known. Of Heracles' other meetings with Centaurs, at least one involves saving a woman from sexual assault. This is the famous story of the Centaur Nessus, who was eventually the cause of Heracles' own death.

According to the tale, Nessus was a Centaur who ferried travelers across the river Euenus, a function that was his exclusively. One day, when Heracles came to cross with his wife, Deianira, Nessus attempted to rape her but was killed by Heracles before he committed the deed. Nessus, however, took his revenge before he died by giving a vial of his blood to Deianira, telling her to use it as a love potion. Later, when Heracles' love for her appeared to be waning, Deianira, in order to re-store his interest in her, sent him a robe smeared with this blood. Instead of reawakening Heracles' desire, the robe caused him to burn with a slow agony that eventually resulted in his death—his transformation, that is, from a mortal to an immortal state.[20]

Though Heracles never appears as the wearer of a facial mask, when he bends over as a hunter, as he clearly does in many representations, the lion's skin that covers his own, and from whose mouth his own head protrudes, indeed becomes a mask of the most powerful sort (Pl. 28). In fact, our knowledge of him as an obvious—not to say disingenuous—impersonator makes his connection with the Centaur Nessus especially interesting and consequential for the interpretation of masks, for, nota-bly, Heracles puts on a second skin to pursue his exploits, yet it is an-other sort of second skin—one that he cannot remove—that causes his death. Because Heracles remains clearly untransformed by wearing the skin of the Nemean lion, one might say that Heracles the hunter pre-figures those who wear masks as deceitful disguises. In this case his con-flict with Nessus may be interpreted as a confrontation between two antithetical sorts of masks—the former that of a unique individual per-forming a social role, the latter that of a metempsychotic transformer. Because, moreover, the "skin" that accounts for Heracles' release into the world of the immortals is imposed upon him by a Centaur, it is useful to inquire whether Heracles resembles, as the Centaurs do, any foreign fig-ures or themes.

Heracles has with some success been described by Dumézil (1970b, 96ff.) as an Indo-European warrior figure, but his extensive development as the most popular of Greek heroes has made specific correlations with other figures quite difficult. On the one hand, examples of his most fa-mous posture as the slayer of the Centaur Nessus (pls. 29 and 30) uncan-nily resemble the representations common down to Roman Imperial times of the slaying of the cosmic bull by the Indo-Iranian and -European Mitra (Roman Mithras; Pl. 31). Mitra is a very ancient figure and the pri-mary god of the Vedic pantheon; he is, as Dumézil has shown at length, the embodiment of contract and the sharer of divine sovereignty with Varuṇa.[21] Certain practices of the Roman Mithraic cults, such as incuba-tion in an underworld cave and initiation by a series of stages or trials,

Plate 28. Heracles and Cerberus. Attic red-figure belly amphora by the Andokides Painter, ca. 520–510 B.C. As Heracles, in the last of his twelve labors, stoops toward Cerberus, the head of the Nemean lion becomes his mask while its impenetrable skin covers his body. Paris, Louvre F204. (Photo: Musées Nationaux.)

also parallel the structural focus of Heraclean legend. Heracles is trained by the Centaur Chiron, whose home is a mountain cave, and the completion of his trials, which leads to his joining the gods, is an exemplary initiation. The warrior function, so important to the legend of Heracles (Dumézil 1970b), is honored, too, by the Mithraic disciples. As god of light and of the sun, Mithras is represented by the solar disc, in which is symbolized his role as vanquisher of the demons of darkness. In addition, both Heracles and Mithras begin as humans and only later obtain divinity. Both, in a sense, die and do not die.

The most concrete reference to an Indo-European people in the mythology of Heracles, and, hence, the best proof that the Greeks knew

Plate 29. Heracles slaying the Centaur Nessus. Spartan ivory relief, ca. 670–660 B.C. Heracles is shown exacting the revenge for Nessus's assault on Deianira. The blood of Nessus, given to Deianira before the Centaur dies, will later cause the hero's death. Athens, National Archaeological Museum.

Plate 30. *Neck,* Heracles slaying Nessus. *Body,* Gorgons pursuing Perseus. Attic black-figure neck amphora by the Nessus Painter, ca. 610 B.C. Heracles appears in the pose in which he is commonly depicted killing Nessus. Below are shown two running Gorgons; the Medusa is shown headless on the left. Athens, National Archaeological Museum, no. 1002.

Plate 31. Mithras slaying the cosmic bull. The flourishing of the cult of Mithras during Roman Imperial times resulted in the many examples of the Indo-Iranian god depicted in this pose. Marble bas-relief, Bologna. (Photo: Museo Civico Archeologico di Bologna.)

something of the Scythians, comes from the genealogy given by Herodotus (4.9f.). According to his story, Heracles traveled to the land of the Scythians; there, while he slept, his mares went astray. He found them in the care of a viper-maiden who bore him three sons. To the third son, Scythes, is attributed the name of the Scythians, and he was said to have fathered the line of Scythian kings. This legend may be taken to indicate that certain Greeks probably had at least a vague factual knowledge of Scythian religion, since it seems that the Scythians did indeed honor such a maiden (Pl. 32).

In other respects, however, Heraclean legend is so distinctly Greek that specific analogies with foreign ideas can seem contrived, as often do the attempts of the Greeks themselves to establish foreign connections for their heroes. This problem, though, should not detract from the possibility that many elements of his legend, such as the role of the

Centaurs, have correspondences in a shared Indo-European past, even though it does caution us against drawing any strict analogies that would imply that he was anything but wholly Greek. It is clear, in any case, that Heracles is deeply embedded in the mythology and imagination of the Greeks, and one must recognize that the details of his persona evolved according to the demands of the Greeks and their changing conception of themselves. The fate of Heracles, therefore, seems to combine an attention to Indo-European warrior themes (Dumézil 1970b) with a mythology that is peculiarly Greek.

Lastly, it is Heracles' uneasy alliance with the gods that makes his case so difficult to understand. He is alternately favored and harassed by the greatest of heavenly beings. Though as a warrior he is usually shown as exceedingly powerful, he suffers from persecution because he is unluckily born of the intrigues of Zeus. More problematically, the Greek legend does not altogether accord with its presumptive Indo-European character. Hera, wife of Zeus and heavenly queen—who, as we have seen, is involved in the origin myth of the Centaurs—continually plagues Heracles ("renowned through Hera") because he is the offspring of Zeus's union with Alcmene, granddaughter of Perseus. When Zeus announced

Plate 32. a, Scythian gold bridal decorations. Frontlet plate and cheek pieces from Great Tsimbalka, 4th c. B.C. b, Gold embossed plaque from Kul Oba, 4th c. B.C. Both illustrate a serpent goddess. The figure in b holds a sword and a severed head in a heraldic pose.

to the gods that a descendant of Perseus would rule over all the Perseidae, Hera in her jealousy hastened the birth of the mediocre Eurystheus, son of Sthenelus of Mycenae, who was also a descendant of Perseus. It was Eurystheus who, as king of Tiryns and Mycenae, imposed the famous twelve tasks upon Heracles. The problem here is twofold. First, we see that Heracles is intimately tied to almost everything that is important in early Greek kingship: he was not, as some say Dionysus was, a foreigner (at least not by this genealogy). Second, even though, for example, Heracles was instructed in the sciences, or, more correctly, initiated into the knowledge of them, by the Centaur Chiron—whose abode was in Thessaly—his twelve labors persistently involved him in routing rather than worshiping or sacrificing anthropomorphic creatures. Among these creatures we find not only dangerous and wild ones, but also the friendly Centaur Pholus, who killed himself by dropping one of Heracles' arrows on his foot, and Chiron, the hero's teacher, who was accidentally shot by Heracles and relinquished his immortality to be relieved of the pain. The fact that their deaths were accidents emphasizes the irresponsibility of the gruff Heracles, who, in a moment of rage, was even capable of slaughtering wholesale his own children.

Like all warriors, however, Heracles found his tasks thrust upon him without regard to his own wishes, and this bearing of the burden of duty must account for his heroic popularity. Interestingly, his carrying out this social duty also accounts for the mask he wears almost continually throughout his exploits. This mask is the skin of the Nemean lion that Heracles was charged to kill, whose horrific face thereafter rested on the head of the hero. In the following chapter I will discuss in more detail the role of the lion in the iconography of Greek masks, especially with reference to the Gorgon, which corresponds mythologically with the Centaurs and with Heracles in several particulars.[22] It is important here, however, to remember that in the mask of the warlike lion, Heracles takes on the social role that opposes him, as the slayer of Centaurs and router of the followers of Dionysus, to that mask responsible for a true transformation. He is a hunter, and as such relies upon the duplicity of his disguise. Whether he timidly or aggressively wears the lionskin (Pl. 28), or whether he hides his aggressiveness in a meek disguise, his effectiveness depends on that duplicity. As Canetti has pointed out,

> Any hunter has control over himself and his weapon. But a masked hunter also controls the figure of the animal he represents; he has power over both which he exercises continuously. He is, as it were, two creatures simultaneously and keeps a firm hold on both until he has achieved his purpose. The flux of transformations of which he is ca-

pable is arrested; he stands on two sharply circumscribed sites, the one *within* the other. (Canetti 1978, 370–71)

Incapable until death of true transformation, Heracles is forced to maintain the duality marking him as the most popular Greek mythological personage and a true tragic hero: a proud warrior who is also a wanton destroyer and glutton, persecuted to the point of madness, tormented but truly a tormentor—a raging warrior whose internal conflict marks him as the archetype of the dualistic individual (see also Burkert 1979, 120). In Heracles we see the most compelling example of a social mask that cannot be trusted but which, nonetheless, must be worn.

Centaurs, Ambivalence, and Curing

Legendary though the conflict between Heracles and Nessus may be, a more significant exception to the noted absence of Centaurs and Satyrs in Greek mythology is the important presence of the Centaur Chiron (Pl. 20).[23] He not only was depicted as wise and just—a marked contrast to the usual lasciviousness of the Centaurs—but was also well known as the teacher of many famous Greek figures. As well as being the tutor of Heracles, Achilles, Jason, Actaeon, Castor, and Pollux, he was also the instructor of Asclepius in the arts of healing. Pindar and Sophocles (among others) refer to Chiron's role in teaching Asclepius, "the hero who warded sickness of every kind" (Pindar, *Pythian* 3.7). Asclepius, the god of medicine and therefore its traditional father, was sent to Chiron by Apollo—also a capable healer—after the child's mother died. Asclepius embarked thereafter on a career that at times proved him a perceptive curer of mental disorders,[24] while at others showed him so strong at curing physical ailments that he was ultimately killed by the thunderbolt of Zeus, who feared that in raising the dead to life Asclepius would free the human race from the bonds of death.

The curing attributes of the Centaurs have been used by Dumézil as evidence for their Indo-European and particularly shamanic character. Laín Entralgo has written that

> it is not hard to find shaman-like traits mixed in at times with "oriental" elements in a goodly number of Greek figures, institutions, and legends . . . such as that concerning the Centaurs. (Laín Entralgo 1970, 75)

In describing Pythagoras as a "Greek shaman" because of his belief in the primary importance of apotropaic treatments for the "expulsion of disturbing daimôn" and of cathartic treatments for the restoration of the patient to a state of initial purity (ibid., 76–77), Laín Entralgo suggests (ibid., 74)—as Dodds, Eliade, and Burkert, for example, also do—that the Greek contact with Thrace and the Black Sea no doubt introduced the Greeks to shamanic practices, and perhaps even brought shamanism in some form into Greek culture itself.

To such a list of authorities we could add many other names, including those of some ancient Greeks, who maintain a belief in the particular connection between the sources of apotropaic or cathartic cures and the Eastern origins of gods such as Dionysus, or to his companions, the Satyrs and Centaurs. Kerényi, for example, thought that there might be some special relationship between Asclepius and Dionysus deriving from a more general connection between the physician's chthonic and warriorlike role as a hero and vanquisher of diseases and the Dionysian symbols of death, regeneration, and recovery that are the essence of his seasonal sacrifice. Kerényi thought that this relationship was reflected both in how close some curing centers were to Dionysian theaters (e.g., at Athens) and in how close the tombs of several hero-physicians (*hērōes iatroi*) were to Dionysian sanctuaries (Kerényi 1959, 70ff.).

But whether or not the cults of Asclepius or of Dionysus and his Satyrs had anything to do with foreign influences, the important point in the transformation of the mask's role is that the Greeks regarded these influences as genuinely foreign. As a result of this attitude, there arises as we proceed through antiquity quite a controversy between skeptics and adherents as to whether cathartic healing actually worked. From the sixth to the fourth centuries B.C., the frequent warnings against the mystery religions came both from the stage, as would be expected of comedy, and from the philosophers of the day, as in the criticisms of Heraclitus (e.g., frr. 5, 14, and 15).[25] One interpretation of this suspicious attitude toward the efficacy of cathartic cures might therefore be that the ludicrous and comic role of the Satyrs in Greek art became increasingly emphasized in conjunction with the rise of classical civilization and its political and social institutions—that it was natural in this context to place the ecstatic proclivities of the Satyrs and Centaurs in some unfavorable light. One might equally argue that the radical rejection of things non-Greek—and what could be more barbarous than an unruly Satyr?—was part of a growing sense of Greek national identity and of the tyrannical manipulation of festival performances and their highly political focus.[26]

Cogent though these lines of reasoning may seem, they cannot provide a totally convincing historical picture. The cathartic treatment of illnesses, for example, continued to evolve in a shamanic fashion even in the midst of advancements in Greek scientific knowledge, the popularity of cathartic curing centers for a time growing in tandem with Greek skeptical thought.[27] Even at the Asclepieion at Pergamum, the zenith of institutionalized cathartic therapy,[28] we find, in contrast to the growing body of received medical ideas, a structure for curing that preserves the primary symbols of the ancient curers' myths.[29] Nor, more importantly, can Greek political or social history provide us with any adequate idea of what it was in the Greek mind that made the Satyrs, Silens, and Centaurs so important to the Greek popular imagination and so much a part of the beginnings of drama. Here we must realize how much the skeptical tradition influenced not only later Greek thinking but the analytical tradition we inevitably resort to in the study of the preclassical. To trust in the efficacy of cathartic sentiment is to understand that the spirits who are the real transformers respond to active performance and demonstration more positively than to supposed, internalized beliefs. Ecstatic rites by definition rely on maximal sensory experience,[30] so that treating them at a skeptical distance cannot diminish the importance of their participatory demands. In short, one cannot deny ecstatic worshipers their belief that such rites are the most appropriate way of averting disasters in a world motivated by a plethora of spirits, gods, and natural forces capable of individual volition and ever present in a potentially infinite number of forms.

The key to understanding the performative character of preclassical ritual—that is, its relation both to Greek attitudes toward catharsis and to later theatrical convention—is, again, ambivalence. Ambivalence is a fundamental condition and not a mere curiosity of the Satyrs and Centaurs. It accounts for the ability of the Centaurs to provide wise counsel—Chiron is the supreme example, although wisdom was a common attribute of the Silens—even while they themselves, at the same time, treat wisdom with complete disregard. It is crucial in the earliest forms of Greek drama, because the ambivalent behavior of the Satyrs themselves became the currency of both tragedy and comedy. Finally, ambivalence is not only Satyric but also shamanic; there are many remarkable genealogical or typological connections between the masks and social roles of the Satyrs and Centaurs and circumstances emphasizing a curative power that is ambivalent. On a genealogical level, this ambivalence is epitomized in the parallel themes of killing and curing and of the curers who were originally, as were the sons of Hippocrates, members of the same family, wherein the healing arts were handed down, in true shamanic fashion, from father to son. Curing is an inherited property whose secrets are affirmed in the Hippocratic oath; likewise, warriors, who, too, are experts in the knowledge of wounds, may be versed in the curing arts, a wisdom both lethal and beneficial. Machaon, the son of Asclepius and the first surgeon, was a *hērōs iatros* who, like Heracles, died and did not die, whose warlike name reminds us that "wounding and being wounded are the dark premises of healing" (Kerényi 1959, 76).[31] Chiron, who was wise enough to teach the children of the gods, taught his wisdom to healers and warriors alike, but in the end traded his own immortality for relief from the pain of a warrior's arrow. Even the absoluteness of immortality is something the master of ambivalence and the healing arts can deny. Nothing is beyond the one who controls the mask, who cures illnesses and vanquishes enemies as the purveyor of the ambivalence that is the essence of cartharsis and of ecstasy—not even the ultimate choice of Chiron, who finally even succeeded in curing himself of being eternal.

· 4 ·

Perseus and the Gorgon Head

The Medusa's Story

If the Satyrs epitomize the lesser daimons populating Greek mythology, then the Gorgon Medusa surely represents for the Greeks the archetypal apotropaic beast. Like the Satyr mask that displays the primordial essence of an ambivalence combining human and beast, the masks of the grotesque Gorgon—as the examples from Sparta and Tiryns clearly show (pls. 9b, 9c, and 34)—exhibit an ancient and fundamental Greek idea. The Gorgon's facial features are significant not only on a psychological level; historically, they derive from one of the oldest and most important examples of an ancient tale surviving in classical mythology. This tale is that of the hero Perseus, who slew a monster and used its visage to vanquish both his own enemies and those of the Greek people.

It is impossible to determine the precise age of the Perseus-Gorgon story. Though Perseus may have, as Nilsson argues,[1] several Mycenaean correlates, we can safely say that the legend we are familiar with was well known at least by the seventh century B.C.[2] Indeed, the traditional story of Perseus and the Gorgon sisters was complete already at the time of Hesiod (*Theogony* 270ff.), whose dates are unknown but who may have lived as early as the eighth century B.C. Homer, too, mentions the Gorgoneion, the fearful face (*Iliad* 5.741; 8.349; 11.36; *Odyssey* 11.634), often enough that there is reason to suppose that the legend about the head being taken was familiar to his audience. There is no certain evidence, however, that the Perseus-Gorgon story goes back to Mycenaean times, although the hero's name is found in Linear B inscriptions. Thus, the question remains unanswered as to whether the legend is exclusively Greek, whether it, for example, came into Greece as the result of the Thraco-

Plate 33. Perseus with the Medusa head. Attic red-figure pelike by the Pan Painter, after 480 B.C. Munich, Staatliche Antikensammlungen und Glyptothek, no. 8725.

Phrygian invasion of Asia Minor (ca. 1200 B.C.) and of the general flow of
Indo-European culture into the Mediterranean, or whether the story
arose in Greece sometime in the beginning of the first millennium B.C.
Artistic evidence points to the legend's presence in the middle of the seventh century B.C.; and if we also take horrific Gorgon-like faces, such as
those from Tiryns (Pl. 34), as evidence, we might push this date back to
the eighth century.[3] As, however, the situation becomes very uncertain if
we seek confirmation for the myth's existence in an earlier era, we need
not look beyond the eighth and seventh centuries B.C., the time that the
literary records and the first artistic representations of the Gorgon cer-
tify her place in Greek culture. Thalia Howe notes that Perseus-Gorgon
tales do not appear with any frequency before the second half of the seventh century B.C., at which time the episode "suddenly begins to appear
everywhere" (Howe 1952, 81). This era, therefore, is where any discussion of the Gorgon and her masks should begin.

     According to the most common version of the story, which corre-
sponds to information given by Hesiod, Perseus was the son of Zeus and
Danaë. Danaë's father, Acrisius of Argos, confined Danaë in a brazen
tower because an oracle had warned him that he would be killed by his
grandson. But Zeus entered the chamber as a shower of gold that landed
on the lap of Danaë and sired Perseus. Upon discovering that his daughter had given birth to a son, Acrisius had Danaë and Perseus put in a
coffer and set adrift on the open sea.[4] As one might expect, this part of
the story has been given a variety of interpretations—in part because
Perseus was confined with his own mother, but also because historically
people were thus cast adrift in widely varying circumstances. Indeed,
this practice was known to Greeks as a means of ridding themselves of
unwanted relatives and children. The act could also have been recognized, however, as a means of disposing of the dead. And there are more
obscure uses: the Etruscans, for example, are said to have employed it as
a way of banishing hermaphrodites. The journey of the oceanic coffer offers us the image of a rite of passage complete with liminal sexual, social, and metaphysical categories—in the transmigrational death that
leads to another life, and in the rite of passage that results in the transference of kingship. In this last case, the Gorgon's death and the hero's
use of her visage—her mask—lead directly to the fulfillment of the
oracle's prophecy and the ascension of Perseus to the throne.

     The first stage in this transition ends when Perseus and Danaë ar-
rived at the island of Seriphus, where the coffer was brought to shore in
the net of the honest fisherman Dictys. Polydectes, who was the brother
of Dictys and king of the island,[5] developed a passion for Danaë and en-

Plate 34. Gorgonesque helmets from Tiryns. Late 8th or early 7th c. B.C. These masks represent what are probably the earliest known examples of the Gorgon type. They have been compared to the grotesque masks or mask molds of Artemis Orthia (pls. 9–12) and were, like them, probably connected to a masked performance in honor of a Gorgon-masked goddess. Athens, Deutsches Archäologisches Institut, neg. nos. 1051, 1388, 1369.

deavored to rid himself of Perseus, who was by then a young man and protective of his mother. During a banquet, Perseus was tricked into agreeing that he would grant the king anything, including the head of the dreaded Medusa ("queen"), the only one of the three Gorgon sisters who was mortal.[6] Perseus was held to his word and soon embarked upon his quest, which he accomplished with the assistance of Athena and Hermes. Athena helped Perseus force the Graiae ("old gray women"), who were sisters to the three Gorgons,[7] to divulge directions for reaching the nymphs. It was from the nymphs that Perseus obtained his magical implements, although in some versions the Graiae themselves, ensconced in the remotest parts of Libya, provided them. These tools included winged sandals for fleeing from the Gorgons, the helmet of invisibility that facilitated his retreat, and the wallet that enabled him to hide the Gorgon head and avoid its lethal stare. Perseus coerced the Graiae by stealing the one eye and tooth that they shared; these Hermes returned to them after Perseus had slain Medusa. Such a reliance upon magical accessories distinguishes Perseus from other Greek heroes, and it has often been suggested that this is evidence of an Eastern origin for his myth. Gilgamesh, the popular Near Eastern hero whose legend can be traced back to Sumerian mythology of the third millennium B.C., slew the monster Huwawa (Humbaba) in a tale resembling the story of Perseus and the Gorgon. Gilgamesh, moreover, along with other similar Mesopotamian figures, regularly used magic. Perseus's sickle, which he is often shown using to take the Gorgon's head despite his carrying a sword, had, likewise, a significance in Asia Minor (Ward 1910, 163, 211); in the case of Perseus, however, there may be a simpler, indigenous explanation, given the prominent roles played in his story by Athena and Hermes. Both these figures continually display their magical skills even if they do not offer the use of them to individuals directly (e.g., Athena puts on the helmet of Hades in order to become invisible and help Diomedes in *Iliad* 5.844–45).[8] It would also seem incorrect to maintain that apparent folk motifs, such as the presence of magical elements, should necessarily be indicators of high antiquity, as the revival of certain cults demonstrates that mythology does not always evolve away from magic, from the simple to the complex, or from the imagery of peasant societies to the overpopulated hierarchies of kings and gods. The assumption that such changes are always diachronic is clearly untenable. Nonetheless, one should note that the story of Perseus is richer in magical elements than the tales of other heroes, for in the least this is part of the complexity of detail and the richness of visual imagery permeating the entire episode.

After obtaining his magic implements, Perseus flew off fully equipped to the shores of Oceanus, where he found the Gorgon sisters asleep and proceeded to take the head of the mortal Medusa as she slumbered. She awakened only enough to utter her horrific shriek, from which an etymology for the word "Gorgon" has been derived. The Sanskrit correlate of the Greek *Gorgō* is generally agreed to be *garj* (जर्ज्),[9] meaning "to emit (a deep or full) sound," "sound as distant thunder," "roar," "thunder" itself, or "growl."[10] There are, in addition, many related words that build upon this radical, such as *garja*, meaning "(roaring) elephant," and *garjana*, "crying, roaring, rumbling (of clouds), growl, grunt, passion" (lexicographers); "battle" (lex.); "excessive indignation, reproach" (lex.).[11] These meanings are very important not only because they give us some grasp of the scope of the Sanskrit word, which is broader still than is here indicated, but also because, as we shall see, they offer an interesting guideline for the examination of related concepts in other cultures.

Although some artifacts show Medusa running headless, according to surviving legend only her two immortal sisters fully awakened and took up the pursuit of Perseus. The most significant feature of the taking of the head is that Perseus had to accomplish the act by looking at the Medusa's reflection in a mirror image on Athena's shield, for the Gorgon's glance turned all who beheld her into stone. The legitimacy of the Gorgon's face as a warrior's apotropaic device is thus affirmed, since it is the reflection in the shield of Athena the warrior that makes possible the taking of the head itself and since, in art and legend, it is also her shield that bears the head as its device—first warding off and then embodying the face's power. The difficulty of the heroic task is, thus, compounded by Perseus's need to avert his gaze, a difficulty emphasized in that Athena herself has to guide his arm for the fatal deed. On the one hand, the necessity of the goddess's help certifies the power of this archetypal apotropaic mask—so potent that even all the available magic cannot enable a hero to perform the act unassisted. More importantly, though, this necessity cements the cooperation of the goddess and hero forever, so that the act becomes a sacred one—as does each occasion of Perseus's removing the severed head from the magical wallet and holding it out before him. The apotropaic visage is, thus, god-given, and its use sanctioned by a sacred force.

Having taken the Medusa's head, Perseus thrust it into his wallet and, putting on the cap of invisibility, outwitted the two remaining sisters, who pursued him. Meanwhile from the Medusa's neck sprang her children, the giant Chrysaor and the horse Pegasus. Their legendary birth has led to a good deal of speculation about the relationship of the Perseus-Gorgon tale to other forms of ritual death in which the direct result is birth or revivification. The focusing of the myth on the head and face of the monster has resulted in some very interesting hypotheses (Croon 1955, for example) about the possible wearing of a Gorgon mask as the mask of an underworld daimon, and the probability that Perseus also originally had some connection with masks and with death rites, if not rites of fertility. That the Gorgon likely was ritually associated with death and revivification is also suggested by an iconographic association between Gorgons and the wrathful Mistress figures of Asia Minor, figures that blur the distinction between creator and destroyer by oddly combining regeneration and asexuality. The role of asexuality in, for example, the worship of Cybele[12] has its corollary in Greek mythology both in the loss of sexuality that leads to regeneration (e.g., *Theogony* 176ff.) and in the death that, in the Medusa's case, causes birth. Likewise, the fact that the Gorgon is frequently depicted as an androgyne and in the pose so often assumed by Near Eastern Mistress figures with known seasonal significance strengthens the argument for their symbolic association. But at the same time, we must be careful not to draw such analogies indiscriminately. Since to connect fertility with the cycle of death and rebirth or resurrection is probably the most widespread of all ritual associations, seeing too much in the Perseus-Gorgon story will reduce it to an almost meaningless generality.

Psychoanalytically, it was this curious detail—the taking of the head and the resulting birth of the giant and messenger horse—that prompted the interpretation of the myth by Ferenczi and Freud. According to them, the head represents, by the process of replacement, the female genitalia and in that capacity functions as a *vagina dentata*. In general, such an interpretation of apotropaic monsters may find support in the recurrent role of Gorgonesque demons (especially Near Eastern ones) as either the purveyors of bad birth or apotropaic protectors of birth.[13] In actual fact, however, the Freudian view offers a very incomplete interpretation of the specifics of the Perseus-Gorgon legend. The mirror- and mask-related details of the story and their possible effects on the self-image of Perseus offer more interesting interpretative prospects. It is not at all impossible that what Perseus actually sees in the shield is his own mirror image and that what the episode suggests, therefore, is his coming to terms with his complete self-image. To Croon's connection of the Gorgon with masking may, therefore, be added another interpretation based upon the role of Athena's shield as mirror. Likewise, the Gorgon's character and the imagery of avulsion and disjunction associated with it need not only have a single Freudian interpretation. The many androgynous representations of the monster suggest that its exaggerated expression is both masculine and feminine and, indeed, similar faces, abundantly utilized in Indian and Indonesian iconography, often incorporate an explicitly masculine symbolism. On the structural level, the confusion of a specific sexual orientation is precisely what is intended; it calls attention to sexuality as such and, thereby, enables it to be isolated. The combined processes of avulsion and petrifaction, therefore, as much permit the isolation and literal solidification of the Gorgoneion symbol as they present any single sexual idea. Such ambivalence does not mean that the Gorgon's sexuality should be deemphasized—for the monster is as much a sign of fertility as of death, as much a giver as a taker of life—but rather that, in order to be powerful, the image must itself embrace contradiction and that as a symbol it must stand alone, emphatic and archetypal, isolated and irreducible.

Of equal significance are the story's heroic aspects and their political consequences. Homer calls Perseus "preeminent among all men" (*Iliad* 14.320) as much because of Perseus's political activities after taking the head as because of the decapitation itself. Thus, while taking the Gorgon head is the central part of the Perseus-Gorgon story and the dominant artistic theme of the legend from the seventh century B.C. onwards, the story of Perseus and the Gorgon is by no means over once Perseus has made his escape. Unlike the trials of Heracles, drawn out as they were in a series of independent episodes, the life of Perseus, once he had slain the Gorgon, followed a series of dependent narrative events. The Gorgon head, that is, became a vehicle for rectifying past injustices and restoring a fair and equitable social balance; once in the hands of Perseus it became a positive force. Thus, after the Gorgon episode, Perseus returned to Seriphus by way of Ethiopia where, using his new powers, he rescued Andromeda from being sacrificed to the sea monster Cetus and married her. Back in Seriphus, he took revenge upon Polydectes by turning him and his entire entourage into stone. Having accomplished these feats with the Gorgon head, Perseus placed Dictys, the fisherman and honest brother of Polydectes, on the throne. This adjudication of kingship and of related fraternal disputes echoes the struggle of his grandfather Acrisius, who is said to have argued, even in his mother's womb, with his brother Proetus. It was left to Perseus to rearrange their split kingdom; this was the final matter of kingship he had to resolve before establishing his own permanent kingdom at Tiryns. Before doing so, however, he had yet to return his magical gifts—the Gorgon face, the ability to fly, and the power of invisibility—and complete the cycle of transition that would enable him to inherit his grandfather's throne.

With Hermes' aid, Perseus gave back the magical implements he borrowed from the Graiae. To Athena he offered the Gorgon head. According to different versions, she mounted it either on her breastplate or on her shield. Here we see the permanent establishment of the Gorgon as an apotropaic aegis—i.e., the ambivalent Gorgoneion, at once horrific and deadly, but at the same time capable, in the right hands or in the proper location, of meting out justice. It is Athena who symbolizes this power, uttering her war cry as she springs from the head of Zeus; it is she, as the patron of princes and warriors, who shields Athens from all danger. It is also Athena who has been characterized as theriomorphic, carrying the curiously Gorgonesque epithet γλαυκῶπις ("wide-" or "bright-eyed").

Perseus completes his kingly transition by returning with his wife and mother to Argos, traveling by way of Larissa in Thessaly. There, on foreign soil, he accidentally killed his grandfather Acrisius with a discus during funerary games held in honor of the local king. Perseus, unwilling to take up the throne he had inherited, effected an exchange with Megapenthes, the son of Acrisius's twin brother, Proetus. Perseus received Tiryns in exchange for Argos, a point of particular significance since it was Tiryns that Acrisius first won from Proetus but Proetus took back with the aid of a foreign king. The final cycle was thus completed by the return of Tiryns to Perseus. The struggle of two brothers, who were said to have fought in the womb and in their quarrels to have invented the shield, was thus resolved by the hero who, with the aid of the patroness of war, killed the monster and controlled the apotropaic visage. The problem of the birth of the original twins who had to struggle with each other for the kingship was resolved by the invention of the apotropaic visage as a warrior's implement and by the intervention of a warrior goddess to whom the original head was presented. In the end, Tiryns was returned by the son of Proetus to Perseus, grandson of Acrisius, inventor of the sacred Urmask, transformer and transformed.

Iconographical Considerations

The most salient features of the Gorgon head are its bulging or glaring eyes, gnashing tusks, a protruding tongue, and snakelike hair, or at least the appearance of snakes in some aspect of her decoration (pls. 35 and

36). These features, as well as the frequent appearance of pierced ears and a beard (Pl. 51),[14] are the iconographical elements commonly associated with the Gorgon head from as early as the eighth century B.C. onward, with the preponderance of examples from the seventh and sixth centuries B.C. However, not all of these features need be present to constitute a Gorgon. The Gorgon from the Temple of Artemis on Corfu (Pl. 37), for example, does not have prominent tusks or a beard, and, as in some Corinthian examples, a snake extends from each side of her head, while two others make up her belt; there at her waist, they are wound in a caduceus certifying her affinity with other chthonic healers and fertility figures. These variations, however, are not mentioned to suggest that the Gorgon's iconography is very flexible. Any Gorgon will exhibit at least the majority of the above-mentioned details, so that as a class Gorgon faces are easily recognizable and distinct from any other visage in Greek art. Additionally, as we shall see, there are other, less frequent—but no less significant—features that figure prominently in representations of the Gorgon. These include her grossly foliated skin, the absence of corners on her mouth, as in some later theatrical masks, and, in many cases, single or multiple dots on her forehead. All of these features provide us with excellent clues as to the nature of her persona.

It has often been hypothesized that the Gorgon derived from an effort to represent some wild animal or that it was reminiscent of the fearful theriomorphic masks common to primitive peoples (Wundt 1908, 168ff.). Howe (1954, 209–10) provides an excellent summary of the theories that developed in the late nineteenth and early twentieth centuries, many of which are no longer acceptable. Modern scholars have looked less for typological analogies and more for linguistic and archaeological evidence that might connect the Gorgon to foreign—especially Egyptian and Near Eastern—prototypes.[15] In fact, the Egyptian influence on Near Eastern iconography was so considerable in the first half of the first millennium B.C. that it is sometimes difficult to argue for specifically Egyptian as opposed to more generally Near Eastern influences on the Gorgon. Combinations of the Egyptian Bes with Gorgons and with Near Eastern winged monsters are common (Boardman 1968, 27–44), but attempts to make a positive comparison between the Gorgon and the Egyptian Bes often come down to very general considerations: they both have foliated skin, large ears, flat noses, beards, and frequent mythological associations with birth.[16] In the hands of the Greeks and Near Easterners, the two forms may well have been combined; but Egyptians favored static, if not tranquil, representations, whereas the Gorgon's frenzied, wrathful nature and her Mistress of the Animals pose are, as

Plate 35. Various depictions of the Gorgon. *a,* From lion-vase, Syracuse, Protocorinthian; *b,* from Macmillan aryballos, handle ornament, Protocorinthian; *c,* Chigi oinochoe, Protocorinthian; *d,* metope, Thermon, late 7th c. B.C.; *e,* clay relief, Syracuse, late 7th c. B.C. Despite minor differences, all display glaring eyes, gnashing teeth, hairiness, and an extended tongue. Payne 1931, Fig. 23.

we will see, more akin to the attributes of Eastern Great Goddess figures, particularly those of Asia Minor. The connections between the Gorgon and the Near Eastern *potnia* figures are manifold; in these connections we find metaphysical references that correspond to both mythological and iconographical variations that the Gorgon actually exhibited. Furthermore, by establishing such relationships between myth and iconography we better delimit both the Gorgon concept and the nature of the Gorgon's association with other well-known deities and daimons.

In examining the evolution of Gorgon imagery, there is also the larger question of how extensively the development of the Greek philosophical tradition influenced attitudes about the Gorgon's role. One of the most remarkable iconographical transitions ever to be recorded is the

Plate 36. Athena wearing Gorgoneion. Attic red-figure belly amphora by the Andokides Painter, ca. 525 B.C. Athena appears wearing the Gorgon head, or Gorgoneion, as a protective aegis. Berlin, Antikenmuseum, Staatliche Museen Preussischer Kulturbesitz, no. F2159.

Plate 37. a, Gorgon from the Temple of Artemis, Corfu. Ca. 600–580 B.C.
Athens, Deutsches Archäologisches Institut, neg. Corfu 554. *b*, Reconstruction
of central part of west pediment sculpture program. One of the best examples
of Early Archaic sculpture. Kantor 1962, Fig. 16.

Plate 38. The Gorgon as Mistress of the Beasts. *a,* Detail of bronze chariot from Castel San Mariano, Perugia, ca. 550–540 B.C. Munich, Staatliche Antikensammlungen und Glyptothek, Kop. 720r, 1. *b,* Detail of shield arm-piece. Olympia, first half of 6th c. B.C. Kantor 1962, Fig. 17. While the pose of the Gorgon differs in these two examples, in both instances she is flanked by lions in the classic Mistress of the Beasts pose.

change of the Gorgon head from a hideous apotropaic visage to a most mysteriously beautiful face (see frontispiece). This humanizing change began in the fifth century B.C., and it is tempting to suspect that it resulted at least in part from the incommensurability of the classification of ambivalent daimons with a reasoned and critical philosophical viewpoint. The skeptical tradition of modern philosophy does not trace itself much beyond the sixth century B.C., so that it follows closely upon the time that the Gorgon and the Perseus-Gorgon story enjoyed their greatest popularity as well as the time that theater as we know it arose in ancient Greece. That the Gorgon should come to be represented as a wolf in sheep's clothing, if not as an altogether sad and tragic figure, stands in remarkable contrast to her earlier role. Prior to this transformation, her entire conceptualization hinged upon her ghastly appearance, while her earliest examples show that on a classificatory level her iconography was freely applied to related concepts such as the Centaurs or Mistress figures that might have benefited from the association.

Originally, therefore, Perseus and the Gorgon clearly shared with local deities and other related figures a very widespread and varied mythology. Gorgons were represented in many different ways. One might say that they constituted a polythetic class of beings (Needham 1975) united solely by the several variations of the Perseus-Gorgon story and the apotropaic visage—beings so popular that their images were often employed associatively and sometimes in a very uncritical, if not indiscriminate, manner. We find evidence for this varied application of the Gorgon's iconography in vase paintings, in sculptures, and in masks. In these instances especially, we recognize the very broad and polythetic nature of the class of beings surrounding the seventh-century Gorgon and connecting her with other figures, such as Artemis or the Centaurs, who might share any one of her imagined attributes. The polytheistic and animistic ideas that flourished before the classical era may have encouraged very flexible and associative attitudes toward masks and the daimons they brought to life. For this reason, anthropologists can, perhaps, make an important contribution, since there are many analogous cases to be compared cross-culturally that display similar attitudes toward the organization of the visible manifestations of the spiritual world.

The problem of the historical transformation of the Gorgon and the rise of the skeptical tradition brings us to consider how Greek an idea the Gorgon is. It has often been stated, as a reaction to an overzealous search for foreign origins in early Greek thought, that the Gorgon is an entirely Greek notion arising only in Greece, the manifestation of purely Greek ideas. The fact that we have not uncovered the Perseus-Gorgon story in its exact formulation elsewhere supports such a statement. So does the fact that we do not find any precisely duplicated representations of the Gorgon in Mesopotamia before these faces first appear in Greece. This evidence seems to confirm the supposition that the Perseus-Gorgon story and the image of the Gorgon first achieved their completed form in Greece in the eighth or seventh century B.C. This evidence, however, does not explain some features of the Gorgon image, certain of which are better understood by a comparative look at popular foreign ideas; indeed, some features of the Gorgon's representation seem to be modeled on an iconography that is clearly foreign.

The most obvious instances of foreign influence occur where early Gorgons are conflated with the images of other daimons or gods. Some of the very earliest representations of the Perseus-Gorgon myth, such as the aforementioned Boeotian example, show Perseus taking the head from a Gorgon-Centaur—that is to say, from a Gorgon attached to a horse's body. While the Gorgon-Centaur illustrated in Plate 22 is probably the best-known example, Boardman shows others (e.g., 1968, 35), and even a cursory look at the fabulous bestiary of Asia Minor illustrates how an interest in hybrid creatures is pan-Mediterranean.

As in the cases of the Satyrs, Silens, and Centaurs, there is a clear intention in Greek mythology to identify the Gorgon with other fabulous monsters whose powers the Gorgon ought rightly to possess. It is a question of attaching through iconography, and of legitimizing through mythology, images and relationships that in themselves are forceful. The power of the Gorgon rests in the fact that it can do what all lesser and similar creatures can do and that in addition it can do much more. "Gorgon," then, becomes a chain complex, a polythetic class, to which images of power are attached. When Hesiod relates what must have been the popular belief that it was Poseidon who mated with the Medusa to conceive the horse Pegasus and the giant Chrysaor (*Theogony* 280ff.), it is as if all of the powers of Oceanus and the underworld are being united, for Poseidon is both the god of horses, magical and real, as well as god of the sea. And when Pliny the Elder characterizes the Gorgons as members of a wild and exceedingly hairy race (*Natural History* 6.200), he is connecting them with all of the strange and fabulous wild men that populated the shores of Oceanus—both the edges of the imagined Greek universe and the edges of the Greek imagination itself. Small wonder, then, that the Gorgon Medusa should be a Great Goddess as well.

It seems that the whole question of influences demands to be looked at afresh, for once we are able to overcome the intensely nationalistic and intellectually egocentric cast that occasionally appears in the study of

iconography, we enable ourselves to attı.bute to the Greeks some awareness of the fact that they were not living in a cultural vacuum. The por-
trayal of the Gorgon as a *potnia thērōn*, or Mistress of the Animals, is
clearly analogous to several Near Eastern figures (see, e.g., Pl. 39), and
there is nothing to militate against the Greek desire to have their own
Gorgon be equal or superior in power to these demons of the Near East,
to compete and win out, if you will, on similar iconographic terrain.
Kantor, for example, in an excellent study in comparative iconography
(1962), presents several drawings illustrating how images of the Gorgon
as a Mistress of the Beasts recall various representational styles from
Asia Minor. The figures in plates 37 and 38 illustrate Kantor's point. Plate
38*b*, in particular, shows the two beasts in a pose common to them
throughout the Near East, though the most popular depiction has the
central figure holding them by either their hind- or their forelegs, as in
Plate 39.

One might object to considering such iconographic variations and
argue that these variations are not Gorgons at all. Such an objection,
however, could not be supported, because clearly the Greek Gorgon
grew out of a class of beasts that exhibited many common properties. It
is therefore essential to consider the wider implications of these properties in order to understand the Gorgon; we cannot simply look to the
later Greek representations and argue that they are not derivative. One
can allow the Greeks their inventiveness without refusing to be a com-
parativist. Indeed, comparison becomes all the more consequential when
we look to the distribution of the Gorgon within the Greek world. From
Sicily and Etruria in the West to southern Russia in the East, the Gorgon
seems to have been integral to the iconography of the most widely dis-
persed settlements. Moreover, the fact that her most famous examples
were found in major trade centers and in cities along Phoenician trade
routes has led frequently to speculation that she must have been connected with them—either partially deriving from iconography trans-
mitted by the Phoenicians, or designed as a representation of some general class of barbarians of which, perhaps, the Phoenicians were a part.
A brief list of geographical locations where Gorgons figured prominently
makes such an idea quite attractive. Places like Corfu, Rhodes, Syracuse,
and Tarentum were all known to Mediterranean navigators, of whom the
Phoenician traders were certainly the most ambitious. Additionally,
the presence of imported raw materials such as ivory in many of these
sites indicates that trade with foreigners—and mainly Phoenicians—
was undertaken. Homer (e.g., *Iliad* 23.740–45; *Odyssey* 15.415–16) speaks
of the Phoenicians as bringers of valuable and ornate objects—objects

Plate 39. Cybele. *a*, Scythian silver and gilt mirror-back from Kelermes, South Russia, 6th c. B.C. *b*, Detail of the Kelermes mirror shows Cybele holding two lions in the classic Mistress of the Beasts pose. Leningrad, Hermitage Museum. (Photo courtesy Thames and Hudson. Drawing by Mrs. Scott.)

Plate 40. The Lion Goddess. Hydria from Meikirch-Grächwil, Switzerland, 6th c. B.C. Bern, Historisches Museum.

about whose background we may suppose the Greeks knew only as much or as little as the circumstances of trade made possible.

Whether or not the Gorgon has a Phoenician connection, it is clear that by the seventh century the image was becoming central in Greek civilization and art. Her prominence in artifacts from Corinth is evident from the period of Early Archaic art (Payne 1931, 79). In these first

Plate 41. Graeco-Scythian gold phiale from Kul Oba, South Russia. Early 4th c. B.C. Rosette pattern with Gorgons, Scythians or Silens, boars or panthers, and decorative volutes. Below are dolphins and fish. Leningrad, Hermitage Museum. (Photo courtesy Thames and Hudson.)

Plate 42. Etruscan bronze lamp. Mid-5th c. B.C. Illustrated is the bottom of the famous oil lamp from Cortona. Here the Medusa head becomes the focus of the composition. On its periphery are sixteen lamps whose bases are decorated with flute-playing Silens and with winged Sirens. Cortona, Museo dell' Accademia Etrusca.

Plate 43. a, Detail of Orientalizing vase painting, Syracuse. Ca. 640–625 B.C. Payne 1931, Fig. 12. In this detail, the Gorgon head takes the place of the feline head seen on Corinthian bicorporates of the same period, as shown in *b. b*, Black-figure Corinthian wine-jug. Ca. 600 B.C. London, British Museum, No. 60.2–1.18.

Plate 44. Ziwiyeh gold plaque from the Scythian tomb treasure in Iranian Kurdistan. 7th c. B.C. Though deriving in some respects from Assyrian art of the seventh century B.C., this plaque may in its depiction of a leonine bicorporate be more favorably compared to certain Luristan pinheads and, more specifically still, to Greek bicorporates from Corinth, Crete, and even Sicily. New York, The Metropolitan Museum of Art, Fletcher Fund, 1951, no. 51.131.1; Joseph Pulitzer Bequest, 1954, no. 54.171. All rights reserved. The Metropolitan Museum of Art.

Plate 45. Cretan bronze helmet decoration from Afrati. Late 7th c. B.C. Two snakes are here intertwined in the form of a caduceus, below which is depicted a feline bicorporate. New York, Norbert Schimmel collection. Drawing courtesy Norbert Schimmel.

pieces, we see reflections of monsters that correspond quite definitely with fantastic creatures from the East (compare Pl. 43 with Pl. 44). Thus, while Plate 43*a* is a Corinthian type found at Syracuse, its similarity to an example found in a Scythian royal tomb at Ziwiyeh in Iranian Kurdistan dramatizes the importance of motifs from farther east. This similarity is also demonstrated through the presence of bicorporates—that is, one head with two bodies—in pre-Achaemenid Iran and in Greek locations such as Crete, where an Assyrian influence is notable.[17]

There was, furthermore, no hesitation on the part of the Greeks to speculate about the monster's homeland. Though the Gorgons were thought traditionally to reside on the shores of Oceanus, this did not stop the ancients from systematically trying to place them in the then-known world. The precise location of the land of the Gorgons varies among both Greek and Roman writers, though all agree that the monsters originated in a far-off land, most frequently in Libya (e.g., Euripides [*Bacchae* 990ff.]; Herodotus [2.91]; Pausanias [2.21.5,6]). As for Perseus, the Greeks quite openly tried to relate him to the Persians: they were so eager to do so that they gave his eldest son the name Perses, calling him the ancestor of the Persians. In this way, they certified the Eastern connection but spared themselves the disgrace of being the descendants, rather than the ancestors, of the Persians.

Thus, even if Perseus and the Gorgons were a Greek invention, the Greeks themselves would certainly have had us believe that they pertained to much that was not Greek. From an anthropological perspective, the importance of this fact cannot be overemphasized, because while it does not tell us any more about who invented the Gorgon, it does show that the Greeks were at first willing to look to other cultures and that what they thought they discovered there became important in defining their own ideas. This curiosity about what is foreign reveals an interesting cultural attitude anthropologists have elsewhere widely reported. Anyone, for example, who has seen this assimilating tendency at work in Hindu cultures—especially in places such as Bali, where the foreign origins of the religion are recognized and even at times admired—will understand how it subverts our popular notions about genius and invention. Both a horror of and a fascination with other cultures led the Greeks not to take lightly foreign analogues to the archetypal imagery of horror and fear that is the essence of the Gorgon head.

If indeed the mythology of the Gorgon focuses on a Greek fascination with things exotic, then to insist that she is an entirely Greek invention is not only to undermine the spirit of her depiction, but also to avoid the obvious social facts. As early as the tenth century B.C., the Phoenicians had expanded their trade routes into the western Mediterranean. By the ninth century, they had firmly established themselves at Carthage, a city soon to be known as the richest in the world; they had traded as far west as Cadiz and, by arrangement with the Assyrians, throughout Mesopotamia and as far east as India; their reputation as traders and their sailing ability allowed them to have regular contact with Egyptians, Assyrians, Persians, Scythians, Medes, and Greeks, and, by extension, with most of the peoples between the western Mediterranean and India; the quality of the objects that they traded in was legendary. In sum, to resist accrediting them with bringing their sophisticated cargo to the eager Greeks, or to assume that this trade was not sought after, is to overlook both some overwhelming historical facts and as well what the Greeks themselves stated to be the case. All the way up to the fifth century, when Phoenician Carthage reached its zenith and the Greeks halted Persian expansion, we see wave after wave of influence extending from farther east. First trade arrived through the intermediary Phoenicians until they were overcome by the Assyrians. Later the Medes and Babylonians overcame the Assyrians; and, finally, the Persians overcame the entire Near East so that their empire extended from the Bosporus to India. The evidence for this influence is recorded in the so-called Orientalizing period of Greek art during the seventh and, to a certain extent, the sixth century B.C., the period in which the apotropaic Gorgon rose to prominence in all of Greece. The successive waves of imperial expansion from the East, made easier by the age-old routes of Phoenician trade, meant naturally that the Greeks became increasingly familiar with foreign ideas and artistic images. By the fifth century we see that knowledge of foreign peoples is much less fantastic in character—so much so that Herodotus (7.60–88) not only knew the numbers and nationalities of the Persian forces, but was able to distinguish in considerable detail their modes of dress, manner of combat, and peculiarities of habit. From his account we see also how the Persian army was truly an international force. Among the battalions that accompanied the much-admired Cyrus and his successors, Darius and Xerxes, we find Syrians, Parthians, Arabians, Ethiopians, Libyans, Phrygians, Thracians, Lydians, Bactrians, and Indians.

This international nature of the Achaemenid Empire could have made a significant contribution to the diffusion of the apotropaic iconography of which the Gorgon is a part. It is, however, important in assessing this issue to remember that prior to this time the Greeks had already been trading directly with the Assyrians from settlements on the Levant Coast and that by the eighth century B.C. both trade and warfare between the two civilizations were occurring on Cyprus (Dunbabin 1957, 24ff.). Iconographically, figures of Syrian origin in bronze and clay— "easily recognisable by the wide deep-set eye sockets, the prominent nose and chin, and the upward tilt of the face" (ibid., 37)—appear at Greek sites as early as the ninth century. The fact that objects of Assyrian origin have also been found in Etruria attests to the widespread influence that this nation exercised, no doubt through the Phoenicians. More importantly, already in the mid-eighth century we find the appearance of ivory in Greece, often—as at Athens (ibid., 39)—displaying Syrian subjects. In short, by the late eighth century and the first half of the seventh century B.C. the Greeks possessed no small knowledge of Assyrian artifacts. This meant, naturally, that they became increasingly familiar not only with Assyrian art, but also with the art of those peoples with whom the Assyrians traded. The Greeks of this time knew not only of the bronze bowls decorated with bestial images that were the specialty of the Assyrians' neighbors the Urartians, who occupied modern-day

Armenia, but also of works from as far away as Luristan in Iran, where bronzes combining Assyrian elements, the art of the steppes, and the stylization characteristic of the ancient Shang bronzes of China have been found. Thus, when we look to seventh-century art in Greece, when the Late Attic Geometric style gives way to the plethora of fantastic monsters we associate with the Orientalizing period, we realize how contrived an iconographic study of the Gorgon is if it limits itself to Greece proper. The Gorgons, Centaurs, Sphinxes, Boreads (winged men), Chimaeras (lion-goat-snakes), birds mixed with panthers and lions, and humans mixed with any of these all become part of a fantastic bestiary from which the Satyrs and Gorgons evolve. To the Greek imagination, surely, we should attribute much of this development, but not without placing it within the wider perspective of which it is a part. It is, therefore, necessary to look more carefully at the Gorgon as, first of all, a natural autonomous icon to which the Greeks may have had access. By doing so, we may both assess what characteristics might have been indigenously ascertained and compare more specific iconographic peculiarities of the Gorgon to certain Oriental figures.

The Gorgon as a Leonine Creature

A comparison of the lion and the Gorgon is warranted not only because the lion shares many physiognomic features with the Gorgon; the fact that art from the Near East, especially from Assyria, is dominated by lions and leonine hybrids increases significantly the probability that the Oriental lion was influential in the evolution of Greek art, as does the function of both lions and Gorgons as apotropaic forces. While it is possible that the lion was at one time indigenous to Thrace, the Greeks were unlikely to have known very much about its habits from firsthand observation. This lack of any detailed knowledge about the lion is frequently cited as an explanation for why the Homeric lion is never said to roar (Dunbabin 1957, 46). It is clear, however, if we accept the etymology given above, that the Gorgon was in essence an apotropaic beast capable of a terrific roar. That the lion's roar did not pass into Homer reaffirms the idea that the Gorgon, if connected with the lion, was likely to have been a transposition of a foreign monster—a leonine beast named for its terrific roar.

It is generally accepted that the earliest seventh-century Greek representations of the lion are copies or imports of North Syrian Neo-Hittite examples of a small short-maned animal.[18] By the mid-seventh century, however, this version gives way to the long-maned, so-called Assyrian lion, common in Corinthian art of this period (Payne 1931, 53ff.)—an influence on Greek art that Hopkins calls "particularly striking" (1934, 345). From the excellence of Assyrian representations of the lion, we realize just how familiar and important it was to that culture. Its role in art is reflected in its role in the lives of the Assyrian kings, who kept parks specifically for lion hunts, illustrations of these events being common in Assyrian art. Under such circumstances the animals could be studied quite closely. The differing sizes of the lions' manes may, moreover, simply reflect such differences of habitat, since the mane is said to grow longer in captivity, though it might equally result from the depiction of the smaller variety of Asian lion once common from Africa to Central Asia, a type known not only for its smaller size but also for the shortness of its mane.

The similarities between the lion and the Greek Gorgon may be grouped according to natural physical resemblances directly connecting the two and resemblances between the Gorgon and those mythical leonine creatures from Asia Minor that are very much a part of the Orientalizing period in Greek art. Because these latter creatures are dominant figures in Assyro-Babylonian religion, they are usually the first to be compared with the Greek Gorgons and the Perseus-Gorgon story. For example, several Babylonian monsters are iconographically represented with a lion head and wings such as are typical of the Gorgon, and scholars have for some time (e.g., Meyer 1914, 113–14) remarked the tendency of the Gorgon to be represented *en face* while running (see, e.g., Pl. 46) or in a half-kneeling pose quite common in Near Eastern representations (Hopkins 1934, 346ff.). The fact that the Babylonian monster Humbaba is only represented full-face, and often in this running or half-kneeling pose, is worth noting; more interesting still, in comparing Humbaba to the Gorgon, is the tendency also to represent the Babylonian monster by the head alone (ibid.). This fact—that both monsters were commonly known by their heads alone—has its parallel in the analogy between the Perseus-Gorgon story and the Gilgamesh-Humbaba epic. Both monsters were decapitated by a hero-ruler assisted by a supernatural or theriomorphic force—in the case of Perseus, the goddess Athena; in the instance of Gilgamesh, the tamed wild man Enkidu. This analogy, combined with the Assyrian influence on Cypriot art and Humbaba's Levantine connections—Humbaba was said to be the guardian of the cedar forests of either Syria or Lebanon—has been taken by scholars such as Hopkins (1934) as an indication of the Gorgon's Assyrian-Babylonian origin; most, however, feel that the faces do not look

Plate 46. Gorgon figures from early Corinthian vases. (Cf. Pl. 43.) Notable here are not only the variety employed in depicting the Gorgon head, but also the excellent example of the Gorgon running *en face*—the obvious solution to the problem of how one maintains the apotropaic qualities of the Gorgon while composing a pictorial narrative. Payne 1931, Fig. 24.

enough alike to prove a connection, that their superficial dissimilarities rule out any such theory.

The question of whether the Gorgon derived specifically and solely from Humbaba ultimately must be left to archaeologists and historians of the period. The structural similarities of the legends are close enough, however, to suggest that they may belong to a class of parallel stories. One analogy in this parallel that has not received its due and one that has considerable anthropological importance is found in the relationship between the apotropaic mask, or aegis, and the sovereignty of the clan controlling it. As we have seen, the final result of the exploits of Perseus is the establishment of the Perseid dynasty. Gilgamesh is also a king, born of the union of a divine being and a mortal who is later deified, and his conquest of Humbaba was so directly relevant to the maintenance of the dynasty that Humbaba's face was tied to regal divination. The one characteristic that appears to have distinguished Humbaba from other monsters was that his face was represented as a continuous line; it thus became a graphic illustration of the entrails employed in divination (Pl. 47). "If the entrails are like the face of Humbaba, a rebel [or: "tyrant"] will rule all the land" (S. Smith 1924, 110) is an omen cited on inscriptions referring to this face. Thus, the single line tracing the face of Humbaba states that there exists a necessary relationship between the social threat the face signifies and the kingly act necessary to avoid social chaos. The victim's sacrifice forestalls imminent catastrophe and the appearance of Humbaba's face in its entrails is the sign that chaos may be winning out.

To the possible meaning of Humbaba we will turn shortly, but first it is necessary to see that, iconographically, Humbaba is not easily connected to things Greek. Features such as the deep grooves of Humbaba's face are extremely general in character and are not, in themselves, sufficient evidence for associating Humbaba with mask types from Sparta (pls. 9–12) and Tiryns (Pl. 34). Such grooves may as much represent faces in old age as they could the entrails of sheep. The ambiguities of these general characteristics, their ability to suggest more than one iconographical connection, were certainly known and exploited by the Greeks. The Graiae, for example, the gray old women from whom Perseus acquired the magic single eye and tooth, were meant to be sisters of the Gorgons, figures who shared, though perhaps in only the vaguest of ways, some common features. These grooved faces may, equally, be meant to signify some general feline connection (e.g., Pl. 48). Indeed, such grooves, as a natural feature of a lion's muzzle, seem far more relevant to the iconography of the Gorgon head, and especially when com-

Plate 47. The face of Humbaba. Clay, Babylonia, ca. 700–500 B.C. The foe of
Gilgamesh is depicted here in its divinatory form. The monster's face is rendered as one continuous line of entrails that have a prophetic character: "If the
entrails [of the sacrificial animal] are like the face of Humbaba, a rebel will rule
all the land" (Smith 1924, 110). London, British Museum 116624.

bined with other physiognomic attributes of lions and Gorgons. Fangs
and, frequently, a protruding tongue are no doubt the most obvious
points of comparison, particularly in view of the latter's importance in
the earliest Protocorinthian images of lions (early seventh century) and
their neo-Hittite models (Akurgal 1968, 176ff.). On the other hand, such
generally monstrous features are shared by so many beasts and depicted
so frequently that one cannot easily employ them in making specific comparisons. Other, less obvious elements of iconography, however, allow

Plate 48. Babylonian demon. Terra-cotta, ca. 2000 B.C. In this example from the Yale Babylonian Collection, a foliated face calls to mind not only the entrail face of Humbaba, but also the grotesque masks from Sparta and Tiryns. YBC 10066.

more specific associations between Gorgons and lions or, more likely, leonine monsters. Among the less obvious details of leonine physiognomy that, it might be argued, are represented on the Gorgon are the two hairy marks or superciliary dots on the lion's forehead (Pl. 49). This at first may seem a curious detail to call attention to; I hope, however, to show that it provides some specific information about the Gorgon's nature.

The fact that the Greeks most likely had no knowledge, or at best

Plate 49. Elsa. Superciliary tufts are clearly apparent. From *Born Free,* by Joy Adamson. Copyright © 1960 by Joy Adamson. Reprinted by permission of Pantheon Books, a Division of Random House.

very little knowledge, of any real lions has not kept this beast from being the favored choice for the Gorgon's origin (see Goldman 1961); in fact, their very lack of understanding goes a long way toward explaining some of the more curious reinterpretations of iconographical elements. Early Greek depictions of lions clearly exhibit the Greeks' awareness that the animal's forehead was to be decorated with some form of protuberance (Pl. 50), though precisely how many marks ought to be indicated, in what location, and for what reason seem sometimes to have escaped them. Homer in the *Iliad* (17.133–36) says with reference to the lion, "he draws down the whole of the skin of his brows, concealing his eyes," an expression attributed to lions "lest they should be frightened by the weapons and desert their young" (Eustathius, *Commentary, ad loc.*). If we may judge from the variation among early representations, such speculation must have been common. Later, in classical times, writers theorized about the relationship between an individual's character and physical appearance and how humans might be compared with animals in these respects. The first such treatment that is in any way systematic is the Pseudo-Aristotelian manual (ascribed to Aristotle or his school) *Physiognomonica*. Especially important in the animal-human comparisons of this manual are the lion and panther (Evans 1969, 5),[19] and the author remarks "gleaming eyes" in particular (*Phgn.* 809b). The disposition of the brows was important enough to Pollux that he included it as a defining feature of masks, though what an attention to the brows of the preclassical lion may have been meant to indicate is difficult to ascertain. That the marks do appear, however, certifies that Greek artists knew that the forehead tufts of the real lion ought to be represented by bumps or dots. But our realization that these forehead marks are not, if we may judge from other representations, a standard facial decoration in the preclassical era and the fact that they occur exclusively on lions and Gorgons[20] suggest indeed that there is a direct connection between the lion and the Gorgon especially—that, for example, the protective function of the Gorgon as Athena's aegis is analogous to the heraldic function of lions as gate protectors throughout Greece and the Near East.

Plate 51 shows two Gorgons by the Attic painter Kleitias (Fales 1966, 25) and one by Lydos. Two show the forehead marks as two dots; the other seems to indicate the superciliary vibrissae with two curled lines. All three closely parallel the marks of the lion both in reality and in its frequent depictions in Assyrian (pls. 52 and 53), Iranian (Pl. 54*a*), and Scythian art (Pl. 54*b*).

Conversely, Plate 55 at once suggests an association—though an uncertain one—between the two creatures. Here what appears to be a panther is depicted with a Gorgon, much as on the famous chariot from

Plate 50. Limestone lion of Mene-
crates. The lion's superciliary tufts of
hair are depicted here as two round
globes. That this detail is often attended to in some stylized way is
remarkable, especially as the shape
and actual location of the marks are
often inaccurately rendered. Corfu
Museum.

a

b

Plate 51. *a*, Gorgoneion by Kleitias.
Attic black-figure fragment. Paris,
Louvre C167b. *b*, Gorgoneion by
Kleitias. Attic black-figure stand.
New York, The Metropolitan Mu-
seum of Art, Fletcher Fund, 1931,
no. 31.11.4.
c,
Gorgoneion by Lydos. Attic black-
figure plate. Munich, Staatliche
Antikensammlungen und Glyp-
tothek, no. 8760.

The placement of the superciliary
marks on these three examples suggests a possible connection with
leonine iconography. All three date
from around the middle of the sixth
century B.C.

c

Plate 52. a, Gilgamesh and lion cub. Detail from a large figure from Khorsabad, the capital of the Assyrian king Sargon II. 8th c. B.C. The lion cub held by the hero Gilgamesh displays prominent superciliary protuberances. Paris, Louvre HO 19861.16. (Photo: Musées Nationaux.) *b,* Assyrian lion face. Lapis lazuli and faience inlay. Nimrud, ca. 715 B.C. In this Assyrian limestone handle of a standard or dagger, the superciliary marks are inlaid and highly contrasted so that they become a dominant iconographic feature. New York, The Metropolitan Museum of Art, Rogers Fund, 1954, no. 54. 117.20.

Plate 53. Roaring lion. Detail of wall painting from Palace of Til Barsip, 8th or 7th c. B.C. Even in profile the superciliary mark of this roaring lion is visible. Drawing after Lucien Cavro, Paris, by Mary Ryder.

Plate 54. *a*, Bracelet in electrum with leonine heads. Luristan, 8th–7th c. B.C. Paris, Louvre A020136. (Photo: Musées Nationaux.) *b*, Scythian lion plaques. These nearly identical Scythian gold plaques show a special attention to the superciliary marks. Berlin, Staatliche Museen, no. 30221f.

Plate 55. Ajax preparing to commit suicide. Attic black-figure belly amphora by Exekias, mid-6th c. B.C. On his shield is a Gorgoneion with two vertical, rather than horizontal, marks; above it is shown what appears to be a panther with two appropriately placed marks. Boulogne-sur-Mer, Musée des Beaux-Arts et d'Archéologie, no. 558.

Monteleone now in the Metropolitan Museum (Pl. 56), but their positions are reversed. Especially interesting on the Greek example is the appearance of superciliary dots on both the panther and the Gorgon; while the panther's are in their natural position, however, those of the Gorgon are vertical. In other words, a clear distinction is made between the two beasts, so that while they both have the marks, the Gorgon's do not copy those occurring naturally on the panther. This contrast clearly indicates that the marks on the Gorgon are not simple imitations of a natural feline feature and that they in all likelihood had some specific meaning of their own. I am aware of only one other location in the Mediterranean where these vertically arranged superciliary marks occur on horrific or apotropaic faces, that being on terra cotta masks from Phoenician Carthage (Pl. 57). Because they resemble the masks of Artemis Orthia, Picard (1964, 62) considers these votive masks, some of them recovered from

Plate 56. Chariot front from Monteleone. Etruscan bronze relief, ca. 550–540 B.C. The Gorgon and feline faces appear on a shield but in the reverse position from that on the Exekias belly amphora (Pl. 55). The lower, feline face exhibits two prominent superciliary marks while the Gorgon above it is unmarked. New York, The Metropolitan Museum of Art, Rogers Fund, 1903, no. 03.23.1. All rights reserved. The Metropolitan Museum of Art.

Plate 57. Terra-cotta mask from Carthage. This Punic mask has been compared to those found at the Temple of Artemis Orthia in Sparta. Especially curious are the two vertically arranged superciliary bumps. Tunis, Musée du Bardo.

graves, as imports. Regardless, though, of whether they were made abroad or by foreign craftsmen within Punic Carthage, it is clear that they are of a quality uncommon in objects manufactured there. Though I cannot go as far as Picard does in saying that they are identical to the masks from the Temple of Artemis Orthia (1964, 69),[21] the resemblances certainly are striking. Like the Greek votive masks, they have furrowed skin; like the Gorgon, they frequently display very prominent forehead marks that probably have some apotropaic significance (Stern 1976, 118) and that should relate, through their kinship with Near Eastern cults, to the same Orientalizing tradition upon which the Gorgon draws.

Though the superciliary marks were common on Athenian representations of Gorgons in the sixth century B.C., they are not restricted to Attic figures. Nor do the marks, when they are employed, only occur in twos. Gorgons are often decorated with one or, more frequently still, with three superciliary marks. This flexibility, combined with the fact that the marks are restricted to Gorgons and leonine creatures, makes one think that this is a distinctive feature with a particular meaning—a meaning that, moreover, may have been carried over from another tradition. In support of the idea that marking the forehead had a specific meaning is the fact that even some representations of lions—especially those of Assyrian and Phoenician provenance—are marked by an indentation or hole, a mark that is unlikely to derive from the depiction of their superciliary vibrissae, but one that might be two-dimensionally represented by a dot. A good example is the bronze head of a lion or panther[22] from Crete, now in Athens (Pl. 58). This figure is important for our study not simply because of the curious marking of the area between the eyes, but because, as Rodenwaldt points out, it, like other Cretan bronzes and like Corinthian vase paintings, shows definite Assyrian influences (Rodenwaldt 1939, 2:145–46). Indeed, this type of grossly foliated face, with a pronounced forehead indentation, is common in images of Assyrian demons (Pl. 59).

Though in several examples these indentations appear to be related to the curious horns so common on Assyrian monsters (pls. 59 and 60),[23] some are clearly, as in the Cretan example, attributes of the lion. Excellent representations of Assyrian lions whose foreheads are marked by a single fillet are two famous Nimrud ivories dating from the eighth century B.C. (Pl. 61). In these nearly identical plaques, we find early proof that the forehead of the Assyrian lion could be marked in a stylistic way that carried a decorative or symbolic rather than a representational meaning.[24] Moreover, since scholars have agreed that some of the Nimrud ivories exhibit a Phoenician influence, and may even have been made by Phoenician artists, again we must note the possible role the Phoenicians had in the dissemination of a leonine iconography from Oriental lands to the world of the Greeks. Bearing in mind, therefore, the potential role of Phoenician trade in the diffusion of iconographic motifs, the significance of apotropaic lions, Gorgons, and votive masks during the preclassical era, and the thrust of military events in Asia Minor from the seventh century B.C. onward, we ought now, for comparative purposes, to turn to the Near East.

Plate 58. Bronze lion or panther head from Crete. This small head shows an attention to the forehead but, as in a number of Assyrian representations, focuses on a single central mark. Athens, Deutsches Archäologisches Institut, neg. Nat. Mus. 4096.

Plate 59. Assyrian demon heads. Such heads show how the superciliary marks may result from the open-ended "horns" so common on these figures. (See also Pl. 60.) Whether they converge in one mark or remain separated as two, they often enhance the foliated appearance of the face itself. Boardman (1968, 38) has suggested the possibility that these horn marks may be connected to the decorated foreheads of Gorgons. Paris, Louvre A02490 and A01197.

Plate 60. Babylonian divinatory plaque (front and back views). Early 1st millennium B.C. The demon Pazuzu lurks behind the plaque, which is divided into
two registers. At the bottom, the female lion-headed demon Lamashtu is
shown holding two snakes in a heraldic pose. Behind her are a patient in bed
and, above, *ashipu* priests, who would treat the patient, wearing lion masks.
Baghdad, State Antiquities and Heritage Organization.

Plate 61. Ivory plaques from Nimrud. 8th c. B.C. These two plaques probably
represent the strongest, if not the earliest, statement concerning the iconographic significance of the lion's forehead. Here there can be no mistaking the
decoration of the forehead for a natural trait. London, British Museum 127412
(detail); Baghdad, State Antiquities and Heritage Organization.

The Gorgon Reconsidered

Having reviewed in very general terms the network of iconography to which the Gorgon seems particularly related, we may now ask to what extent, if any, she may be envisaged as an Oriental beast. To explore this question, we must look more closely both at Humbaba and at related Near Eastern beasts. Most attempts to clarify the possible connection between the Gorgon and Humbaba involve another Near Eastern intermediary—namely, the goddess Cybele in her Mistress of the Animals role. In part, this is because of the structural amenability of the Gorgon—as the Greeks themselves felt—to Mistress of the Animals or *potnia thērōn* figures as well as to Near Eastern leonine demons.

We can be certain about the iconographic conflation of these types not only by virtue of the aforementioned examples of Gorgons as Mistress figures; we can also find many Near Eastern, and possibly even Indo-European, figures in this pose. By far the most complex and controversial example of these combined forms is the seal of Shaushshatar, king of the Indo-European Mitannians (Pl. 62). Here we have what appears to be the Vedic pantheon depicted with both Humbaba and a winged, lion-bodied Mistress or Master of the Animals recalling certain Assyrian figures such as the demon Pazuzu (Pl. 63). Though the pose itself is extraordinarily widespread and ancient, and though the Shaushshatar seal is far too early (1450 B.C.) to provide any useful comparisons for the Gorgon, the likelihood that it conflates figures known from different traditions and that it utilizes a popular heraldic format make it an especially compelling example.

In myth, the Near Eastern conflation of the legends and iconography of different Mistress of the Animals figures makes their possible connection to the Gorgon seem more likely, though not certain. Here, especially in the legend of Cybele and Attis, we may observe a mythological network that offers some interesting clues to the polythetic nature of Gorgon imagery. More specifically, the analogy of the story of Perseus to that of Attis, Cybele's eunuch and lover, urges us to look to the lions accompanying Cybele either in their heraldic Anatolian pose, or pulling (as do the horses of Mitra) the chariot of Time.

Cybele is, as I have mentioned earlier, the Near Eastern Great Goddess figure who shares with some early Gorgons not only the Mistress of the Beasts stance but, specifically, a pose wherein she is accompanied by lions. While the heraldic and symmetrical juxtaposition of lions to either side of the goddess is a common format, as it often is for the Gorgon, in

Plate 62. Seal of Shaushshatar. Cuneiform tablet found at Nuzi, northern Iraq. Ca. 1450 B.C. This seal depicts a Pazuzu-like figure in the Mistress or Master of the Beasts pose surrounded by what appears to be a mixture of Indo-European and Near Eastern deities. Among these figures may be (top left) Mitra slaying the cosmic bull, (to the right of Mitra) Humbaba, (top right) Varuna as the god of waters, and (bottom left and right) the Nasatya twins. *a,* Drawing after Barnett by Mary Ryder. *b,* Photograph of original seal © President and Fellows of Harvard College for the Harvard Semitic Museum.

Plate 63. Pazuzu. Bronze, Assyrian, first half of the 1st millennium B.C. Though as the king of evil spirits he is essentially a horrific figure, Pazuzu may, like Humbaba, become a tame, protective demon—a particularly striking role when we consider not only his ugliness but also his potentially dangerous nature. Paris, Louvre MNB.467. (Photo: Musées Nationaux.)

Plate 64. Attacking lion exhibiting superciliary marks. From the chariot of Cybele, north frieze of the Siphnian Treasury at Delphi, ca. 530–525 B.C. Delphi Museum.

some quite magnificent examples the lions can play a more complex narrative part (Pl. 64). In mythology, the function of the lions is to announce Cybele's arrival with their horrific roar, especially during seasons of furious transformation—the moments of ecstatic dancing, when her duties as a time goddess are paralleled by the lion's solar significance:

> When the autumn and winter storms start to blow, and the trees bow under the vigour of the wind gods, the Goddess is riding through the forest. Then she is the wild and restless Goddess who gives no rest to other beings, men, beasts and plants. Nature, like the Goddess, is in ecstasy. (Vermaseren 1966, 26–27)

Like the Greek Gaea or Rhea the Phrygian Cybele has as her consort a eunuch; in Phrygia, this eunuch is Attis, whose emasculation was self-inflicted and whose followers were often priest-eunuchs as well (see n. 12 above). The introduction of Cybele into Greek mythology was made possible by her identification with Rhea, making her, therefore, not only the daughter of Earth personified (Gaea) but the equivalent of Zeus's mother—that is, the grandmother of Perseus.

Since both the Greeks and the Romans seem to have known less about the details of the birth of Attis than about the rest of the myth, it is at first difficult to see why preclassical Greeks would tend to depict the

Medusa as a *potnia thērōn* figure. Vermaseren, however, building upon a textual comparison published by Hepding in 1903, provides an interesting description that underlines the connection between the Gorgon and the underworld demons of the ancient Near East. From the Eleusinian priest Timotheus, by way of Arnobius (*Adversus nationes* 5.5.7), and from Pausanias (7.17.9–11, citing Hermesianax), we learn of a legend—and apparently the only traditional legend—of the origin of Attis. It sounds like a remarkable conflation of the births of Perseus, Gilgamesh, and Mithras, and so possibly a tale that could link the Gorgon to the Near Eastern epics. Like the Perseus-Gorgon myth with its story of Zeus's shower of gold that enters the brazen tower and impregnates Danaë, the Phrygian tale began with Zeus or Jupiter losing his seed while attempting to impregnate the rock that was the Great Mother:

> In Phrygia there is an enormous rock . . . near Pessinus known by the name of Agdus which took the form of the Great Mother. While she was sleeping Jupiter wanted to make love to her . . . , but the Goddess refused and Jupiter, struggling to obtain . . . her, lost his seed. . . . According to Pausanias, however, Zeus lost his seed while sleeping. The Goddess is the *petra*, the mountain, the venerable Terra Mater. Now, against her will, in the tenth month she brings a bisexual being into the world whose name, Agdistis, is derived from Agdus. We must note that Agdistis, like Mithras, is born from the rock (*petra genetrix*). . . .
>
> Because of his bisexual character the new creature has the power to create by himself, to have offspring without the aid or intervention of any other being—he may be divine or mortal. Hence Agdistis has an *insana et furialis libido et ex utroque sexu*. He does not worry about the gods or mankind and he believes that he is the most powerful being in the world. In many respects he has the traits of evil god[s] in Iranian and Indian literature, and the jealous gods now use similar tricks against him. When the other gods in the divine council are too fearful and hesitate Liber, or Bacchus,—possibly in order to obtain immortality (though this is not stated)—arranges to tame him. . . . The water in the spring where Agdistis drinks is mixed with wine. When Agdistis sinks into a deep sleep . . . after having drunk this mixture, Dionysus ties Agdistis' virile parts to a tree [or: his own foot] with ropes . . . , awakening the wild god *ipse se viribus eo quo vir erat privat*. From the blood the earth conceived a pomegranate tree with fruit (*malum cum pomis punicum*) (Arnobius), or an almond tree which bore fruit in due time (Pausanias).
>
> The daughter of the "king," or of the river Sangarius, whose name is Nana, takes them and puts them in her lap. . . . Only Pausanias recounts that the fruit immediately disappeared, but both Pausanias and Arnobius relate that the virgin daughter then became pregnant. Although Nana's father tried to kill his daughter, the Great Mother saved the future son before his birth. When the child is born Sangarius still does not understand how this happened, he gives order to expose it. (Vermaseren 1966, 3–5)

Here we see a myth combining the idea of a sexless or self-fecundating monster that is indicative of chaos or—as is Humbaba or Kronos, who eats his children—of tyranny, and whose drunken emasculation by the hero Dionysus produces the seed that falls into the virgin's lap. "Attis was born from the seed of Agdistis, which was changed into the fruits of a tree, to an unmarried daughter of Sangarius" (ibid., 6). As in the Perseus myth, where Acrisius tries to rid himself of his heir,

> Sangarius' role in the drama is that of a king who does not acknowledge his illegitimate grandson as a future successor. . . . (ibid.)

The thematic parallels between Greek and Near Eastern myths—between tales involving Medusa, Humbaba, or Agdistis—are by this legend made readily apparent. While none of the stories is exactly comparable, many important parallels may be drawn between any two of the three cases. The themes that illustrate these parallels include the conquering of an androgynous or sexually ambiguous monster that threatens social or cosmic stability; conquest by emasculation or decapitation; the assistance provided in that conquest by some non-human, divine, or theriomorphic agent; conflict among members of the same lineage; and birth through a shower of seed that creates an unwanted grandson. While there are still other parallels that may be construed, these seem most relevant to the peculiarities of the Perseus-Gorgon legend.

If influences as such are to be argued between Near Eastern and Greek mythology, then the differences between the birth of Attis and the Perseus-Gorgon story suggest more in the way of influences than would direct copying, since structural inversion is a more likely reaction to the barbarous ideas of others than is the copying of their absurd practices. Viewed from this perspective, the structure of the above version of Attis's birth does provide some possible explanation of why the Gorgon might have assumed Cybele's heraldic imagery and, in general, the Near Eastern Mistress pose. On the symbolic level, the Perseus-Gorgon story is, indeed, something of a structural inversion of the Near Eastern myth, the Greek hero decapitating the Mistress figure in reaction to the Near Easterners who are emasculated in her name. The character of the monster Agdistis, moreover, provides a possible indication of the relationship between the leonine figures of Asia Minor and those that arose at various times in Mithraic religion. It is worth noting here that the theme of a sexually ambivalent leonine figure personifying time is so common in the ancient Near East[25] that attempts to find a source for the later so-called lion-headed personage of Roman Mithraism have regularly focused on these Oriental monsters (Barnett 1975, 466). The sexuality of the Mithraic lion-headed personage is frequently obscure enough that scholars are led to believe that it was deliberately meant to be ambiguous. Interestingly, the Mithraic devotees were known to dress up in masks (Pl. 65; Hinnells 1975, 309; Vermaseren 1963, 101, 168), at one level to wear the mask of a lion, and, of all things, to partake of a baptism whereby, according to Tertullian, Mithras makes a mark on his initiates' foreheads.

While it may be said that the Gorgon has many Near Eastern corre-lates, there are several problems that impede our seeing her as directly derivative of some Near Eastern image. First, as has been pointed out, the Mistress of the Animals model is extremely ancient and very com-mon. This means that legends employing the popular figure could have evolved quite independently at any location from a much earlier source and that proposed links between, for example, such names as Cybele, Kybebe, Kubaba, and Khumbaba resulted from a conscious association of preexisting figures rather than a linear transmission of a monster or a deity from one tradition to the next.[26] A similar case could be made for Perseus since his name is known in Mycenaean times and since the root *per-* may be related to many concepts such as the words for Lithuanian and Slavic head-idols,[27] the Etruscan *phersu* or, for example, the Greek *Persephonē*. Here again we must recognize that a common class of ideas

Plate 65. Mask wearers at Mithraists' meal. Drawing of limestone relief found at Konjik in Herzegovinia, probably 4th century A.D. At the far right is seen a person wearing a lion's mask (Leo) and at the left another in a raven's mask (Corax). Two other initiates stand to either side of the central figures (Mithras and Sol). Vermaseren 1963, Fig. 26.

need not imply influences. In fact, it seems more likely that quite the opposite is the case, that the peculiarities rather than the common features—inversions rather than imitations—are our best signs of a simple influence from one culture to the next.

Another problem is that while the legends of the Gorgon, Cybele, and Humbaba demonstrate remarkable structural parallels, the truth is that they just are not the same: Humbaba is a forest creature; the Gorgon Medusa inhabits the shores of Oceanus and is one of three sisters; and while Athena may have had a theriomorphic origin, she shows very little resemblance to Gilgamesh's wild-man friend, Enkidu. The list could go on, but quite clearly, while the legends may be said to be of the same type, they are in important respects extremely dissimilar. On the basis of these problems alone we might dismiss the idea that the Gorgon was not an entirely Greek invention. There is, however, another avenue of influence that to my knowledge has remained unexplored. This is the hypothesis that the Gorgon of the preclassical era is figured, at least in part, by superimposing Indo-Iranian and even purely Indian ideas on an earlier goddess figure, or on a Perseus legend, already known to the Greeks. The evidence for this view is, I think, significant; for it can be supported by iconographical comparisons as well as by mythological parallels, sociological structures, and historical trends. Let us begin by considering the name of the monster Humbaba.

While differing ideas have been presented to explain the meaning and origin of the name Humbaba, its most obvious source may be found in the language of the Elamites, the Babylonians' eastern neighbors who periodically raided Babylon from the Zagros Mountains and conquered Babylonia in 1100 B.C. The Elamites spoke an agglutinative language about which not a great deal is known. Nevertheless, the fact that the Babylonians and Elamites waged war upon each other over several centuries could easily explain the Babylonian association between the monster Humbaba, the name of an Elamite king (Khumbaba), and the idea of political tyranny. These associations are especially probable given the fact that Elamite kings were known to be deified within their lifetime (Ghirshman 1954, 67) and that King Khumbaba apparently introduced Elamite deities into Babylon, giving rise to the legend whereby he is slain as a monster by the hero Gilgamesh (Sykes 1930, 1: 59). Thus, Babylonians could not only come to associate foreign gods and rulers with demons—a cultural "influence" if ever there was one—but be assured in that conviction by the awareness that the Elamites could have a tyrant whose name was akin to one of the most popular members of the Elamite pantheon (Khumban).

The presence of Indo-European words in Mesopotamia, though of less importance in the second millennium B.C., grows in significance with the invasion of the Medes and Persians in the early first millennium. The existence of such words is of importance because it makes possible the connecting of the name "Humbaba" with a fundamental Indo-Iranian concept. The word *kumbha* is Sanskrit for "a jar, pitcher, [or] water pot" (Monier-Williams [1899] 1970, 293); metaphorically, it may also designate a pot that contains something sacred (e.g., *soma*, a demon or god), an embryonic container (i.e., a womb), or a round object that suggests containment and fertility (e.g., the superciliary protuberances of rutting elephants).[28] While Humbaba may not strike us as a particularly cogent analogue to the Gorgon, the word *kumbha* is archetypal enough in the Indian imagination that the question must be asked whether there are any significant Asian parallels for the Gorgon. To this question we must ultimately answer yes; but first we must ask how it would have been possible for any image or idea from such distant lands to have reached Greece in the preclassical era—long before we can be certain of any regular contact between Greeks and Persians, not to mention Greeks and Indians. One possible avenue of contact must surely have been through the Phoenicians, who had established themselves as traders between Babylonia and the Mediterranean in Mycenaean times and were well known to the Greeks of the early first millennium B.C. Even Greeks themselves were known to be on the Tigris at the beginning of the seventh century B.C., when they manned Assyrian ships fighting the Chaldaeans on the coast of Elam (Sykes 1930, 1: 41–42). It is, therefore, reasonable to assume that Greeks could have been exposed to themes from farther east at this early date, since Babylonian and Assyrian contacts with Medes, Persians, and Scythians could easily have resulted in the Phoenicians' relating new ideas, vague though they may have been, to the West. This is not to say that the Phoenicians did bring any ideas that were fundamentally new to Greece (though, of course, this argument is regularly made), but only that they could have had some influence. Here, I am merely establishing a structural ground for looking farther east, not a factual basis for discrediting Greek inventiveness.

An Indo-Iranian origin of Khumbaba is strongly suggested by other considerations. First, Khumbaba is mentioned as a god along with the gods Shuqamuna and Shimalia, both of whose names are Kassite.[29] Second, *kumbha* surfaces in Avestan religion; there we know of the immortal Khumbya, the "jar" demon, the "son of the jar" (Yasht 138). Iconographical considerations make analogies between Greece and the Zagros more compelling. The apotropaic marked forehead is manifest throughout

Indo-Iranian art and religion. The symbolism of the forehead was important not only in the worship of Mithras,[30] but also in the ancient religion
of the Magi,[31] when sacrificial victims were killed by a blow on the forehead (Zaehner 1961, 169), and throughout the entire history of the Parsees. To the present day, the symbolism of the forehead is important in
Avestan religion, as, for example, in the iconography of the "four-eyed"
dog—a sacred dog so described because of the mark or "eye" on its forehead above each natural eye. This animal figures in both the symbolism
of sexuality and that of death, the darker side, so to speak, of birth and
revivification. The four-eyed dog is central not only to the Zoroastrian
bareshnum, or Great Purification, but also to funerary rites, where it is
meant to sense through *sagdid*, "dog sight," or "the seeing of the dog,"
the condition of the deceased. Four eyes, in other words, had especially
to do with ascertaining the point of transformation from life to death. In
this respect, the four-eyed dog functions as a marker of boundaries. Its
role is apotropaic, protective; it counters the effects of the evil eye and
determines the exact threshold, as it were, of transformation:

> One can scarcely separate the funerary *sagdid* from the belief in the two
> dogs which, according to Videvat 13.9, keep the Bridge of the Retributor
> and which in turn have their opposite numbers in India (Rig Veda
> 10.14.2; Atharva Veda 18.3.13) in the two "four-eyed" dogs, messengers
> of the death god Yama. (Duchesne-Guillemin 1966, 59)

The four-eyed dog is generally associated with the dangerous jour-
ney across water to the kingdom of the dead; four-eyed dogs guard the
heavens (Boyce 1975, 116–17).[32] Though the dog was a sacred figure in
Iran, it was not without its dark, even profane, elements.[33] In India, this
profane nature was also apparent. The four-eyed dog not only protects
Yama, god of death, while he plays his flute beneath a "fair-leafed tree"
(*RV* 10.135.1), but is especially associated with the harlot's trade: in the
Taittirīya Brāhmaṇa, the year of the *aśvamedha* begins when the son of a
harlot is ordered to slay a four-eyed dog and pass it beneath the legs of
the sacrificial horse (P. Dumont 1948, 455). The act was meant to drive
away evil, but it was also a transition into a sacred event, a sacred time
and space. The rite of fertility was thus sanctified, and the transition
was thus accomplished through the actions of one who himself was the
symbol of profanation. Again, evil not only drives away evil, it also re-
vivifies the sacred—a fact that is clear in ancient India from the relationship of the dog to the rebirth of the solar year.[34]

Now, the four-eyed dog's possible symbolic parallel to the image of
Humbaba becomes more likely on a closer look at the word *kumbha*. In

Sanskrit the root *kumb-* means "to cover"—not only in the sense of placing a lid on a jar, but also in that of encircling, of marking out a perimeter, "an enclosure round a place of sacrifice."[35] It is the imagery of sacrifice and containment that connects the monster Humbaba with the Sanskrit word for "bowl," providing a container, a boundary, within which the demon is manifested; for like the contained entrails that displayed the face of Humbaba, the Sanskrit term is also used—especially as it concerns the worship of Durgā—to distinguish the horrific image contained in a bowl. In Sanskrit, moreover, the word *kumbha* means, as noted earlier, a superciliary mark on the elephant, that swells when the animal is sexually excited. *Kumbha* thus means not only "jar" but also the frontal globes or prominences on the elephant that swell in the "roaring" (cf. Latin *rūgīre*) or rutting season. The significance of the word *kumbha* rests, then, not only in the fact that it is part of both sacrifice and containment, but also in the fact that it is apotropaic and that it has everything to do with both the forehead and sexuality. From the function of Humbaba as a demon of bad birth, to the iconography of the superciliary mark, the word *kumbha* incorporates both the idea of delineating and protecting sacred space and that of the cycles of sexuality and birth, of death and revivification.

· 5 ·

The Third Eye

Iconological Considerations

In considering what might possibly have been the iconographical and ideological influences of Indian art on the West in the first half of the first millennium B.C., the greatest difficulty we encounter is the lack of Indian artifacts for the period. While there is a considerable amount of textual evidence from this era of Indian history, oddly there are virtually no important works of art surviving from the entire period between the Indus Valley civilization (ca. 2500–1500 B.C.) and the Maurya Empire— that is, until about the fourth century B.C. The usual reasons given for this absence of artifacts are that the Aryans did not build permanent sacrificial altars and that what art they did produce was likely to have been made of perishable materials (see, e.g., Taddei 1970, 46). Such reasoning is remarkable when one considers the material interests of other cultures of this period and the fact that small, transportable, but not unnoteworthy artifacts have been uncovered at nomadic sites from China to Europe. However this absence may in the future be accounted for, we must nevertheless concern ourselves in the study of Indian art with the iconography of a period later than that of preclassical Greece. A combination, however, of later artistic and earlier textual evidence will enable us to reconstruct the dominant features of the facial iconography of the period under consideration.

It has long been argued that the earliest post-Indus Valley sculptures from India—that is, the so-called lion capitals (Pl. 66) of the Maurya period (ca. fourth to second centuries B.C.)—show the direct influence of the Achaemenid Empire of greater Persia (sixth to fourth centuries B.C.)— an influence seen also in art styles that may have come to India from Iran

Plate 66. Lion column. Lauṛiyā Nandangaṛh, near Nepal. Maurya period, 243 B.C. It has been suggested that such pillars were in fact erected during an earlier era for Brahmanical or zodiacal purposes and that the placing of the lion of Buddha on the top was a means of reinterpreting the symbolism of an earlier pre-Buddhist cosmology. (Photo: Archaeological Survey of India.)

during the early third century B.C. by way of the envoys of the cos-mopolitan emperor Aśoka (Rowland 1977, 64).[1] The problem of where these lions came from is, however, complicated by our inability to place them in an existing artistic tradition—a dilemma that has lent favor to the idea that they were copied from Achaemenid Persian originals. In any case, that these leonine forms were readily adopted in Aśokan times obviously indicates an Indian predisposition for them. Again, diffusion depends upon a compatibility of disposition, and the notion that a par-ticular motif is simply invented by one group and then taken up by an-other is a severely limited and unsatisfactory commentary on the human imagination. The consequences of a broader consideration of Indian art may be seen in Gajjar's assertion that the iconography of certain Indian leonine figures—the Sarnath lions among them—is as much in accor-dance with Assyrian and Hellenistic sculpture as it is with the art of Achaemenid Persepolis, and that any account of Indian iconography must admit the fundamental significance of certain symbols in both early Vedic and West Asiatic mythology:

> Maurya sculptors evidently chose their forms not from Persepolis, but from a tradition cognizant of ancient Occidental art as well as of Vedic symbolism. In effect, details in the treatment of Asokan animals reveal as many similarities with Mesopotamian art in general, as with the Per-sepolitan protomes in particular.[2] (Gajjar 1971, 87)

A similar comparison with special reference to Greek and Indian notions of the horrific and apotropaic face, likewise, deserves to be explored, not only because of the importance of such images throughout Indian his-tory and art, but also because the Greek Gorgon can be shown to corre-spond more closely to Indian religious themes and iconographic motifs than to those of any other non-Greek tradition.

In addition to their heraldic qualities, set up as they were as regal monuments, the Maurya pillars have, as Irwin has argued (1976), a spe-cific sexual symbolism in which the column is united with the *terra mater*. Because these monuments were intentionally placed in moist, fer-tile soil, they were, in this view, understood as symbols of divine sexual union—of column and *kumbha*, the vessel or womb (Pl. 67). To this simple image is added another great theme in Indian art: the churning by the gods of the ocean primeval, the occasion on which the gods created *amṛta*, the Elixir of Immortality so honored in the Vedic hymns.

Lions, sacred vessels, and themes of divine union are images that have a primordial and archetypal character. But it is not yet clear why the iconography of the forehead would be part of the *kumbha* concept. How could such a peculiar detail be part of a class of ideas so otherwise immediate, so general, so intuitively related? Indian iconography provides only one possible answer, one image that has the symbolic complexity, traditional importance, and the archetypal character to class it among these other great symbols. That image is the third eye, the inward eye of higher perception that is also a powerful external force.

Without a body of icons that would give direct knowledge of how Indians represented their deities in the period between the eighth and sixth centuries B.C., it might appear impossible to pursue a comparative iconographic study. However, combining what is historically known about Indian religion of the early first millennium with its vast literature makes it possible to demonstrate a continuity of archetypal imagery— imagery that in other historical periods would manifest itself in the plastic arts. Though the study of Indian art of much of the pre-Christian era can only be the study of what Coomaraswamy has called "an iconography without icons" (1927b, 293), there is sufficient evidence to indicate that the third eye was an important feature of Indian religion in the first half of the first millennium B.C. The first Buddha, Gautama, born in the

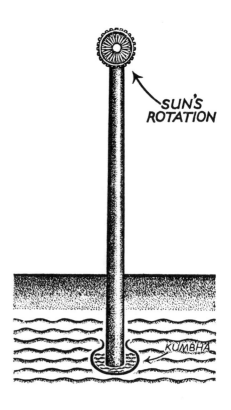

Plate 67. The Cosmic Pillar resting in the primeval *kumbha.* On its capital is an icon (sun, lion, bull) symbolic of the primordial impregnator of the sacred vessel. Drawing by Margaret Hall. Courtesy John Irwin (from Irwin 1976, Fig. A).

sixth century,[3] is traditionally said to have had a third eye that took the form of a hairy mole at the center of his forehead. Known as the ūrṇā, it was a distinctive powerful mark that later became one of the magic signs (lakṣaṇā) appropriate to representations of him[4]—of a warrior king, of prince turned monk, of the vanquishing fire of Agni that is also the inward fire of enlightenment.[5] Even though the Buddha is not represented in art before the Gandhara period of the late first century A.D.—when Hellenistic influences first gave rise to plastic images[6]—and even though known images of the Buddha displaying the ūrṇā are later still, the fact that the lion is an early symbol of the Buddha (Rowland 1977, 67), that the Buddha was thought to have in fact been a warrior, a Kṣatriya rebelling against Brahmanical superiority,[7] suggest that the ūrṇā is not distinct from his leonine characteristics as a warrior, any more than it is distinct from the vanquishing features of the third eye. There is a considerable interest, indeed, from the Vedas onward, in relating the imagery of the eye to leonine and apotropaic manifestations of certain deities; what is more, there is also a connection between the forehead and Great Goddess figures, and the forehead and the yogic āsanas, the meditative postures that can be traced all the way back to the civilizations of the Indus Valley, to at least one thousand years before the Buddha's birth.

Leonine Manifestations of the Eye

The growth of Indian mystical philosophy and the religious trend toward a more spiritual, theistic form of worship eventually combined to transform the notion of the third eye into an almost purely transcendental principle (Zaehner 1962, 10). It even came later to represent an inner consciousness, a spiritual quality in contrast to physical experience, an inner or transcendental eye. But however complex may be this spiritualistic perspective, its symbolic background is clearly more complex still and involves an inner enlightenment that is also an outward, material manifestation of the senses, a world-conquering physical strength. Thus, while inwardly directed, it represents an enlightening, higher form of perception; in its outward manifestation it is as fire, whose wrath is, in the words of Karapātrī, the power of all physical destruction:

> The frontal eye, the eye of fire, is the eye of higher perception. It looks mainly inward. When directed outward, it burns all that appears before it. It is from a glance of this third eye that Kāma, the lord of lust, was burned to ashes and that the gods and all created beings are destroyed at each of the periodical destructions of the universe. (Daniélou 1964, 214)

In its completeness, therefore, the third eye signifies not only the more recent emphasis in Indian thought on spirituality and abstinence, but also on all-devouring material destruction. The third eye both abstains and consumes, both enlightens and destroys. Such a paradox is central not only to the mythology of the third eye but as well to the complex solar imagery and the proliferation of solar deities characterizing the Vedas.

The third eye is, in essence, the synthesis of the other two, and for this reason the sun is glorified as the symbol of a single all-seeing eye. Likewise, the vision of the Vedic solar deities is usually described as the function of a single eye—such as in the orderly, "friendly" sun-eye of Mitra (Gonda 1972, 77), or Sūrya, who, since his name designates the solar orb as well, is the most concrete of solar deities:

> The adorable light of Sūrya in the sky is as the face (anīka) of great Agni ([RV] 10, 7³). The eye of Sūrya is mentioned several times (5, 40⁸ &c.), but he is himself equally often called the eye of Mitra and Varuṇa . . . or of Agni as well (1, 115¹); and once (7, 77³) Dawn is said to bring the eye of the gods. The affinity of the eye and the sun is indicated in a passage where the eye of the dead man is conceived as going to Sūrya (10, 16³ cp. 90¹³. 158³⁴). In the AV. he is called the "lord of eyes" (AV. 5, 24⁹) and is said to be the one eye of created beings and to see beyond the sky, the earth, and the waters (AV. 13, 1⁴⁵). He is far-seeing (7, 35⁸; 10, 37¹), all-seeing (1, 50²), is the spy (spaś) of the whole world (4, 13³), beholds all beings and the good and bad deeds of mortals (1, 50⁷; 6, 51²; 7, 60². 61¹. 63¹⁴). (Macdonell 1897, 30)

Even in cases such as that of Varuṇa, where the god has two hands, feet, and arms, the single face is characterized by the vision of a single eye:

> The eye of Mitra and Varuṇa is the sun (1, 115¹; 6, 51¹; 7, 61¹. 63¹; 10, 37¹). The fact that this is always mentioned in the first verse of a hymn, suggests that it is one of the first ideas that occur when Mitra and Varuṇa are thought of. The eye with which Varuṇa is said in a hymn to Sūrya (1, 50⁶) to observe mankind, is undoubtedly the sun. Together with Aryaman, Mitra and Varuṇa are called sun-eyed (7, 66¹⁰), a term applied to other gods also. (Macdonell 1897, 23)

As the sun itself is thus compared with the face of Agni, so too is that of Varuṇa (ibid.; RV 7.88.2). The association of the solar face with the face of Agni is particularly significant in the development of Indian facial iconography since fire, the manifestation of Agni, is also epitomized in the third eye. Because Agni, as fire, is the accomplisher of divine sacrifice, he is the great priest; he is the great seer who, as messenger and intermediary between gods and mortals, brings the former to the soma sacrifice. Thus, as the sacrifice of soma is received by the fire of Agni, the fire, the eye of Agni, the all-seeing eye of the sun, becomes symbolic of sensation—whether this sensation be exalted, ecstatic, and hallucinatory, or fiery, roaring, and destructive. Such an ambivalence is not only, therefore, characteristic of the Vedic notions of the divine, but is also fundamental to an understanding of the third eye. It is manifested in the iconography of deities and demons and is realized through masks on the world-stage that is its outward visual construct.

The fact that the third eye and the *ūrṇā*, or hairy mole, of the Buddha occur singly rather than in pairs would seem to weigh heavily against a leonine iconographic connection. Once the reconciliatory role of the third eye is realized, however, the necessity of its singleness becomes self-evident. It symbolizes unity because it manifests either its inner or outer aspect. It represents the deliverance from irreconcilability because oppositions are resolved through it. It is ambivalent in its capability, but decisive and conclusive. It is a symbol of opposition, but of opposites reconciled through the winning out of one force or the other. The face, the mask, becomes the intermediary, the arbiter between these two inner and outer oppositions, and the lion its iconographical symbol. The lion symbolizes this opposition not only because of its natural ambivalence as protector and destroyer, but also because the mythological character of the beast as well as the physiognomics of its representation are models of ambivalence. That strong protectors may also be wrathful destroyers is a theme emphasized not only by the ambivalence of such fire gods as Agni and Indra, but also in the latter's role as a warrior and in the destructive aspects of the dominant three-eyed Hindu figures of Viṣṇu, Śiva, and Durgā.

Just as in those creation myths of the world that divide divine power into a dual order—a dual symbolic classification—so too this order may be, conversely, controlled or undermined through the actions of an ambivalent figure equally capable of manifesting itself in one or the other of two previously opposed forces (Banerjea 1956, 477). The lion, which symbolizes the visual externalization of sensible experience, thus comes to represent the concerted outward consequence of the fire that is the third eye, the outward manifestation of its internal, invisible opposite. The symbolic dualism of the lion's natural superciliary protuberances becomes reconciled in the oneness of the solar symbol that, in lighting the world, sees all and makes all apparent. The symbolic marks become reconciled in the single eye, just as the two outer marks of the *nāman* may conjoin to form a central line. The lion's roar, the roar not only of Agni and Soma, but also of the warrior Indra, the power of the sun itself, is the terrifying roar, the *garjana*, of the Gorgon. The lion's eye, like the Medusa's and the Brahman priest's after imbibing the sacred *soma*, can kill at a glance (*Maitrāyaṇī Saṃhitā* 4.8.2). His tongue is that of Agni or of Kālī, who creates by destruction. While in the plastic arts the association of lion and sun is apparent in such images as the Aśokan columns, it is even more apparent in Vedic mythology. There, divine leonine ambivalence is common, though perhaps nowhere else so aptly rendered as in the figure of Indra.

Since Indra is the warrior who drinks *soma* in order to kill the archetypal dragon Vṛtra,[8] both Soma and Indra become vanquishers identified with a roaring, scorching, leonine fire. This fire is the face of Agni symbolized in the third eye, the eye of the fire itself. The association between Agni and Indra is so close that more than any other divinities these two are joined into a compounded force. Indra is described as the winner of light (*RV* 8.78.4), the one who burns Vṛtra like the sun (*RV* 8.12.9), the great god of battle and the guardian whom the warriors invoke (*RV* 4.24.3). He fights as does a lion (*RV* 4.16.14); he is even the lover of Ahalyā, the wife of the warrior Gautama. Indra, therefore, is the warrior *par excellence*, a fire that is both the sun and the eye of Agni, one who devours the ecstatic *soma* and who roars as the vanquishing lion.

Though the third eye may possibly derive from pre-Aryan solar worship (Banerjea 1956, 428, 430),[9] its appearance throughout later Hindu iconography shows how compatible it was with Vedic cosmology. In fact, the third eye's appearance to the present day as a common attribute of Viṣṇu and Śiva preserves not only its Vedic solar imagery but also its leonine outward character. This fact is especially interesting since these gods grew from an origin that was also Vedic into the most important of modern Hindu deities.[10] Though, as Zimmer reminds us, the details of their myths have been reshaped over time, Viṣṇu and Śiva are very ancient personifications of principles of power that are at least as old as the Vedas (Zimmer [1946] 1972, 178ff.); their popularity, or the popularity of gods much like them, among the non-Aryan tribes of India suggests that they are as much pre-Vedic as they are the tribal Indian adaptations of Aryan figures.

In assessing the significant leonine elements of Indian gods, one must begin by recounting Viṣṇu's leonine manifestation since, in fact, the fourth incarnation (*avatāra*) of Viṣṇu, whose name means "the penetrating" (see Jouveau-Dubreuil 1937, 57), is explicitly called a man-lion (*narasiṃha*: "half-man, half-lion").[11] The story from the *Bhāgavata Purāṇa* begins with an evil king, Hiraṇyakaśipu, whose name means "golden garment" or "golden vesture." Hiraṇyakaśipu was an arrogant and boastful man who had managed to be granted invulnerability by Brahmā, which unfortunately only exacerbated his impudence.[12] Hiraṇyakaśipu, who is described as a demon, had a son named Prahlāda, who was a devout worshipper of Viṣṇu. The father tried to discourage the son from his devotion and became increasingly incensed by the son's pious attitude. Because of the protection of Viṣṇu, the father's attempts to punish and even kill the son were all in vain. In a final effort to dissuade Prahlāda, Hiraṇyakaśipu began mocking the son's claims that Viṣṇu was omnipresent, and, demanding to know whether Viṣṇu was present in the stone pillar of that very building, kicked or punched it violently. To vindicate himself, save Prahlāda, and punish the impious king, Viṣṇu burst from the pillar of the temple in the form of Narasiṃha and tore Hiraṇyakaśipu to pieces.

The story of Narasiṃha is of great interest from a structural or transformational point of view. The event occurs at twilight; Viṣṇu bursts from a pillar that is a threshold—"neither inside nor outside" (Daniélou 1964, 169)[13]—and the incarnation itself is half man, half lion: *nara* (man) and *siṃha* (lion). As Banerjea points out, "the face is only [as in other *avatāras*] that of an animal (here, that of a lion with shaggy manes), all the other parts of the body being human" (1956, 415), so that transformation of faces, as in the wearing of masks, is central in the Hindu attitude toward appearances as manifested in the outward response of the third eye. This relationship, as we shall see shortly, is made explicit in the leonine manifestation of Śiva.

The other noteworthy features of the story of Narasiṃha are its great age and the fact that "man-lion" was an epithet of warriors. As Daniélou points out, "The cult of the man-lion is an ancient one. In the man-lion, valiance is worshipped as an aspect of divinity. This is a cult meaning for kings and warriors (*kṣatriya*)" (1964, 169). O'Flaherty has also called attention to the age of this figure, suggesting that the actual historical development of Narasiṃha

> preceded, and perhaps inspired, Śiva's *śarabha* form. The way in which the Man-lion appears, emerging from within a stone pillar, to save his devotee from a murderous demon may also have inspired the famous image of Śiva appearing from within the stone *liṅga* to save his devotee from the god of death. (O'Flaherty 1975, 195 n. 21)

The time sequence in the myth may, therefore, reflect a historical transformation that follows the mythological situation. After having destroyed the demon (*asura*) Hiraṇyakaśipu, Narasiṃha's destructive spree went unabated and threatened the earth's peaceful inhabitants. To combat this madness Śiva took on another leonine form (see Banerjea 1956, 488), that of the Janus-headed Śarabha, attacked Narasiṃha, caught hold of him and tore him up; the skin of Narasiṃha, he wore as his garment and the head was worn on his chest or, as some accounts have it, on his *makuṭa* [crest] as an ornament. Viṣṇu came to his proper senses and retired, after praising Śiva, to his own abode. . . .[14] (Gopinatha Rao 1914–16, 2, 1: 172)

In this role, Śiva's behavior reminds us of that of Heracles—or perhaps of Athena—in making a cloak of the skin and a crest or aegis of the head. The Śarabha legend, however, as an accretion of the Narasiṃha story, in no way diminishes the power of the man-lion image, for, as we shall see, Śiva's own most powerful image, the *kīrttimukha*, is the direct analogue of Narasiṃha. What is more, we see throughout the history of Hindu iconography the Narasiṃha image evolving into several distinct and well-known manifestations (Gopinatha Rao 1914–16, 1, 1: 145–61). In fact, an association between the Narasiṃha legend and Indian religious drama is certain in eastern India, where performances in honor of the Hindu god formerly involved human sacrifice. The onetime prevalence of such sacrifices among the forest tribes, such as the Gonds' to their tiger god, suggests not only that the Hindu ritual drama may derive from an aboriginal practice, but also, as is sometimes suggested, that lion gods such as Viṣṇu are of aboriginal or at least non-Aryan origin. As for why this beast should persist as a manifestation of the Hindu divine form, the literature provides ample mythological reason that "this fearful man-beast is the greatest being wandering on the earth" (*Nṛsiṃha-pūrvatāpinī Upaniṣad* 2.13; see Daniélou 1964, 169). As for how this image passed from the Vedas to the modern day as a dominant facial type and frequent mask form, we must examine the lion as a manifestation of Śiva.

Like Hiraṇyakaśipu, Jalandhara was also a tyrant demon. Jalandhara had accumulated so much kingly power that he sent Rāhu, the monster "whose function is the eclipsing of the moon" (Zimmer [1951] 1974, 175),[15] to challenge Śiva himself.[16] The challenge concerned Jalandhara's megalomaniac intention to make Śakti,[17] Śiva's own love and the mother of Skanda, the god of war, his own bride.[18] As soon as Rāhu delivered Jalandhara's demand, however, Śiva responded in a characteristically leonine way:

From the spot between his two eyebrows—the spot called "The Lotus of Command" (*ājñā-cakra*), where the center of enlightenment is located and the spiritual eye of the advanced seer is opened—the god let fly a terrific burst of power, which explosion immediately took the physical shape of a horrendous, lion-headed demon. The alarming body of the monster was lean and emaciated, giving notice of insatiable hunger, yet its strength was resilient and obviously irresistible. The apparition's throat roared like thunder; the eyes burnt like fire; the mane, disheveled, spread far and wide into space. (Zimmer [1951] 1974, 180)

Rāhu, terrified by this man-lion manifestation, pleaded with Śiva for protection.[19] Interestingly, Śiva, now separated from his man-lion manifestation, requested that his creation feast on itself rather than on Rāhu; forthwith it began by eating its own feet, legs, arms, torso, and neck, until all that remained was its face. What remained in effect was the mask, the Face of Glory, or kīrttimukha, so called because this self-consumed manifestation was to Śiva also a pleasing self-interpretation. Zimmer describes this pleasure as deriving from Śiva-Rudra, or Śiva's Vedic world-conquering name, rudra—"The Howler," "The Roarer,"[20] who is responsible for the cosmic fire that periodically annihilates the universe:

> gratified by the vivid manifestation of the self-consuming power of his own substance, he smiled upon that creature of his wrath—which had reduced its own body, joint by joint, to the nothingness of only a face— and benignantly declared: "You will be known, henceforth, as 'Face of Glory' (kīrttimukha), and I ordain that you shall abide forever at my door. Whoever neglects to worship you shall never win my grace." (Zimmer [1951] 1974, 181–82)

Thus, the kīrttimukha, like the pillar from which Narasiṃha bursts, represents the point of transformation between the outer world and the inner sanctum. It is as much a metaphorical mask, therefore, as it is an auspicious device for the protection of true believers such as Prahlāda. In fact, as I shall argue in the next chapter, it especially becomes mask-like when its various manifestations are considered as a class. We shall see how its iconography signifies a specific sensation and how the autonomous image this mask represents is grounded in the senses. We must, however, first ask what connection there might be between Indian gods and Greek notions of ambivalent leonine daimons.

Foreheads

There exists much ancient evidence that indicates the aesthetic importance and magical significance of decorating the body with cosmetics. Red dyes, for example, commonly applied to the fingers, toes, and the face, were used from a very early date. At the time of the Indus Valley civilization, colors employed in the decoration of the body were believed to have magical properties (Chandra 1940, 63). Not only were cosmetics offered to the great Celestial Serpent, but specific colors, also, were employed to indicate different mental states—a belief that has remained important in Indian iconology to the present day:

> Black, for instance, is associated with evil passion and it is supposed to be imbued with an efficacy which is powerful enough to drive away evil

spirits; it is used by some sections of the Indian people to guard against
the evil eye at marriages, deaths, etc. (Chandra 1940, 63)

In fact, the Vedic etymology of Kālī, the fierce goddess who is Śiva's consort, confirms not only the antiquity of the belief that black was an apotropaic color, but also the association between the apotropaic color and
the iconography of the horrific monster face. In Vedic times, the word
kālī was associated with the seven tongues of Agni, who used them to
devour oblations of butter. According to the *Muṇḍaka Upaniṣad* (1.2.4),
these tongues include Kālī and Karālī.[21] Thus, while Agni is the focus of
the Vedic ritual hymns, Kālī, "the black," is the terrifying manifestation
of the horrific devouring tongue. Agni, born of wood and consumer of
wood, is said to make the forest black with a lick of the tongue. Conversely, as a beneficent force, Agni is the rising sun and the source of
enlightenment. This complex solar imagery of devastation and enlightenment—of an ambivalent deity who is a destroyer but also a source of
inspiration—underlies the notion of the third eye. This same imagery
also assures the close connection between the solar fire of Agni and the
facial features of the lion since, from Rome (Vermaseren 1963, 119) to India (Macdonell 1897, 93), the lion's wide-open mouth mythically accounts for the scorching heat of the sun.

From where, then, might we suppose the concept of the third eye to
derive? According to the Purāṇas and Upaniṣads the three eyes refer to
the sun, moon, and fire respectively—a combination for which Śiva is
particularly known. His horrific and erotic imagery is continually expressed in his relationship with the Goddess; love and fear are complementary aspects of their relationship, his third eye shining forth when
his other two are covered by Pārvatī in love or in anger (O'Flaherty 1969).
The third eye is a fire like the sun, a fire that is internal and external,
latent and manifest, dark and light. Like the twenty-four-hour path of
the sun and the behavior of all powerful Hindu deities, the third eye is
enlightening on the one hand and dark and destructive on the other.
That the solar attribute is the prerogative of several Vedic deities (e.g.,
Sūrya, Mitra, Varuṇa, Indra, Agni, Soma, and Śiva) is evident in the difficulty with which figures on early artifacts are positively identified.
This widespread use of the eye, however, should not suggest that it is
indiscriminately appropriated in the representation of any deity or that
its symbolism is very general and undefined. From the beginning of both
Indian and Iranian iconography, the sun is not only destructive but is
symbolic of fertility and birth, so that it naturally becomes identified
with Great Goddess figures whose consorts, the lions, and whose heraldic posture identify them as such. In fact, one Iranian figure displays a

rising sun on her forehead at what becomes the location of the third eye (see Ghirshman 1964, 421 n. 61). Likewise, the decoration of the forehead in the worship of solar deities in India is an early practice, and we must therefore ask what is peculiar to ancient Indian mythology that would account for such images of divine paradox. The answer is to be found in the ecstatic sensibility and in particular in the connection of the eye not only with destruction and fertility but with the psychoactive *soma*.

In Luristan, we see several examples where *soma*—or *haoma* as it was known in the Avesta[22]—is connected with fertility, as when it is offered to Ashi (Yasht 17); indeed, it was believed to be life personified. Imbibing the blood of the bull mixed with *haoma* (*soma*) provided both immortality and ecstatic enjoyment to the followers of Mithra. Like *haoma*, the Indian *soma* was the god of life (Vermaseren 1963, 17). It was a plant; it was also a god.[23] *Soma* had milk as an admixture and was said to be a rain or milk that fell from the moon. It was likened both to the seed of the sacred bull and to the nourishment of the heavenly cow (Zaehner 1966, 21). As Macdonell remarks, "Soma is said to flow clearly with a stream of honey like the rain-charged cloud" (1897, 107). *Soma* was both the embryo of the waters and a kind of fertile honey. Not only was *soma*, or *haoma*, said to bring on immortality and an entry into pure light, but, like the eye of Mitra and Varuṇa—which is the sun itself—*soma* was a wise seer (*RV* 8.68.1). In other words, it not only made visions possible, but was vision itself.

That *soma* is connected with honey is itself interesting, since *soma* may also be the honey-mead that provides vision and immortal light, exhilaration and immortality. *Soma* and mead are connected as intoxicants and also as mythological equivalents (Macdonell 1897, 105). This possible equation of hallucinogen and mead not only shows how crucial sensory exhilaration was for Vedic religion; it also raises some interesting questions about the etymology of the hallucinogen's name. The word *soma* derives from the crushing process by which the drug was prepared; indeed, the other gods are said to have conspired to kill King Soma by crushing him with stones. As an elixir it was metaphorically connected with mead and with honey, so that the words were somewhat synonymous:

The term *madhu*, which in connexion with the Aśvins means "honey" or "mead," comes to be applied, in the general sense of "sweet draught," not only to milk (*payas*) and ghee (*ghṛta*), but especially to the Soma juice (4, 27[5]; 8, 69[6]). Mythologically *madhu* is the equivalent of Soma when the latter means the celestial ambrosia (*amṛta*). Conversely, *amṛta* is frequently used as an equivalent of ordinary Soma (5, 2[3]; 6, 37[3] &c.; VS. 6, 34; ŚB. 9, 5, 1[8]). King Soma when pressed is *amṛta* (VS. 19, 72).

Another expression is *somyam madhu*, "Soma mead" (4, 26[5]; 6, 20[3]). Fig-
uratively the Soma juice is called *pīyūṣa* (3, 48[2] &c.), milk (9, 107[12]), the
wave of the stalk (9, 96[8]) or the juice of honey (5, 43[4]). . . . The juice
is intoxicating (1, 125[3]; 6, 17[11]. 20[6]) and "honied," *madhumat* (9, 97[14]).
The latter expression simply means "sweet," but as applied to Soma
originally seems to have meant "sweetened with honey," some passages pointing to this admixture (9, 17[8]. 86[48]. 97[11]. 109[20]). (Macdonell
1897, 105)

Since *soma/madhu* is also produced by the churning of the primordial waters, and therefore related to the archetypal *kumbha*, it might be pertinent to ask if *madhu* and *kumbha* may be compared to anything Greek.
Such a comparison may be questionable, first, because we have virtually
no evidence of any contact between Greeks and Indians in preclassical
times; and second, as noted earlier, because what we lack in early Greek
texts we lack in Vedic and Brahmanical icons. The first problem need not
give pause, however, since no direct contact would have been necessary
for ideas to have been exchanged. Greeks need not have known Indians
to know something of their ideas; one need not have met the individual
responsible for initiating a rumor for its information, spurious or otherwise, to affect one, nor need one understand the etymology of a word to
be using it, or not using it, in its original sense. For the second difficulty,
we must ask how much the Indian icons we do know of resemble early
Greek ones, and, if they are similar, whether there is enough evidence to
argue that the same or similar images were also known in India.

It is hard to see a modern depiction of Durgā, Kālī, or any one of the
Great Goddess forms without being struck by her iconographical similarity to the Greek Gorgon (Pl. 68). One cannot help but be amazed that
a creature so identically depicted—from the snakes around her head, to
her bulging eyes, gnashing teeth, protruding tongue, and the mark on
her forehead—could exist in such entirely different historical contexts
separated by thousands of years. But is the similarity only the result of
the archetypal nature of this face? In order to see how she may have assumed this form at an earlier time, we should first especially examine
the history of the forehead mark that she shares with other figures. For
the moment, that is, it is necessary to look not only at the iconography of
the Great Goddess in India, but to the other two great Hindu deities, Śiva
and Viṣṇu, since one cannot address the history of Hinduism without
pointing out the androgyny that, though mainly an attribute of Śiva,
may be seen in the iconography of all three figures.

Androgyny and the worship of trinities or of deities with two consorts are structural factors of utmost importance in Indian religion. The
consequences of these interrelations for both the facial iconography and

Plate 68. The Goddess (Kālī, Durgā, or Pārvatī), consort of Śiva. In this modern representation of the Indian Goddess, we see how closely her iconography parallels that of the Gorgon—tusks, tongue, snakes, eyes, even her forehead. Moor 1810, Plate 27.

the mythological interrelations of major deities are considerable. Śiva is no doubt the best modern example of an androgyne, since the Goddess is often perceived as an emanation of him. Conversely, both Śiva and Viṣṇu are frequently understood to be mounts of the goddess Durgā (van Kooij 1972, 33); aspects of one figure can be assumed by another according to the perspective of the worshiper. The river Ganges, for example, is worshiped as the trinity, Brahmā-Viṣṇu-Śiva from the *Gaṅgāvataraṇa* point of view, as a threefold river, and as the Goddess herself in Bengal. Likewise, what is iconographically significant for one may be, with certain variations, assimilated or subsumed by another figure. A Mistress of the Beasts may appear in the same pose employed by a Master, and specific elements like the *tilaka* or *nāman*—the mark on the forehead frequently associated with the third eye (O'Flaherty 1969)—may take on a wide variety of shapes while representing sectarian variations on a single theme (Pl. 71).

Let us look at the case of Viṣṇu. He is not only the man-lion *par excellence* in Hindu mythology; his similarity to the Gorgon is indeed much closer than a mere mythological comparison might suggest. The most common attribute of Viṣṇu is the mark, worn on the forehead both by the god and his followers, called *tirunāman* or *nāman*. Today, there are two basic kinds of *nāman*; their names signify the way they are joined together:

> The *Vadagalai* gives the *Nâmam* [*nāman*] the shape of a U, and the *Teṅgalai* prolongs the white mark just on the nose and takes the form of a Y [Pl. 69]. . . . [The *nāman*] consists of three vertical stripes; the middle one is red, and is called *Tiruchurnam* (holy chalk), because it is made of a

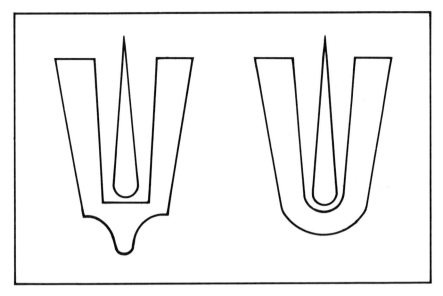

Plate 69. Nāman (Teṅgalai and Vadagalai). This mark, commonly made on the forehead, is used as a sectarian mark and is frequently associated with the third eye. After Jouveau-Dubreuil 1937, Fig. 16. Drawing by Mary Ryder.

Plate 70. a, Vaiṣṇava Brahman (South India). *b,* Vendor of Vaiṣṇava *nāman* clay. Thomas 1960, figs. 125, 140. (Photo: India Pictorial Features.)

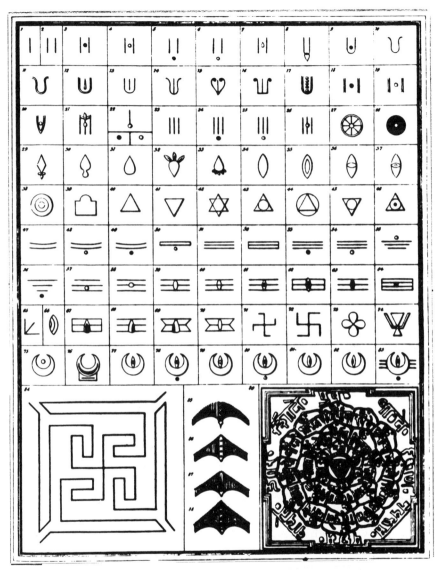

Plate 71. Hindu sectarian marks. The chart shows the wide variety of marks that distinguished the many major and minor sects of the late eighteenth century. Moor 1810, Plate 2.

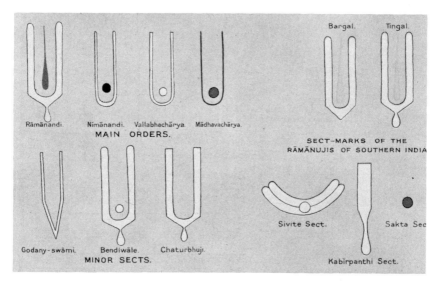

Plate 72. Hindu sectarian marks. Although, as can be seen in Plate 71, sectarian marks have evolved an elaborate iconography, these are the common sectarian marks of the twentieth century (main orders and minor sects). Russell [1916] 1969, vol. 2.

mixture of lime and saffron. The other two stripes on each side of the first are much broader and are joined below. They are white and are called *Gôpichandana* [Pl. 70]. (Jouveau-Dubreuil 1937, 58)

The iconology of the *nāman* is historically quite complex, as a look at the various Hindu sectarian marks illustrates (pls. 71 and 72), and these marks have clearly undergone transformation over time. The especially consequential point in the iconology of Viṣṇu, however, is not simply that the *nāman* indicates particularly his role as Lord of the Beasts, which he shares with both Śiva and the Goddess, but that in this regard he is notably leonine—either in his own manifestation as the man-lion Narasiṃha or as a deity depicted precisely in the Lord of the Beasts pose—with the *nāman* prominently delineated and flanked by two lions (Pl. 73). In this capacity he resembles the Goddess, who is regularly compared to foreign Mistress figures such as Artemis (Darian 1978, 69–78) and Cybele (Bhattacharji 1970, 82–92, 158–77), since Durgā is noted for her leonine consorts. From the point of view of those who advocate her worship, both Viṣṇu and Śiva are her mounts; she thus becomes the ultimate feminine force. Structuring the major deities in this way is not only the basis of Śāktism—the more or less licentious worship

of the female principle—but it also suggests that the cults of both male
and female deities may center around archetypal themes (e.g., Śāktism
is generally a very female, black—that is, "left-hand"—form of worship,
and the lion, even when manifested as the Narasiṃha *avatāra* of Viṣṇu, is
decidedly "left-hand" [van Kooij 1972, 30]). Likewise, the leonine aspect
of the forehead is not only tied to Viṣṇu as Narasiṃha, but is an even
more significant part of Śiva and of the idea that the Goddess is a manifestation of his androgyny (see Kramrisch 1981, 197ff., especially 228ff.,
and O'Flaherty's comprehensive study of androgyny [1980b]). When the
Goddess playfully covers Śiva's eyes, his fierce third eye, the eye of fire,
appears and burns the Himālaya, since everything would be enveloped
in darkness if he did not gaze upon it.[24] Likewise, in the *Liṅga Purāṇa*
(1.41.7–9), Śiva springs as a fierce, enormous androgyne from the forehead of Brahmā:

> His androgynous body had been conceived in Brahmā's mind. When it
> emerged from Brahmā's head, it was terrifying to behold, glowing like

Plate 73. Rāmānuja, founder of Vaiṣṇavism. Mysore. A modern example of
Viṣṇu in the heraldic Master of the Beasts pose. Thomas 1960, Fig. 71. (Photo:
India Pictorial Features.)

the sun, hot because of Brahmā's anger and because it was the shape of Rudra, who is Fire. (Kramrisch 1981, 200)

As for the Goddess's own forehead, we find that it is indeed the source of life itself:

> Śiva did not create mortals. He stood by as the Great Goddess, his Śakti, who stemmed from him gave Brahmā the power to create women. She gave to him of herself, of her own power (*śakti*) when a Śakti issued from her forehead. (ibid., 225)

Though such speculating leads frequently to complicated descriptions, what is essential to remember is that the divine must necessarily be contradictory and that it may ultimately be represented as a single point (*bindu*)—the substance of both Śiva and Śakti, the resolution of complementary opposites.

We will further discuss the forehead's significance and the complementary and contradictory character of its iconography in the following section; if, however, we are finally to compare the Indian and Greek facial iconography, we must first ask why, during the early days of the Gorgon, we have no clear Indian prototype of the Goddess. The answer is at once complex and simple—complex because dating emendations of the texts is almost impossible when the origins of such major works as the *Rāmāyaṇa* and *Mahābhārata* are disputed by hundreds of years, simple because there were major trends that clearly affected the role of the Goddess at particular times in Indian history. In the Vedic and Brahmanical periods, the periods with which we are most concerned, much popular religion, including worship of the Goddess, is not often discussed in the written materials. This fact does not keep us from recognizing some of the important elements of popular religion, but it does mean that they can often only be seen indirectly:

> The Brahmanic rituals were too technical and the Upanishadic Brahman was too abstract to affect the religious ideas and practices of the masses. . . . Even in Rigvedic times, the ritual was an elaborate and expensive affair in which the rich alone could engage. It was, therefore, not only a hieratic but an aristocratic cult. The real religion of the masses was different. (P. Banerjee 1973, 11)

How different was it? Answering this question is not easy, because the more that is understood about both popular and non-Aryan tribal religion in India, the more one realizes the importance of the worship of the feminine principle throughout Indian history. Goddesses, as Macdonell pointed out long ago, "occupy a very subordinate position in Vedic belief and worship" (1897, 124). Furthermore, the Vedic literature has been widely recognized for presenting a very one-sided view of Indian religion, ignoring, naturally, the pre-Aryan religion that yet continues in the non-Aryan languages and social institutions of South India, in many tribal customs of the North itself, and in much of what is generally referred to as popular religion. "Many of the basic features of Hinduism," writes Marshall in discussing their ancient character, "are not traceable to an Indo-Āryan source at all" (J. Marshall 1931, 1: 77). The well-known exception among early Aryanized texts is the *Atharva Veda*, which contains hymns and charms employed in the daily lives of the ancient Indians. In this sacred text, we find direct references to the philosophical meaning of certain facial icons from the point of view of popular religion; and here, in large measure, we are able to see the structural connection between the various ambivalent, leonine androgynes known in India from the civilization of the Indus Valley to the present day.

Soma and *Madhu*: Aphrodisiacs and Apotropaism

Among the many love charms described in the *Atharva Veda* is one (*AV* I, 34, 3–5) utilized to secure a woman's love by means of a plant, one whose name, *madhu* or *madugha*, is synonymous with the Sanskrit word for honey. Used as an ointment, *madugha* was a powerful attractive force, a compelling sweetness that made possible both the spiritual and the physical oneness of man and woman.[25] Like the third eye, from which *madhu* flows as the Ganges, *madugha* is both mental and physical—not only securing mutual spiritual attraction but influencing the outer world of sensory experience. *Madhu* was, as was *soma*, what motivated the third eye, what caused it to achieve its most extreme sensory state. The terms *madhu* and *soma* are, however, themselves not easily defined.

The Sanskrit *madhu* is part of a large and difficult conceptual complex. Nonetheless, there is a thread of continuity uniting the various terms of which the word *madhu* is a part. Most commonly, the focus of *madhu* terms is, as already mentioned, a kind of sweetness, and in particular a "milky" sweetness. But, in the Vedas, *madhu* refers not only to the honey of a bee, to ecstatic love charms, and to metaphorical sweetness; it signifies, in being used interchangeably with *soma*,[26] an imbibed psychoactive drink. Where the sweetness or milklike nature of the drink was emphasized, *madhu* rather than *soma* seems to have been the more appropriate term, since milk was apparently mixed with the *soma* drug for purposes of making it pleasantly sweet and drinkable. More likely still is the possibility that *madhu* was a separate substance that, because of its psychoactive properties, was interchanged, if not intentionally conflated, with *soma*. The reasons for this assertion are as follows.

The Sanskrit *madhu* becomes the root for a class of notions central to sacrifice, though the list of terms derived from or based upon the word *madhu* is complicated indeed. In addition to its references to honey and sweetness, the emphasis of the term may be conveniently divided into a few interdependent categories. First in importance are those terms relating to rites of spring. Like the role assumed by many Greek underworld fertility figures that relates them to the spring, the Sanskrit *madhu* corresponds to—even means—the spring: "of the first spring month"; "honey connected with spring"; "intoxicated by spring" (*madhumatta*). *Madhu-mādhavī* means, in fact, both "the spring flower abounding in honey" and "a kind of intoxicating liquor." The *madhumāsamahotsava* is the great festival of spring, the *madhumāsāvatāra* the "commencement of spring," and *madhusahāya* "companion of spring, god of love" (Macdonell 1924, 215). The annual role of the sweet, intoxicating beverage is, then, clearly central to the word. But from what source did this intoxicant derive? Here, a second group of terms helps us to be more specific.

Madha (*madhu*) refers to a liquor made of the blossoms of *Bassia latifolia* (Shastri 1959, 660). This so-called Indian butter tree is also called *madhūka*, which is Sanskrit for "bee." The *madhūka* is "a large deciduous tree with thick grey bark found in dry rocky hill regions, valuable for its delicious and nutritive flowers which bloom at night and fall on the ground at dawn. They taste something like figs and are much sought after by bears, birds and deer so that the natives, in order to collect the flowers for themselves, have to guard the trees" (ibid.). The *madhūka's* nocturnal blossom might seem without ritual or symbolic meaning were it not for the significance of related terms. *Madhūtsava* means, specifically, a "spring festival *on the day of full moon in the month of Kaitra* [March-April]" (Macdonell 1924, 215). So here we have linguistic evidence for a spring rite involving intoxication or hallucinogenic ecstasy and a tree, or a forest of sweet trees (cf. *Madhuvana*, "honey woods"), whose flowers are known by the same name as the bee that frequents them—flowers that, moreover, blossom in early spring, fall at night, and are responsible for the intoxicant employed on the first full moon of spring. *Madhusya*—which, however like "Medusa" in sound, is etymologically unrelated—likely meant much more than "to wish for honey," since it would have connoted a psychoactive substance taken at a particular time of year and in particular rituals. Though the function of the tree in these rituals, no doubt, varied, it seems that it was particularly associated either with marriage or with the worship of the Goddess in her terrifying aspect.[27] That, moreover, the tree figured in such practices at an early date is shown not only by the fact that references to *madhu* occur in the *Atharva Veda* in conjunction with love charms and marriage, but also by the fact that we find in the same text the earliest evidence in the Sanskrit literature for the prototype of Durgā, the terrifying Hindu goddess (*Atharva Veda* IX, 9; see Bhattacharji 1970, 166). Today, the blossoms of *Bassia latifolia* are used to make a powerful methylated stimulant, and the Sanskrit word *madhu* forms the basis for various names by which the tree is still known. The drink itself is often compared to brandy or whisky, and the association between *madhu* and types of alcoholic drink is confirmed in the Indo-European etymological connection between *madhu* and "mead."

Identifying the Vedic *madhu* solely with a liquor derived from *Bassia latifolia*, however, leaves crucial questions unanswered, for it is in no way clear how this liquor could account for the various forms of *madhu* described in the Vedic texts. Among the more curious instances already noted are a salve applied in the interest of physical pleasure, a drug employed frequently in women's rites, a licorice substance chewed to encourage prophecy and especially to produce eloquence in disputation, a drink affording warriors superhuman vanquishing power, and, above all, a substance akin to *soma*. *Madhu* and *soma* were not only a source of pleasure; throughout the Vedic hymns they are said to instill a physical power enabling warriors and warrior gods alike to exhibit both superhuman mental concentration and an annihilating physical strength. Indra, the patron god of warfare, is said to have imbibed the sweet *soma* from birth; it enables him to "see"; through *soma*, Indra gains the necessary concentration of strength to kill the monstrous Vṛtra. The "milk of heaven" is said to make the sun rise, to be born for battle. The polythetic imagery of love and warfare, of sweetness and power, of solar vision and solar fire are, thus, all aspects of a complex image; the hallucinogen symbolizes all of these because it is "many eyed"—both a means of achieving heightened inner states and a fixating, petrifying force, the ambivalent light that both nourishes and consumes.

While it is possible that some of these sensations may be caused by an alcoholic drink distilled from *Bassia latifolia*, clearly not all of them can. Where, then, do we look for a clue as to what substance or substances in Vedic times the term *madhu* referred? The answer is simple and perhaps points to an interpretation of horrific facial imagery that is both Indian and Greek; it arises, in India, in a problem of botanical classification.

In the *Manual of Indian Forest Botany*, Bor states that *Bassia* is an invalid label for the genus *Madhuca*. This genus includes, among other members, *Madhuca butyracea*, *Madhuca latifolia*, *Madhuca longifolia*, and *Madhuca malabarica*. Now, as these are different trees, it is difficult to see why the ancient Indians would have, as they did, anticipated scientific classification by grouping them together, until we realize that they are all members of the order Sapotaceae; for members of this order nearly all exude milky sap, and, moreover, the varieties with which we shall be presently concerned do so from flesh-colored cracks that develop in the bark of the tree.[28] By proposing that *madugha* referred in prehistoric times to a tree, or group of trees, yielding milky sap, we come up with some interesting resolutions of the *madhu* puzzle, especially given the Vedic connection between *madhu* or *soma* and milk.

By this time-honored classificatory scheme for sacred trees some ambiguities about the nature of *madhu/soma* may be readily resolved. For example, though *Madhuca* (*Bassia*) *latifolia* is widely used today as a domesticated, ornamental tree, other members of its order conform to ancient testimony that located *soma* or *madhu* solely in the mountains (*RV* 9.46.1). *Madhuca butyracea*, a sub-Himalayan tree, grows at elevations up to five thousand feet. "According to *Mahābhārata* I, 18, the *amṛta* in the cosmic sea is derived from the sap of trees originally growing on Mt. Mandara, admingled with the waters in the process of churning" (Coomaraswamy [1928–31] 1971, 2: 21). Like *Madhuca latifolia*, *Madhuca butyracea* also develops vertical blazes that exude milky sap. Another curious aspect of the ancient use of *madugha* was the chewing of it to win at disputation at an assembly. In this connection, Bloomfield (1897, 274ff.) rendered *madugha* as "licorice"; but another, more obvious, candidate presents itself, since latex derived from certain Sapotaceae forms the basis of chewing gum. Still, we have not yet addressed the more important question of what psychoactive *soma*-like substance the Vedic *madhu* might have referred to. Here, I think, the folk classification not only explains what appear to be textual inconsistencies, but provides some explanation for the hallucinogenic character of the Elixir of Immortality.

Though it is entirely possible that *madhu* refers only to the intoxicating drink distilled from the flowers of *Madhuca latifolia*, several milky plants, classed together as sacred, have known hallucinogenic powers. Many are highly alkaloidal, being used not only to form the basic substance in the manufacture of soaps, but also in the production of medicines, poisons, and hallucinogens. In recent times, evidence has been put forward to suggest that the delusions of flight, of superhuman powers, and of erotic orgies experienced by witches in medieval Europe were induced by tropane alkaloids absorbed into the bloodstream when applied externally to the body (Harner 1973, 125–50 and ref.). Belladonna, henbane, and mandrake all contain quantities of atropine and are capable of being absorbed through the skin and especially through the mucosae. Used as plasters or salves, the drugs derived from these plants have been held responsible for the combined sensations of erotic pleasure and superhuman physical strength. People under their influence not only experience the sensation of flight, but often claim to grow to giant size and to possess the capacity for prodigious physical feats.

Whether or not members of the genus *Madhuca* contain alkaloids of the right type can only be answered after the chemical properties of these trees are comprehensively analyzed. But there is at least enough factual evidence to determine that the folk classification of milky-sapped plants is based upon the real knowledge that some are stimulants. When the gods churn the ocean in the *Mahābhārata*, they are not only calling to mind the fact that the *Madhuca* is in fact employed to make a sweet butter or ghee, but they are also indicating that the Elixir is made by the mixing of all the milky-sapped plants. It was not, in other words, necessary for the ancient Indians to be aware of all of the properties of their sacred plants in order to create something hallucinogenic, since only one ingredient need have the requisite properties for inducing visions.

But how, we may ask, can we be sure of the significance of the folk class itself? While evidence will be provided in the last chapter to show that the classificatory idea is important enough to persist in contemporary Bali, the significance of the classification for early India is attested to by other cross-cultural evidence. First is the fact that the Indian *mahua* (*madhūka*) has a Chinese correspondent, *ma-huang*, which is the word for the alkaloidal drug ephedrine (Wasson 1968, 133; Brough 1971, 361). *Ma-huang* (麻黄), *Ephedra sinica*, is a powerful stimulant used both in ancient times and as an important drug in the modern Chinese herbal pharmacopeia. Ephedrine "causes dilation of the pupils, increase of blood-pressure, increase of heart rate, and relaxation of the muscles of the bronchi and gastrointestinal tract" (Brough 1971, 361; see also Goodman and Gilman 1955, 505–6). In other words, it has precisely the effects that would prepare warriors for battle. Stein (1931) connected the fact that the *Ephedra*, *ma-huang*, was a source of the alkaloidal drug ephedrine with his finding of bundles of *Ephedra* twigs in a Central Asian cemetery (see Wasson 1968, 132–33). The likelihood that the same kind of case could be made in India seems very good, especially given the fact that *Ephedra sinica*, the *ma-huang* of the Chinese, is known in Tibet, where its effects on the body are likened to those of atropine, the basis of hallucinogenic plasters. We already know, in fact, that *Madhuca latifolia* contains alkaloidal traces and *Madhuca longifolia* is employed as a cardiac stimulant. According to Chopra, after the oil is extracted from the seeds produced by the flowering tree, a yellow powdery substance (*huang* means "yellow") can be isolated; it is soluble, as is *madhu* in the *Atharva Veda*, where it is mixed with the fat of a bull. "It is fairly toxic and has a specific action on the heart and circulation, similar in many respects to that of the drugs of the digitalis group [i.e., it is a heart stimulant]" (Chopra 1958, 357). We also know that *Thermobacterium mobile*, one of the microorganisms of the agave in Mexico (Lindner 1933) and the active agent in producing alcohol from a number of plants, is itself a psychoactive stimulant. We cannot doubt that Lindner is correct in suggesting that we look to the so-called Indian butter tree (i.e., *Madhuca latifolia*) as a source of *Thermobacterium mobile*, since we know already from its use that the tree contains, if not *Thermobacterium mobile*, something very similar. We may, therefore, suspect that these trees were, in part, made sacred because of their psychoactive properties; more importantly, we may deduce that the *madhūka* possesses great symbolic value as a tree whose sweet blossoms fall on spring nights and whose bark is milk-exuding and wood flesh-colored. Throughout the remainder of this study, such a symbolic humanizing of certain tree species will be shown to be closely related to the iconography of horrific ambivalent deities; moreover, that this relationship can be evidenced in the symbolic importance and folk classifications of sacred trees will be apparent from their importance not only in India but among Hindus in Bali as well. Finally, if one adds to this symbolic framework the fact that such milky-sapped trees are considered by Indians to be the most appropriate timber source for making wooden *liṅga*s (Gopinatha Rao 1914–16, 2, 1: 77), then the complex iconography of sacred trees, Cosmic Pillars that are temple thresholds, and ambivalent notions of sexuality, ascetic meditation, and the warrior's vanquishing power may all be readily connected.

Judging from the extreme antiquity of the Indo-Iranian Yama legends, from the Iranian condemnation of the evil *mada*, from the connection between Haoma and trees (L. Campbell 1968, 62), from the fact that Yama not only played his flute beneath a fair-leafed tree (*RV* 10.135.1) but also was drinking with the gods within the tree itself (Darian 1978, 52 and notes and references), and from the link between Yama's dogs and the vernal equinox, we may assume that the connection between the worship and carousing at the change of the seasons under some psychoactive stimulant existed from the earliest times among Indo-Iranians. "The word used for Yama's carouses when he has reconquered immortality (*mad-*) is identical with the word used by Zoroaster for the 'drunkenness' (*mada*) of the followers of the Lie . . . " (Zaehner 1961, 132). The Persian reformer thus equated the followers of *mada* with the Lie—i.e., with those who performed the proper rituals with the wrong intentions.

Because, on the other hand, there is no precise equivalent of the Gorgon in Vedism and because, as an icon, the lion is often not as important as other animals in the early Vedic texts, it might be easy to conclude that no Gorgon-like figure was worshiped in India in this capacity. We shall see, however, that this cannot be correct, since there are in fact references in the Vedas and concrete examples later on to non-Vedic figures to which the Gorgon may be specifically compared. But before this problem can be addressed, it is necessary to examine further the connection between *madhu* and the underworld. This relationship is confirmed through several textual examples. I shall restrict myself to three: the *Mahābhārata*, the *Śatapatha Brāhmaṇa*, and the *Rāmāyaṇa*.

In the so-called doctrine of Madhu, two demons, one of which is named Madhu, stole the Vedas and took them to the underworld hell beneath the ocean. In this version, the *Mahābhārata* states that Viṣṇu took on the form of the horse's head to kill the demons, but left the head in the ocean that it might devour oblations (O'Flaherty 1980b, 222–23). That Viṣṇu is manifested as the horse's head is significant since "the Vedas are 'contained' in the head of the sacrificial stallion Dadhyañc" (ibid.). According to O'Flaherty, a later version, in which the demons are assisted by Māyā, goddess of illusion, shows how the story resembles two ancient equine models: one in which a demonic goddess stole and a divine one restored, the other exemplifying a contrast between a stallion that is a positive force and a mare that is demonic.

The second example, that from the *Śatapatha Brāhmaṇa*, shows that the Vedas as essential ritual instructions and the hallucinogenic *madhu* are synonymous. In this case,

> it is said that Viṣṇu's head was cut off by a bowstring and became the sun; the vital sap [*vīrya*] flowed from him. Since Viṣṇu is the sacrifice, the gods went on sacrificing with the headless sacrifice and so did not obtain heaven until the Aśvins replaced the head of the sacrifice. (ibid.)

In a related and truly bizarre episode, the Aśvins approached Dadhyañc about the possibility of learning the secret of the hallucinogenic drug. But since Indra had threatened to cut off Dadhyañc's head if he disclosed the secret, the Aśvins convinced him to let them sever it and put it away for safekeeping, replacing it with another, which Indra duly cut off. The horse's head—a mask?—once removed, was replaced by Dadhyañc's own. In this instance, the question of a connection with the underworld is complex, but suggested by several facts. First is the association between the ancient Indic *aśvamedha*, the great horse-sacrifice, and rites of revivification, occurring throughout the Indo-European world, in which a horse was sacrificed (and symbolically revivified) in connection with banter and, often, with the imbibing of a psychoactive substance. The underworld, in this instance, is the focus of spring rites in which chthonic spirits are impersonated, social rules are suspended, and quantities of drink consumed; here, in other words, is the archetypal *madhūtsava*, where the flower that falls at night becomes part of the first-full-moon spring festival, where the Vedic drug that is the moon affords the occasion for ecstasy.

While the Vedic pantheon cannot itself be characterized as chthonic, Vedic religion certainly shows signs that it assimilated aboriginal religious notions whose emphases were chthonic. These traces become all the more visible in Brahmanism and especially, later on, in the Purāṇas. The Vedas, however, also show vestigial chthonic elements.

The *aśvamedha*, it should be recalled, was, as the most important of all Vedic rites, a rite of unification. Although in later times it became under Kṣatriyan influence the occasion in the *Rāmāyaṇa* to glorify the splitting of kingdoms between twins, it was originally a rite of unification between a sovereign king and the maternal forces of nature. That the queen—that is, the king's main wife—could have attained, and probably did attain, an underworld status in such a context is suggested by various myths pertaining to the *aśvamedha*, but perhaps also by the immense popularity of Great Goddess figures in India from the Indus Valley civilization onward—figures with which gods such as Yama would likely have been reconciled. That the queen had, no doubt, an underworld significance is demonstrated by the chthonic character of fertility—of *kumbha*, earthen container—and by the concomitant fact that *madhu*, according to the *Atharva Veda*, was an especially feminine, dark, and left-handed substance. In other words, the *madhu* of the *aśvamedha* ought to be positively connected with a non-Vedic chthonic idea prevalent in Vedic times among non-Aryan Indians. This interpretation is supported by a third textual example.

In the *Rāmāyaṇa*, a late first-millennium B.C. adulteration of very ancient themes, a mythical king is born of the queen's sacred fertilization at the spring rite. Here, the queen's role as a chthonic fertility figure survives Kṣatriyan emendations of the text once we recognize that the *aśvamedha* was not only a rite for consecrating the *soma* supply, but also the rite at which *soma* was meant to bring on the queen's sacred pregnancy.

Rāma, the great hero-king of the *Rāmāyaṇa*, is said to have been born the holiest of his line because his mother imbibed fully half of all the sacrificial *soma* at the *aśvamedha* at which he was conceived. The word *mādhavī*, too, suggests an underworld connection, since it is not merely a name for the earth, but one which carries the epithet "Vernal Beauty" or "Drinker of Soma" (Shastri 1959, 660). To the present day, this Sanskrit underworld association survives in not only the name of one of India's most sacred cities, but also in the word *madhura*, a temporary enclosure, a sacred space in which humans are possessed by spirits arriving from the underworld (Seligmann and Seligmann 1911, 267ff.). The connection, therefore, between *madhu* and fertility is not only possible from what we may suspect to be the psychoactive potentials of the tree, but from what we know to be its connection to women's rites, to the worship of the female principle, and to the *kumbha*—the container, the womb— that is the earth itself.

This feminine principle is, clearly, deemphasized in the Vedic literature. Likewise, such chthonic leonine figures as Śiva and Viṣṇu have Vedic ancestors that are often not described in leonine terms. To argue, however, that the worship of a feminine principle is entirely non-Aryan— Tamil, Dravidian, or aboriginal—is almost impossible; for there is very little known about the Tamils of South India before 800 A.D., while aboriginal customs went almost entirely unrecorded until the nineteenth century. It is rather the deemphasis of certain kinds of images in the Vedas, combined with our knowledge of their converse importance in the traditional customs of Hindus, that indicates the significant influence of non-Aryan tradition on Indian religion. Viṣṇu's return of the stolen Vedas from the underworld may well be read as a structural assimilation of non-Aryan practices; how much more easily might one confiscate another tradition's cosmology than by creating a myth whereby the *madhu* of the non-Aryan Indians was, supposedly, the *soma* or *madhu* that the demons of another tradition (i.e., *their* deities) stole at some earlier date? By this interpretation, the confusion of *soma* and *madhu* in the Vedas may have been quite deliberate, and Viṣṇu's trip to the bottom of the ocean to return the Elixir brought back a force to the Aryans that they felt was rightly theirs. Interestingly, it is also Viṣṇu whose manifestations, whose *avatāras*, make his post-Vedic image the most masklike of all Hindu gods, the most capable of adopting new images, of accreting other images of power. Once we realize the potential influence that non-Aryans had on the evolution of religion in India, we begin to see how the feminine goddesses came to spend most of their time underground, as it were, in Vedic literature. This fact, however, does not keep us in complete darkness as to the status of ambivalent leonine icons—gods, goddesses, and androgynous deities—in the first half of the first millennium B.C.

While we find evidence of Great Goddess figures—and, interestingly, of tree goddesses—in the Indus Valley civilization (J. Marshall 1931, 1: 51ff.), by the time of the Aryan migration into the Gangetic plains we know that the Goddess was worshiped in the form of the river itself.[29] This worship is reflected in the appearance of the Ganges as a receptacle for the seed of Śiva (as Agni), which, carried down the river to the ocean, becomes the fire-breathing horse's head. That the Ganges should be a container of seed is entirely in keeping with what we know of the mythology and history of the Great Goddess. To the present day she is seasonally worshiped as Kālī or Durgā in the form of a *kumbha* filled with water, and the Kumbha Melā, the great festival of the *kumbha* vessel, is held at Prayāga, the meeting of three rivers (the Ganges and Yamunā, which are visible, and the Sarasvatī, the divine river, which is not). It is a holy confluence already known in the *Ṛg Veda;*[30] given that it is the confluence of the triple Goddess, we may assume that as a sacred place it is more ancient still.

The iconographical consequences of this mythology cannot be underestimated, because they lead us to see how an image very similar to that of the Greek Gorgon arises out of two "left-handed" or "black" forms of Goddess worship. This image is given its most explicit manifestation in the later *Kālikā Purāṇa*, where we read of the practice—witnessed by many early travelers among the aboriginal tribes—of placing a mark (*tilaka*) on the worshiper's forehead with the blood from the head of the sacrificial victim (van Kooij 1972, 22). One need only look at the horrific iconography of a modern-day impersonator of Durgā/Kālī in this capacity to see how closely the Greek idea is paralleled (Pl. 74). That this practice, or some mythological equivalent of it, is indeed very ancient may be deduced from many facts. For example, Kālī, who is both the River and Time, is the "black goddess," whose name is already known in the Vedas as the black or horrific devouring tongue. Second, human sacrifice was known in India into the last century, and in mythology it is the head alone that is revivified—not just the horse's head beneath the ocean that devours oblations, but also the head of Rāhu that becomes the disembodied eclipse-demon for having attended the churning of the primeval hallucinogen by the gods. Madhu is decapitated by Viṣṇu for his part in stealing the secret of the *soma* and perhaps also the "somatic" secret, the secret of how the dead are revivified, how the sacrifice is made complete. In Śaivite legend, we even see an assimilation of blood sacrifice in the appearance of the *triveṇi* on Viṣṇu's forehead. Having cut off one of

Plate 74. Impersonator of the goddess Kālī. This woman is a member of the Bahrūpia class, a group of mendicant actors. The name comes from the Sanskrit *bahu*, "many," and *rūpa*, "form," and refers to the habit of its members of assuming various roles. Russell [1916] 1969, vol. 1.

Brahmā's five heads, Śiva struck Viṣṇu in the forehead with his trident (thunderbolt, *vajra*), causing drops of blood to issue forth from the marks into the waiting head of Brahmā. This attribute of Viṣṇu is particularly interesting because it suggests an adaptation of another "left-handed" aspect of the Goddess.[31] The idea that *madhu* or *soma* resides in the head underlies the second "left-handed" or "black" form of the Goddess's worship that has its analogue in the Gorgon head. In this case, we may ascertain a relationship between the horrific leonine head on the one hand and the imbibing of *madhu* on the other—a relationship made explicit in the connection between yogic iconography, the forehead, and the Ganges.

As has already been noted, the analogy between the *kumbha*, as womb, and the forehead is indeed very ancient. This association, however, also has a specific connection with both the symbolism of *yoga* and that of the Ganges; for the confluence of the three rivers is also the confluence at the forehead, the *triveṇi*, where the three meet and express themselves as either a three-pointed mark—trefoil, triangle, or simply three dots—or the single mark, *oṃ*, that indicates the encirclement of the three. While the textual material that makes this imagery explicit is much later (see, e.g., Avalon 1958; Woods 1927), Tantric *yoga* is often specifically identified with the *Atharva Veda*, and even though we have no body of Tantric images from the era of the *Atharva Veda*, the fundamental yogic ideas are much older than the Vedas themselves. Though written testimony about the popularity of *yoga* and *sāṃkhya* takes us back to about the fourth century B.C., iconographically the different *āsanas* are already fully developed in the Indus Valley period.[32] In other words, though we are without images from the Vedic period, we may safely assume that the triple Goddess was worshiped in the form of the Ganges, and that the womb, the *kumbha* containing the secret of immortality, was equated with the head that wore the mark of fecundity. The *amṛta* is, in other words, according to the symbology of *yoga*, not only in the womb, but in the head as well. This is not to say that the two are symbolically the same, but somehow, in being radically opposed, they are similar.

If, finally, one were asked to draw a figure whose head is a bowl of sacred water, whose face is apotropaic, and from whose forehead a sacred river flows in the shape of an inverted triangle, a Greek artist of the early seventh century B.C. might come up with something very close to a heretofore unexplained Proto-Attic figure—namely, the Early Geometric Gorgons from Eleusis (Pl. 75). Suppose that these figures, of whose faces little sense has been made, are attempts at rendering an exotic legend without the benefit of pictorial models. The bowl-like head, the odd lines on the forehead that look very much like a simple representation of water,

Plate 75. Gorgon from a Proto-Attic amphora found at Eleusis. Ca. 670–660
B.C. In this early representation of a Gorgon we see a very uncharacteristic
face, which nonetheless displays all of her salient features. Note especially the
curious treatment of the forehead. Eleusis Museum.

begin to look much more like the work of a Greek in the act of interpretation. That these lines are the first indicators of the more complex markings
of the Orientalizing and Archaic periods cannot, given the simplicity of
the images, be proven; but it is worth bearing the idea in mind as we
reexamine the evolution of superciliary iconography on Gorgons and the
mythological framework that gave rise to them in preclassical Greece.

Signs of the Mistress

In Bengali tradition, Durgā, the Great Goddess, is still worshiped
during a seasonal festival that marks the transition of the Bengali year
(Östör 1980, 28). As legend has it, her head lies buried in the earth beneath a sacred tree. Known, like the Gorgon sisters, in three aspects, she
is honored as the patron of women's rites (ibid., 17–23). Of greatest importance is the fact that her origin myth relates her explicitly to the fertility
demons of the *Rāmāyaṇa:*

Rāvan, the demon king of Laṅka, was a fervent devotee of the goddess, and he gave men the model for the worship of Durgā as the goddess of spring. Rāvan established the Bāsaṇṭipūjā, and at one time that was the only annual pūjā of the goddess. Once a year people used to worship Durgā in this special way, with all the elaborate rituals, just as Rāvan taught them, the same way the rituals are still performed today. (Östör 1980, 18)

These facts bring us back again to Viṣṇu, since Rāvaṇa and his giant brother, Kumbhakarṇa, were killed by Viṣṇu so that they might escape a curse that had turned them from guardian figures to Rākṣasa demons. It is quite clear that we have here an assimilation of non-Aryan figures through the person of Viṣṇu, for Kumbhakarṇa is not only, by virtue of his name, a vessel demon, but one who sleeps for six-month intervals, the archetypal master of the seasons. Kumbhakarṇa had, indeed, already been once killed, in the form of Hiraṇyakaśipu, by Viṣṇu (Narasiṃha), when Hiraṇyakaśipu struck the sacred temple pillar. The deaths of Rāvaṇa and Kumbhakarṇa in the *Rāmāyaṇa*, therefore, took them one step closer to salvation, so that we find them—as when Madhu and Kaiṭabha stole the Vedas—grateful for having been killed by Viṣṇu and for moving closer to salvation. Things begin to look odder still when we realize that not only was Viṣṇu known as Madhusūdana, or destroyer of Madhu, but that one of his earliest epithets, also, is *urugāya*, "wide-going," or "wide-leaping"—a word that bears the same meaning as "Euryale," the name of Medusa's sister. But what is more remarkable is the fact that Viṣṇu performs his wide leaping in the form of three steps that conform, as do the rivers of Gaṅgā, to the three regions of the universe. He conquers them all, reaching the third, which is the highest region of the gods, wherein lies the fountain of *madhu* (*RV* 1.154.5). It would, therefore, seem arguable that the rise of Viṣṇu as a deity has very much to do with his assimilation of the triple Goddess and that the *nāman* of Viṣṇu has as its origin the apotropaic mark that is also an aphrodisiac—the three intertwining rivers or the staff and caduceus that culminate in the fountain of *madhu* at the forehead.

What, then, is the historical evidence for asserting that the Gorgon may be related to some Indian underworld beasts of non-Aryan origin? First, in summarizing the early Greek case, we know that the introduction of Cybele into Greek mythology was made possible by her iconographic conflation with Mistress figures in Greek mythology. It was clear to the Greeks, in other words, that their own myths of origin were, in certain respects, comparable to those involving sexually and emotionally ambivalent underworld deities among their immediate eastern neighbors. In

India at this time the conception was much the same: the word *brāhmaṇa* itself connoted a sexless power, a union of opposites, while the ideal notion of a demon was hermaphroditic—the embodiment of contradiction, impudent and independent. The sacred and the profane, in this view, differed *only* in attitude, in the structural role—*in the ritual*—they partook of.

But the etymological evidence strongly suggests that a Greek comparison with Brahmanical ritual would require more than a structural analogy; for not only is the name of the Gorgon probably related to the Sanskrit *garj* (meaning "to shout; to emit a beastly roar"), but so also is the generic name for the ecstatic spring festivals taking place in India even to the present day. The name *gājan* (from *garjana*) refers specifically to the shouting associated with the worship of Śiva in the spring month of Caitra, the time of the *madhūtsava*. Its ecstatic nature is realized in dancing and is symbolized both in the image of the *liṅga* (the phallus that is Śiva) and in the springtime association between his worship and that of his lover, Durgā, the Mistress of the Beasts (Östör 1980, 28ff.). As in the worship of Cybele, the behavioral focus of the Caitra *gājan* is both ecstatic and deprecatory, incorporating elements of self-denial and sacrifice. Moreover, the definitive significance of the word *kumbha* in India and the Near East and the widely argued influence of Khumbaba (Humbaba) on Greek legend lead us to suspect that the iconographical similarity between the Gorgon and the Brahmanical Mistress is much more significant than has heretofore been thought possible; the fact that they look so alike, in other words, is more than just analogically convincing.

Beyond her very general beastly appearance—her ambivalent expression that alternately grins and growls, her gnashing tusks and glaring nucleated eyes—there are two features common to representations of the Gorgon that are also common in Indic ambivalent deities. The first is the famous and ancient symbol of the caduceus—the two intertwined serpents. Not only do these relate to the two snakes that often extend from either side of the Gorgon's head—not to mention to the snakes that are the Medusa's hair—but also, in instances in which the Gorgon assumes the role of Mistress of the Beasts—such as on the Temple of Artemis on Corfu—the intertwined caduceus may be represented as a knot in the daimon's belt. It connects her, as it does all who employ it, with a tradition of healing extending from early Babylonia through Greece, with such figures as Asclepius and Hippocrates, to our own culture, in which the staff of Mercury is the physician's emblem. In India, however, the symbol has undergone a different evolution, one that fits more convincingly into the nexus of Gorgon iconology. Here the image of the

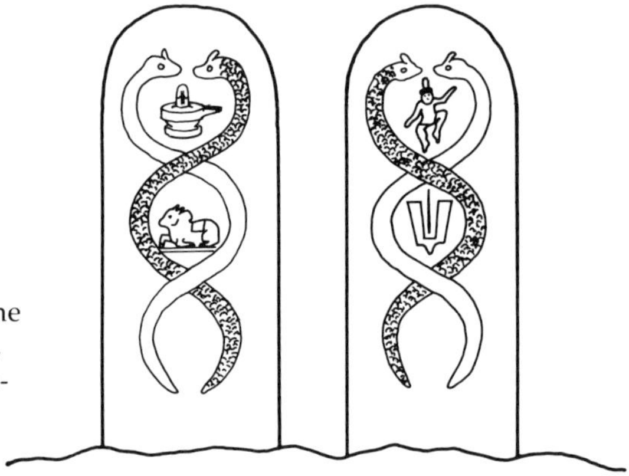

Plate 76. Stone-cut snakes (*nagas*) in the form of the caduceus. On the left, the *liṅga* of Śiva; on the right, the *nāman* of Viṣṇu. After Jouveau-Dubreuil 1937, Fig. 35. Drawing by Mary Ryder.

snake is not connected merely with a revivifying chthonic cure, but with one of an explicitly sexual sort. Besides the yogic and Gangetic motifs, there is also the Tantric explanation, according to which the two snakes are said to encircle the invisible phallus of Śiva. As in the herm of Dionysus surmounted by a mask of the god, the power of the underworld spirit to cure or transform is localized in an image that is frequently phallic. In India this image is not simply the *liṅga* alone, but the *liṅga* of Śiva surrounded by the serpents of the Great Goddess. Their marriage in the spring is evidence that a transformation has been consummated, and the caduceus is the eternal symbol of their union. Iconographically, this union of opposites is also represented by the two snakes and/or divine rivers entwining a third. Physiologically, the two forms are believed to wind around the human spine and connect the base of the spine and the sexual organs with the head.[33] " 'In the Idā is the Devī Yamunā, and in Piṅgalā is Sarasvatī, and in Suṣumnā dwells Gaṅgā. They form a threefold plait united at the root of the Dhvaja [i.e., the sexual organs], they separate at the eyebrows, and hence it is called Triveṇī-Yoga.' . . . These three form one, but considered separately they are distinct" (Avalon 1958, 322).

The second relevant feature is, of course, the *tilaka*, *nāman*, or *bindu*—the Indian superciliary mark whose iconographic background has already been considered at some length. Though at first it may not appear that this mark is extensively used on representations of the Gorgon, there are enough iconographic examples from throughout the Greek world that clearly do not derive from the placement of the lion's superciliary vibrissae to confirm that something more complex was signified.

Moreover, among Orientalized Gorgons this iconography becomes increasingly complex and more clearly defined. We have several images of the Gorgoneion that any Hindu *paṇḍita* would at once describe as *triveṇi* (cf. pls. 77–83)—marks that can each be readily explained by Hindu categories, marks that, additionally, have a specific Yantric meaning. According to Avalon,

> the Male Power-Holder Śiva is represented by a triangle standing on its base. A triangle is selected as being the only geometric figure which represents Trinity in Unity—the many Triads such as Willing, Knowing, and Acting in which the one Consciousness (*Cit*) displays itself. Power or the feminine principle or Śakti is necessarily represented by the same figure, for Power and Power-Holder are one. The Triangle, however, is shown reversed—that is standing on its apex. Students of ancient symbolism are aware of the physical significance of this symbol. To such reversal, however, philosophic meaning may also be given, since all is reversed when reflected in the Waters of *Māyā*. (Avalon 1959, 418)

Plate 77. Gorgons with tridentate forehead marks. Laconian black-figure hydriai, 6th c. B.C. In India, the triadic sign represents not only Unity in Trinity, but, depending on the positioning of the triangle, either the masculine or the feminine principle. *a*, London, British Museum B58. *b*, Courtesy Museum of Fine Arts, Boston, No. 68.698, Frederick Brown Fund.

Plate 78. Gorgoneion with tridentate forehead mark on the shield of Achilles. Laconian black-figure cup from Etruria. Ca. 560–550 B.C. Paris, Louvre E.669. (Photo: Musées Nationaux.)

Plate 79. Attic black-figure skyphos. 6th c. B.C. Paris, Louvre CA1845. (Photo: Musées Nationaux.)

Plate 80. Panathenaic red-figure amphora. By the Berlin Painter, late 6th c. B.C. Munich, Staatliche Antikensammlungen und Glyptothek, no. 2312.

Plates 79–81. Gorgon faces with tridentate forehead marks. In these three examples, the association between the Gorgon face and the three-pointed forehead mark is quite clear. According to Indian belief, the three points describe a triangle that connotes, depending upon its position, either the masculine or feminine manifestation of androgyny. This transformational characteristic is perfectly in keeping with the Gorgon's bearded and unbearded representations.

Plate 81. Attic black-figure amphora. By the Amasis Painter, 6th c. B.C. Courtesy Museum of Fine Arts, Boston, no. 01.8026. Pierce Fund. Purchased of E. P. Warren.

This imagery is also reflected in the relationship of both the *nāman* and the caduceus to Greek eye cups. These drinking cups are quite useful in discussing the Gorgon as an apotropaic visage, since they often, as in plates 82 and 83, reduce her iconography to the most minimal abstraction. The depiction of the nose and the superciliary marks here points unmistakably to Gorgon figures, as does the larger class of ideas of which these motifs are a part. Frequently, for example, they are decorated with Satyrs (pls. 84 and 85) and phallic images (see the base of Pl. 85), and often they are composed in such a way that the Satyr takes up the forehead space where the superciliary mark might otherwise have been (pls. 84 and 85). The most common interpretations of this filling-in between the eyes of the drinking cups resort to aesthetic considerations of balance and proportion. Obviously this cannot be correct, for the iconography of the cups, and the position of the eyes in particular, are connected with various forms of super-sensibility, just as the caste mark or *nāman* identifies that place on the forehead that is said to be the locus of this special sensible power. Such an interpretation would seem to conform perfectly to the representations of the forehead of certain Gorgons and of eyes on Greek drinking cups, especially given the broader iconographic concerns of these vessels. If, in other words, this mark has any meaning at all, it is likely an indication of some specific sensation—a view completely in keeping with the Indic use of the *nāman* and *ājñā-cakra* as sensory loci and one perhaps lending new meaning to the stylized lotus foreheads on certain Greek eye cups (see Jackson 1976, 68).

In India, two symbolic associations make explicit the sensory meaning of the mark. The first regards the year-symbolism of the *nāman*: it is the mark of the devotees not only of Śiva, but also of Viṣṇu in his role of Lord of the Beasts—the pose synonymous with that assumed by so many Great Goddess figures. The use of the mark leads us, in other words, back to the ecstatic seasonal worship of an underworld trinity, whether it be a trinity of three gods or of a single god with two subsidiary figures.

The case of the possible connection between the forehead marking of the Gorgon and the iconography of the lion is more complex. In part, this is because the lion has superciliary vibrissae as part of its natural physiognomy. The two marks or tufts of hair above the eyes, that is, ought to be apparent on any portrait of a lion made by even the most casual observer. The appearance of this leonine trait on Gorgons, however, is probably not accidental since the lion—usually a pair of them—is

Plate 82. An exact replication of the common Gorgon design. Attic black-figure cup by the Amasis Painter, ca. 540–535 B.C. Copenhagen, National Museum, Department of Near Eastern and Classical Antiquities.

Plate 83. The tridentate mark is shown as dots to either side of a central line. Attic black-figure kylix by Exekias, ca. 540–535 B.C. Munich, Staatliche Antikensammlungen und Glyptothek, no. 2044 (8729).

Plates 82–84. Eye cups. These three eye cups exemplify the one other instance in Greek art in which foreheads, like those of Gorgons, are distinguished by some special marking.

Plate 84. A mask of Dionysus in the same location. Black- and red-figure kylix, ca. 530–520 B.C. Baltimore, Walters Art Gallery, no. 48.42.

the consort of the Mistress of the Beasts. Like Cybele or any other Mistress, the Gorgon was flanked by lions when depicted in that role. Lions were said to announce the arrival of Cybele, their *garjana* no doubt the sound that marked the rites of transformation with which they were associated. In India, similarly, they have always been the animals most essential to depictions of the Goddess; they are a major element in representations of Durgā. But can we be sure that the double mark that is natural on the lion has, like the seasonal use of *madhu*, an ecstatic association?

Here again, a closer consideration of Hindu ideas provides us with a second association that is sexual in nature. Among Hindus both modern and ancient, two dots or circles separated by a line form a sign (identical to the mark in Pl. 83) having either an obvious phallic meaning or an androgynous one whereby the right and left are divided by the vertical line into male and female. This more complex idea may be elaborated yet further, as, for example, in the Balinese exegesis on the representation of the *mantras*, the secret sounds by which priests are supposed to produce a divine communion with the gods. According to Covarrubias,

> The synthesis of this is contained in the Word of Words of the Yogis: *Om*, pronounced in Bali *ong*, consisting of the sounds *ah—u—m* . . . Brahma, Wisnu, Iswara, the eternal Trinity manifested throughout the universe: heaven, earth, and underworld; fire, water, and wind; male, female, and hermaphrodite. The symbol for this sound, called *ongkara*:

is composed of an upright dash (*nada*), a *lingga* or phallus; a crescent moon (*arda tjandra*), symbolic of the female creative organ; and the circle (*windú* or *wandú*), symbol of completion—the hermaphrodite—thus the word *ong* is Siwa. (Covarrubias 1937, 297)

This hermaphroditic symbol is not only the symbol of completion; among its other formulations is one of particular interest in the present context. This sign is the *ongkara madhu mukha*, that is, "the *ongkara* with the face of *madhu*." It is represented by two *ongkara*s facing each other:

Like a living being, the *ongkara* has a crown (the upright dash), a fore-head (the circle), eyes (the half-moon), besides a mouth, trunk, stomach, and legs—the various sections of the lower character.

The magic formulas are the essential part of the religious service of the high priests, the often mentioned *maweda*, through which the *pedandas* make the "pure" holy water (*tirta*) used in such profusion in the ritual that the Balinese have come to call their religion *agama tirta*, the "science of the holy water." (ibid., 298)

It is precisely this holy water that in prehistoric—especially in priestly, Brahmanical—times was the venerable *amrta*, the *madhu* or *soma* intoxicant responsible for ecstatic communion with the gods. Thus, the formula originally connected with the priestly completion of *maweda* is represented precisely as the mark of sensation located between two eyes. The Hindu view, therefore, points continually in the direction of spiritual ecstasy, which again suggests that the Greek icons are not accidental.

This ecstatic feature of the eye cups—combining Satyrs, drink, and phallic imagery with the caduceus and *nāman*—calls attention to another interesting development in the growth of the Hindu gods out of the Vedic pantheon. That is the development of Śiva as the erotic ascetic (O'Flaherty 1973), so that he eventually evolves into the best-known and most popular figure of the Hindu trinity. This erotic element means that Śiva not only becomes the most important deity with a third eye on his forehead, but also, as the god of dancing and ecstasy, exists as the "eye" formed by the foreshortened view of the *liṅga* and *yoni* (Pl. 86)—symbol

Plate 85. Attic bilingual eye cup with Satyr mask and Gorgon. In the manner of the Andokides Painter, late 6th c. B.C. Most eye cups, when not employing a tridentate forehead mark, display some Satyric or erotic image. In this case, there is no mistaking the suggested symbolic associations. Oxford, Ashmolean Museum 1974.344.

of the union of god and goddess. Considering, therefore, the concerns these details—caduceus, eyes, Satyrs, and cups for drinking—symbolize in association, we may readily interpret the Greek cups as a near-perfect redaction of an idea that is equally Indian. Thus the combination of motifs as much as the possible Indian origin of the *nāman* leads to this

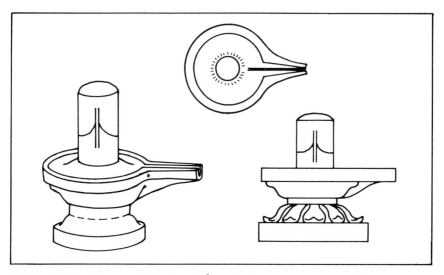

Plate 86. Liṅga. The manifestation of Śiva. As the representation of the joining together of male and female, the *liṅga,* or phallus, is joined to its female counterpart, the *yoni.* Drawing by Mary Ryder after Jouveau-Dubreuil 1937, Fig. 1.

hypothesis and forces us to reconsider the Perseus-Gorgon story with this imagery in mind.

The Perseus-Gorgon story is above all a visual legend. The stare of the Gorgon was fatal, and Perseus himself had to assume invisibility— his is one of the rare Greek myths where magic and magical implements used in modifying appearances abound.[34] Secondly, the Graiae, the three sisters who help Perseus find his way, share, it is said, their one eye at the forehead;[35] it is only when the eye is placed in her forehead that any of them has vision. Third, and in some respects most interesting of all, is the significance of Argos, which has a complex panoptic tradition. Most famous is Argos himself, whose body is covered with eyes enabling him to guard Io when she is turned into a heifer. If we recall that Herodotus claimed that the Persians sacrifice to Zeus and that Argos came to exercise a "benevolent neutrality" toward the Persians,[36] it is interesting to note that

> Three eyes, two ordinary and a third in the forehead, characterized an ancient idol (*xóanon*) of Zeus preserved in a temple of Athena on the Larisa, the akropolis or citadel of the city of Argos. (Pettazzoni 1956, 152)

This detail leads us further to wonder about the nature of the Zeus of the East. Even more remarkable is the explanation given by Pausanias

(2.24.4) for these three eyes—an explanation that sounds much like the three worlds of the Ganges. According to him, the three eyes symbolized the three regions of the universe and their relationship to Zeus, "who in his own person ruled the sky, as Poseidon the sea, and as Hades the underworld" (ibid.).

The connection between the Sanskrit *madhu* and the Indo-European *médhu*, "mead," has long ago been argued (e.g., Macdonell 1897, 114), and Puhvel (1970, 167) has extended considerably the scope of this relationship by showing that the Indo-European term also concerns both ritual drunkenness[37] and the seasonal mating of horses and humans. In Greek, however, while the Indo-European base survives, the =dh= of *médhu* becomes a =θ= (hence, for example, our word "methane"). There is, therefore, no linguistic connection between the Sanskrit and Greek—between Madhu and Medusa. On the other hand, the Greek μέθυ is not the precise equivalent of the Indo-European term for mead. As Buck points out (1949, 389), μέθυ "occurs only as a poetical word for 'wine,' but is the source of the common prose word μεθύω, 'make drunk.' . . ." The Greeks were obviously aware that their μέθυ differed from the intoxicating drinks of foreigners, as is evident both from the Greek "μελίειον (Plut. Mor. 672b of the drink of the barbarians), deriv. of μέλι 'honey'" (ibid.). Looking further into Greek prehistory, we find that the relationship between *médhu* and μέθυ is less clear-cut still.

According to Scheinberg, the early use of hydromel among the Greeks is confirmed by both linguistic and mythological evidence—the latter especially in conjunction with triadic, particularly feminine, deities and with prophetic speech:

> The honey-induced prophetic frenzy of the bee maidens in the *Hymn to Hermes* . . . belongs to a tradition in which divination depended upon the ritual drinking of a sacred, perhaps intoxicating liquid, which opened the human psyche to messages from the divine world by bringing the god within the seer. Corollary to this is a still more obscure tradition, nearly forgotten by Greek mythographers and by the Greek language, according to which the men and gods of earlier times drank honey, mixed with wine or fermented as mead. (Scheinberg 1979, 19)

The significance for the Gorgon of this association between mead and prophecy is considerable. Croon (1955) has argued, as we have seen (Chap. 4), that the connection of the Gorgon with sacred springs, and of the first syllable of the name "Perseus" with underworld figures, suggests a seasonal rite wherein the monster was impersonated with a mask—a hypothesis that becomes increasingly likely in light of the Gorgonesque masks from Tiryns and the similarity between the Gorgon

Plate 87. Leiden, Rijksmuseum van Oudheden.

Plates 87–88. Etruscan black-figure amphoras. Late 6th c. B.C. In these two nearly identical examples, an interwoven caduceus rises between the eyes, where finally the two snakes appear face to face with a dolphin. In India, the serpent power winds around the spine, rising from its base to the head in the form of two snakes that represent two sacred rivers entwining an invisible third.

Plate 88. Courtesy Museum of Fine Arts, Boston. No. 62.970, Frederick Brown Fund.

and other daimons known to manifest themselves on a yearly basis. The association between mead and prophecy, however, is also suggested in two important connections by the Medusa's name. First is the fact that the Greek word μέδω is attested originally as a participle (μέδων) and only later as a verb. Like the Sanskrit personification Madhu, it was used to designate a ruler (first Poseidon, it seems, and then the Gorgon Medusa—that is, the "female leader").[38] If, therefore, scholars are correct about the significance of honey mead in pre-Archaic Greece, it is quite possible that in Greek, as in Sanskrit, the name of the "ruler," the "lord," or "leader" would have been synonymous with the imbiber of hydromel—the sweet, intoxicating, and hence psychoactive drink. Be this, as it may, a speculation, it nonetheless suggests that the Greeks were willing to acknowledge distinct roots for honied drinks—μέλι, which they share with the Hittite *melit* (Sturtevant 1947, 160); and μέθυ, their phonetic reflex of *médhu* (*madhu*, "mead")—and that the period of the early first millennium B.C. may well have seen a transition either in what were recognized as sacred drinks or in the terms used in defining them. When Strabo tells us at the end of the classical age that the Indians, having no bees, obtain honey from trees (15.1.20), we can only wonder about how early the ancient knowledge of *madhu* might have found its way westward—of the roots, blossoms, seeds, and leaves of the honeyed *madhu* already articulated in the Ṛg Veda, of the Sanskrit *madhusya*, "to desire or wish for *madhu*."

As for lions, we have seen how iconographically they are a class of beasts that may be distinguished by certain common characteristics, but one that is not easy to subdivide more accurately. Though they did, indeed, have individual words for lion and tiger, "the Greeks for whom these images were destined were not endowed with the linguistic means to distinguish these different animal species from one another" (Detienne 1979, 37). In preclassical times, the lack of literary evidence makes the task of distinguishing different cats very difficult, and we can only, as Rodenwaldt has done, employ terms, such as "lion-panther" (1939, 2:149), that are suitably hybrid. Detienne's later evidence does, however, point to an association between certain cats and myths concerning both trees and ecstasy. The panther, for example, exuded a sweet odor—given off by its roar—that seductively lured its prey. This perfume, which came to distinguish the panther from other cats, was how it seduced but also how it might be seduced. Its insatiable desire for the aroma of wine, and its desire to drink as much wine as it could, made its capture possible. It was not only consecrated to Dionysus, but it was also directly connected to the mythology of gum-exuding trees. Attracted by their sweet emanations, "panthers come over the mountains of Armenia, cross the Taurus, and proceed toward the gum of the styrax tree when the wind begins to blow and the trees exude their fragrant odors" (Detienne 1979, 39).

The question of actual contacts between Greeks and Indians—when they first began and what effect one had upon the other—are beyond the scope of this inquiry. Whether Greeks had heard anything at all of India in the early first millennium B.C. is totally a matter of conjecture. As for any diplomatic connections, it is not until the sixth century that the Persians could claim, under Cyrus, that their kingdom stretched from the frontiers of Greece to the Indus Valley. Later on, Herodotus has much to say of foreigners: of the people beyond the Argippaei who, like Kumbhakarṇa, sleep six months out of the year (Hdt. [4.25]); of the Issedones, the apparently Tibetan tribe to the southeast of the Argippaei who, as Zenobius also tells us, saved the heads of their dead and covered them with gold (Zen. [5.25]; Hdt. [4.26]), or those who made ritual vessels of such skulls; and of the Arimaspi, warriors who dwelt farther east and to the north of the Issedones and supposedly had but one eye in their foreheads (Hdt. [4.13]). Such being the nature of ancient testimony, archaeologists and historians can alone provide specific details of the first contacts between Greeks and the East, though naturally our records of the first known travelers cannot go as far back as the moments when initial interest arose in learning something of these distant lands—of their unusual beliefs or their material culture—through intermediaries. We must conclude, therefore, by agreeing with Filliozat that it would "not be correct on our part to say that because India and Greece had not known each other very well in antiquity, nothing could have passed from one to the other" (1964, 239). For Filliozat, the question of the ancient contact between India and Greece is as significant as the answer to its specific direction is complex. The focus of the present inquiry has, however, been entirely comparative, both from a structural and an iconographic point of view. And here there is an important comparison that remains to be made.

While we saw that the *nāman*, as the sign of the third eye, achieved in India archetypal status equal to the images of lions and of sacred vessels and themes of divine union, it is not yet clear what kind of meaning the marking of the forehead between the eyes of Gorgons might have had for Greeks. Curious though it may be that each and every kind of Gorgon mark can be readily explained in Indian terms, we do not have explanations from Greece that are in any way as exact as those we have for Indian iconography. But this is not to say that there is no Greek evidence to

Plate 89. Lion Gate, Mycenae. Ca. 1250 B.C. According to Arthur Evans, the Lion Gate derives from an ancient tree and pillar cult. The deity worshiped was believed to reside in this pillar. In Indian mythology Viṣṇu is not only flanked by two lions but in his man-lion *avatāra*, Narasiṃha, he bursts from the column in order to destroy the non-believer Hiraṇyakaśipu. (Photo: Edwin Smith.)

be had. There are descriptions of Gorgons that have, like the Graiae, a removable eye in their foreheads, and of the Medusa, who has but one stony eye that is petrifying,[39] to say nothing of the recurring theme of petrifaction. It seems, in other words, that the idea of a mental power that functions as an externalized force—an insight that is also all-seeing—is so like the *nāman* (third eye, *tilaka*) as to necessitate a structural comparison of the Indian notion with the Perseus-Gorgon legend. And doing so provides some interesting results. In Sanskrit, the word *nāman* means not only "a characteristic mark or sign," but also "name, appellation . . . personal name . . . substance, essence; a good or great name, renown, fame; . . . to give a name, call" (Monier-Williams [1899] 1970, 536). The *nāman*, in other words, is the mark that establishes identity, the Sanskrit cognate of our word "name." While recalling the correspondence between names beginning with *per-* and the underworld suggests one interesting parallel between Perseus and the Gorgon, considering the etymological connection between "Perseus" and "person," one has the sense that the myth is more archetypal still. Looking in the divine mirror, what kind of daimon does the hero overcome? Whose identity does this person see?

· 6 ·

Balinese Faces and Indian Prototypes

Hinduism and Bali: Problems in Interpretation

In this final chapter, I will consider the relationship between iconography and sensation in the context of Hindu art in Indonesia with special reference to the apotropaic iconography of Bali.[1] I have decided to consider this case for three reasons. The first is that Bali has an exceedingly rich masking tradition. The second is that the masking iconography, from the ethnographical point of view, represents a form of Hinduism that, I think, is closer to the Brahmanical tradition than are those Indian forms falling more heavily under the influence of Buddhist transcendentalism. The third reason—which in part explains the second—is what Bosch called the deep reverence of the non-Indian Hindus for Indian tradition. Among the Balinese, this has resulted in no merely antiquarian attention to the epic literature of India, but rather in an active interpretative concern for it.

What Hindu elements there are in Balinese culture constitute probably the best examples for a thesis on masks in the very broadest cultural sense because the entire layer of Hinduism in Balinese culture is arguably an exercise in interpretation; the relationship of Balinese art to another great tradition is not only recognized but at times even exalted, and the Balinese may themselves be said to be interpreters insofar as they are Hindu. That some account of cross-cultural dynamics is necessary is borne out in the anthropological literature; there the problem of Hinduism in Balinese culture has often led ethnographers to the position that to view Bali as a Hindu culture is to oversimplify, if not to be wholly inaccurate. This argument, important in its own right, is not one the present study can examine; to recognize the argument, however, is

Plate 90. Temple gate. Pura Dalem Sidan, Bangli, Bali. Here the horrific *bhoma* monster is seen in its role as protector of the temple gate. (Photo: author.)

immensely important because it indicates how what may be interpreted as Hindu in Balinese culture is itself metaphorically a mask—an attitude toward appearances and visual manifestations that strikes certain ethnographers as peculiarly disjointed from those ideas that might be viewed as indigenous and Indonesian. Here we find in the literature not only a great emphasis on Balinese history, but, in attempting to sort out the various influences, a distinction between the older, casteless form of social organization and the small percentage in modern villages of ranking members from one or more of the upper castes of *brāhmaṇa, kṣatriya,* or *weśya* (the Brahmans, Kṣatriyas, and Vaiśyas of India). On the one hand, it has been argued that Balinese Hinduism, with its idea that the dead are reborn into the same paternal line, is, as a type of ancestor worship, more Indonesian than Hindu; but on the other, one might equally point out that Hinduism is an adaptive religion of a high order, remarkably free of dogma and open to interpretation, and that the Balinese tradition is no less a form of Hinduism than any other. Both of these views are, in part, correct. The idea of a Hindu veneer on Balinese culture is equally a statement about cultural institutions and their apparent superficiality— about the mask as a metaphor for culture—as it is a question of facts; one could, in other words, regard this characterization as an important feature of the masking idea rather than as a criticism about the superficiality of Indian influences on Balinese religion. Indeed, the heuristic importance of the mask metaphor for understanding Balinese culture cannot be overemphasized; for the tradition of Brahmanism suggests, in fact, a connection between the idea of culture and that of personhood and the manifestation of personae. In clarifying this connection, one must certainly begin by recognizing the distinctive character of the Brahmanical view of religion's social role—not only because of its crucial notions about the relationship among such factors as culture, cognition, personality, and possession, but also because it provides us with some interesting suggestions as to why the horrific apotropaic Hindu iconography has survived to the present day in the masks of places so remote from India as the island of Bali.

Of primary importance in understanding the change away from the Brahmanical view is the status given to visual phenomena in general:

> No doubt we are sufficiently aware of the spiritual revolution indicated in the Upaniṣads and Buddhism, whereby the emphasis was shifted from the outer world to the inner life, salvation became the highest goal, and knowledge the means of attainment. (Coomaraswamy [1928–31] 1971, part 1:1)

While in the Buddhist tradition, as Coomaraswamy points out, the search for spiritual emancipation must necessarily have given way to the exigencies of social order and the fulfillment of *dharma*, or social function, one may equally say that world-renouncing tendencies are central to Buddhism. This is ethnographically clear from the way salvation through Buddhism is counterposed to other modes of deliverance—as, for example, to exorcistic cures of a more animistic nature in the pluralistic curing methods popular in traditional Sri Lankan society. I say "pluralistic" because, as the literature clearly shows, the various techniques of curing rely on cosmological perspectives that deliberately distinguish themselves from one another and that explicitly emphasize their incommensurability—Buddhism in Sri Lanka being distinguished from other ways of dealing with the supernatural that more closely resemble sympathetic magic. This, of course, does not mean that the various Sri Lankan cosmologies are either unrelated or unsystematic (Obeyesekere 1966), but only that they may function independently.

I will not here attempt to explain the transition from the Brahmanical theory of society to that of the Upaniṣads and Buddhism, but I should like to call attention to Tambiah's excellent study of the problem (Tambiah 1976). One point in particular is consequential for a thesis on masks and concerns the theory of the *varna*; for while Buddhism of course has its own collective cosmology, its doctrine of the non-self is clearly distinguishable from the Brahmanical idea of a collective personality united through the semi-divine role of the Brahmans (ibid., 35). As Tambiah puts it,

> The real thrust of the Buddhist story is that it is self-consciously an inversion of the Vedic theory of the origin of the varna. (Tambiah 1976, 22)

In Buddhism, social order "occurs together with and as a result of the institution of kingship by the voluntary acts of men," while according to more ancient principles, "varnas are divinely created, and of them the preeminent varna is that of the priesthood" (ibid.). In studying what might be the consequences of the Hindu tradition for the interpretation of masks one must, therefore, realize two things. First, the word *brahman* itself meant, according to Keith, a "holy power"—a power, Zimmer tells us, not only far from intellectual but equivalent to the modern *śakti*:

> for *bṛh* means "to grow, to increase" and, when referring to sounds, "to roar." *Bṛṁhita*, which . . . signifies "made great," when referring to sounds denotes "the roaring of an elephant"—that mighty trumpeting which, whether angry or triumphant, is the greatest of all animal noises. (Zimmer [1951] 1974, 77)

This power or force is epitomized in the use of the word *brahman* to describe a sacred ritual or formula as "the crystallized, frozen form . . . of the highest divine energy" (ibid., 78). The Brahmanical iconography, by extension, represents not only the divine manifestation of a roaring power but also a social structure whereby this power can be manifested in sacrifice.

But the Buddhist deemphasis of sacrifice is not the only obvious indication of the development of a different attitude to presenting the visual, sacrificial spectacle; the common confusion—even, as Dumont tells us, by modern Indologists (1970, 67)—of caste and *varṇa* is indicative of a transformation whereby *varṇa* becomes (incorrectly) synonymous with hierarchy. Dumont maintains, after Hocart and Dumézil, that the apparent hierarchy of the *varṇa*s ought to be seen "not as a linear order, but as a series of successive dichotomies or inclusions" (ibid.). In the original Vedic order there is

> an absolute distinction between priesthood and royalty whereby the king . . . does not sacrifice, he has sacrifices performed. In theory, power is ultimately subordinated to priesthood, whereas in fact priesthood submits to power. Status and power, and consequently spiritual authority and temporal authority, are absolutely distinguished. . . . This fact is older than the castes, and it is fundamental to them in the sense that it is only once this differentiation has been made that hierarchy can manifest itself in a pure form. (L. Dumont 1970, 71–72)

The difference between the ancient Indian and the Buddhist theories, therefore, is that while the former's objective is the realization, through Brahmanical rites, of the divine, the Buddhist emphasis on the non-self in the context of the kingly world demanded an as if Platonic release from the unreality of appearances and ritual. The exceptions to this idea are the Tantric Buddhist practices that, in searching for some immediate identification with the supreme, necessarily focus on the performance of magic and on exorcism—i.e., on realizable experience and demonstration. This fact is especially significant when one tries to understand how the worship of Śiva and Buddha came to be conflated in early Javanese religion, and how, in general, certain aspects of Hindu religious practice could be reintegrated into Buddhism despite an earlier period of separation. Today, the frequent emphasis on the Bodhisattva vow and on the idea that Buddhahood is not likely in the present life necessitates a deemphasis on appearance; thus, even in Tibetan hieratic art, wherein masks are still employed, the belief is common that material evidence for a demon's presence is secondary and that the highest forms of devotion must be practiced without such accoutrements as masks. Here we may see how the Buddhist and Christian attitudes toward the material world are remarkably similar. For this reason, also, religious forms perhaps closest to the Brahmanical ideals are seen in places influenced by Indian religion at an early date—the early notion of *brahman* defining *varṇa* as something distinct from what is now indicated by caste, while expressing itself as the manifestation of a holy, roaring power through ritual.

The second point about Brahmanism that must be recognized in the interpretation of the demonic Brahmanical iconography is that *bṛṁhita* not only signifies "becoming great," but "*bṛṁhayati* in classic Hindu medicine denotes the art of increasing the life-strength in weak people" (Zimmer [1951] 1974, 77). The Brahmans—these "gods in human form" (Grünwedel 1901, 11)—are not only a strength in their own right but a life-strength with curing properties. The power to do battle and to protect is thus, as we have elsewhere seen, a power also to possess, to exorcise, and to cure. As Filliozat describes this ambivalence,

> The equivocal character of gods and demons becomes a commonplace thing in India from the time of the Veda. This can be linked with the general and very important fact that in the Veda many notions have two opposite values, one favourable and the other unfavourable, as it is well attested by the Vedic vocabulary, which is extremely ambivalent. (Filliozat 1964, 45)

What better way, then, to manifest this power could there possibly be than to invoke the Brahmanical power in rituals wherein the priests displayed their divine kinship through the terrifying mask of a demon-god? Specifically, this feature of the Brahmanical power forms the link between the ancient Indian social order and the phenomenon of masked possession in Bali.

Indonesia and the Sources of Monstrous Icons

It has been widely recognized that the Hindus of Indonesia have exhibited a special artistic interest in the monstrous icons of Indian art and architecture. Referring to the occurrence of the Face of Glory, or *kīrttimukha*, in Java (Pl. 91), Zimmer remarks,

> The aboriginal traits in the Javanese people, who became converted to Hinduism in medieval times, delight in these figures, at once awe-inspiring and humorous. . . . They represent the "other side," the wrathful aspect (*ghora-mūrti*), of the well-known and loved divine powers. When properly propitiated, such presences give support to life and ward away the demons of disease and death. (Zimmer [1951] 1974, 183)

Plate 91. Javanese *kīrttimukha*. 13th c. A.D. The *kīrttimukha*, or Face of Glory, derives from a legend of Śiva not unlike that of Viṣṇu's man-lion *avatāra*, Narasiṃha. In Śiva's case, the impudent Jalandhara ("water carrier") wishes to have for himself Pārvatī, Śiva's consort. To this end, he sends Rāhu, the eclipse demon, to demand Pārvatī of Śiva. In response, Śiva sends forth from his third eye a lion-headed demon of such size that Rāhu pleads with Śiva for protection. As the monster needs a victim, however, Śiva orders him to devour his own body, leaving only the protective head or Face of Glory. (Photo: *Rūpam.*)

In drawing attention to the predispositions of the original Javanese, Zimmer is also directing us to see the basic ambivalence of the Hindu pantheon; the aboriginal Indonesians, in other words, could not have accepted Indian religion wholeheartedly unless they were already inclined toward the character of Hindu belief. However, because the substantive focus of Zimmer's comparison is demonic ambivalence and the proper ritual propitiation of such forces, we can better connect the structure of Hindu cosmology in modern Indonesia to Indian religion of a far earlier era; for the manifestation of such forces through ritual is more Brahmanical than Buddhist, and the former is a system already codified in the early first millennium B.C. (the dates usually ascribed to the Brāhmaṇas being ca. 900–600 B.C.). In this period, before the rise of Buddhism, the manifestation of the gods in the persons of the semi-divine priesthood would have readily accommodated some form of horrific iconography—especially when it was in the interest of the priesthood to demonstrate, as in sacrifice, their kinship with these ambivalent deities.

The Brahmanical concern with ritual cannot be distinguished from ideas about social structure, nor can it be distinguished from conceptualizations of the category of the person, of the human body-image. As social structure reflects cosmology, so does it reflect a specific thesis on personality. Such a thesis may particularly find its way into iconography when the religious ideology includes a semi-divine priesthood regularly called upon to demonstrate its divinity through ritual and through sacrifice to a pantheon of conflicting and ambivalent forces. In this sense, Dumont's distinction between the Untouchables and Śūdras on the one hand and the "twice-born" on the other sets up a dichotomy that differs absolutely from the caste system. In the latter, which in India developed out of the *varṇas*, not only does the dual organization of those who are and those who are not twice-born give way to a hierarchy, but on the cosmological plane one may, through the accumulation of *dharma*, escape completely the cycle of rebirth. The idea of the person, therefore, is completely connected to notions of social structure and cosmological order, metempsychosis being, as Grünwedel once remarked, "a further development of the caste system" (1901, 11). Likewise, whether one is reborn into the same ancestral line or escapes rebirth entirely is ultimately a function of whether individuals can influence their progression toward or away from liberation and the supernatural, or whether there is a certain kind of semi-divine category of personhood, someone twice-born, who regularly makes visible through ritual the supernatural to the natural world.

What we may actually know about the first contacts between India and Indonesia is little indeed, though the body of available knowledge becomes increasingly large. The earliest evidence of contact between India and island Southeast Asia are inscriptions dating from the early fifth century A.D. found in West Java and Kalimantan (East Borneo). They, however, can hardly be used as indicators of when Hindu ideas first came to the archipelago, because, first of all, there is no telling how early trade was carried on between Indians and natives of this part of the world, and, second, there is no great body of art objects from before this period to be found even in India itself. Using the fifth century as a contact date is generally thought to be too conservative, especially since Chinese travelers indicated that Brahmanism already prevailed in Java during this period. For Bali, the situation is yet more complex, in part because the earliest datable inscriptions come only in the ninth century A.D., but also because there is a mistaken tendency to equate, as with the so-called original Balinese (Bali Aga), that which is not Javanized in Balinese culture with that which is not Hindu.[2] Bosch rightly believed that the study of Balinese religion was at once the most interesting and challenging type of undertaking both because of the island's vague and enormously complex history and also because of the diversity of its social institutions. Such historical problems are not, therefore, of necessity part of this study. Here the idea is, as it was in the Greek case, to point out structural analogies rather than to speculate over dates of contact.

While we may not be able to determine the reasons for the abundance of monstrous leonine icons in Bali, we may safely say that they greatly depend upon their Indian relatives. I am not concerned here with isolating the many correspondences in detail, since there is an excellent literature on this topic—Bosch (1960) provides a valuable sourcebook—not the least of which are the manuscripts that the Balinese themselves are constantly interpreting. The questions, rather, that this study seems most fit to consider are those relating to the structural and ideological role played by this iconography and to the relationship of the apotropaic mask, as a natural autonomous symbol, to notions of appearance and the roles of individuals as manifested in social personae. In this regard, two elements of the Balinese masking iconography must be considered. The first is that the horrific iconography is itself transformational. Bosch's admirable study shows in great detail how plant forms, in particular the lotus stalk, may be transfigured representationally into an open mouth, and then into the aquatic *makara* monster, and how two of these *makaras* may be juxtaposed heraldically to either side of an arch (*toraṇa*) atop which appears the enigmatic *kīrttimukha* (pls. 91, 92). Bosch himself em-

Plate 92. *a, Kāla* (Time) monster. Candi Puntadewa, Java, 9th c. A.D. The frame of this niche, so characteristic of doorframes of the Central Javanese period, shows a *kāla* monster, the "all-devourer," spitting foliage that ends in two stylized *makara* monsters. Archaeological Survey of Indonesia.

    b, Kāla-makara antefix. Borobudur, 8th c. A.D. The apotropaic expression of arrest is frequently rendered architecturally by omitting the lower jaw entirely or by suggesting that a threshold is itself the monster's mouth. Courtesy H. W. J. Bosch.

phasizes the need to recognize the transformational and hierarchical characteristics of these icons. In comparing the attitude of Hindu observers with that of Westerners, he remarks that, in general, the latter "are not accustomed to recognize animal shapes in plants" (Bosch 1960, 43). More important, of course, is the fact that the iconography is recognized as intrinsically transformational and that the nexus of this transformation is, ideally, a horrific apotropaic face. This nexus is the second element of the Hindu-Javanese and Hindu-Balinese iconography that is crucial to masking, since, as we shall see, the motif of the horrific face provides a structural mediation that is also an archetypal refinement of sensory experience.

    To understand the possible significance of this horrific manifestation, we must, according to Bosch, address the relationship between visual phenomena and abstract ideas in Indian thought—that is, the degree to which visual phenomena form the foundation for abstract ideas

(Bosch 1960, 58–59). In the beginning, the progenitor Prajāpati, who is Ruler of the Creatures, impregnates the primeval waters and thus gives life to the golden germ synonymous with Agni. Since Prajāpati is in part mortal and in part immortal—according to the *Śatapatha Brāhmaṇa*, he has a mortal body and immortal breath—the germ of life that springs from his mouth (*Śatapatha Brāhmaṇa* II, 2, 4, 1) is the first manifestation of Agni, the fire of life; and it is the first manifestation of the paradoxical Brahman-Prajāpati, the absolute appearance of a single being possessing two natures,

> manifested and unmanifested, mortal and immortal, immanent and transcendent, of this side or of beyond. (Bosch 1960, 59)

Life itself is, thus, interpreted as the visible manifestation of an otherwise unmanifested Prajāpati or Brahman. The waters are taken to be the place of germination and what is germinated is the essence or immanent force, *rasa*. The purest *rasa* is the sap of plants, which is the "embryo of the waters":

> From the rain and from the water in the soil they draw rasa for their growth and sustenance, they are reared from rasa. The sap of each plant is rasa but the sap of Soma, the king of plants, is rasa in its strongest concentration, its purest essence. The same substance is moreover found in cow's milk in rain, dew, mead (*madhu*), blood, semen virile, and liquor (*surā*). (Bosch 1960, 60)

The waters are both protective and creative, and their essence or *rasa* is the germ manifested in Agni and Soma. According to the *Mahābhārata*, "the whole world is made of Agni and Soma" (VIII, 34, 49), and both are manifestations of the two sides of divine being:

> Brahmins well versed in the Vedas know the two bodies of this god (Mahādeva), one terrifying (*ghora*), the other mild (*śiva*), and these two bodies in turn assume various forms. The terrifying body is like fire, the thunder and the sun; the gentle and mild body resembles dharma, the water and the moon. One half of his being is Agni, the other half is called Soma (Mbh. XIII 160, 44).[3] (Bosch 1960, 61)

The paradox in the Brahmans is not only, therefore, a sexual paradox, but a paradox of the manifested and the unmanifested. In the power, *brahman*, is embodied the capacity for manifesting the outward terrifying body that signifies Agni's ritual participation in the *soma* sacrifice. Life is the visible; it is Agni; it is fire. And *rasa*, feeling, is its immanent force—invisible and latent when of the unmanifested "other side," horrific and manifested when of this world. Such sophisticated dualism necessitates that the unmanifested Brahmanical force periodically manifest itself in this world, and, as the result of this presupposition, visible phenomena are at the foundation of common knowledge. This being the case, one would anticipate that apotropaic faces, so much a part of both mythology and the plastic arts, would no doubt contain much knowledge. In fact, the sophisticated character of the horrific apotropaic visage is made apparent by the way in which it becomes the binding image for several different but interrelated symbols, in such a way that the theory of *rasa* completely permeates the iconography of the plastic arts. In architecture, in the performing arts, and in the human body-image itself, *rasa* provides the theoretical basis for one's self-definition, for one's social role, and for the lasting images one constructs to attest to the vision at whose foundation is feeling, immanent force, *rasa*.

The Senses Manifested as an Apotropaic System

While it may be the case that the leonine face is attributed a mythological role directly related to the external manifestation of the senses, we have yet to ask whether there is anything special from a strictly perceptual and sensory point of view that might account for this image and the role such faces assume as mask forms. It will be helpful in this regard to examine the sensory organs of the face as individual iconographic elements and then to consider the composite face as a complete expression.

Though the bulging, nucleated eyes of many apotropaic images may have a phallic character (Deonna 1965, 61),[4] the eye has several metaphoric and symbolic relationships with other organs of the body and is as well the primary facial organ for registering and signaling states of emotion.[5] The most widely distributed iconographical manifestations of eye imagery are pupils dilated in emotional arousal—and, of course, in response to diminished light—and the freezing open of the eye, when the overt presence of the whites exaggerates the nuclei, in fear, surprise, anger, and, in general, moments of arrest (Pl. 93). These arrestive images are of immense importance for iconography because they indicate just how visually similar are the representations of emotional states often defined as radically different. In visual terms, however, these categories need to be questioned, since all such faces have the net result of arresting the onlooker, petrifaction being a weapon of Gorgons and Durgā alike. What, then, is the origin of this divergence between the visual impression and the verbal description of these arresting emotional states?

Since the time of Darwin's *The Expression of the Emotions in Man and Animals* (1872), the argument over ontogeny and phylogeny in facial ex-

Plate 93. The expression of arrest: surprise and anger. In the instant before fear turns to fury, we see how arrest mediates between emotional states. (Photo courtesy Tapio Nummenmaa.)

pressions has taken on various forms. Experimentally, the argument has ranged from Birdwhistell's idea that no expressive gesture or movement has a universal meaning to Ekman's position that, while both seem to be at work, ontogeny should be favored over phylogeny (1979, 199)[6] to the opinions of ethologists such as Lorenz and Eibl-Eibesfeldt—the latter of whom feels that the presence of certain facial gestures among infants with impaired perceptual faculties indicates, as Darwin maintained, the presence of some fundamental, phylogenetic mechanism. The inescapable difficulty with the study of bodily communication and that study's traditional reasoning is that in the case of heightened emotional expression—such as in the donning of an apotropaic face—one is not only rarely sure of what exactly is being communicated, but one might even argue that the meaning deliberately involves the thwarting of a specific message. As with Lewis Carroll's Cheshire Cat, there is a deliberate attempt to seize the very expression that indicates the ambivalent, yet highly arresting, stage between a laugh and a frown, or between fear and aggression—the point, in other words, of emotional transformation. Thus, instead of debating the innateness of a specific message, one could equally argue that the leonine apotropaic face is, first, the natural symbolic manifestation of the most intense sensory experience and at the same time that it commands attention precisely because it thwarts our apprehensions about what its meaning might be. Such expressions involve, in other words, a specific message, but it is a message that does not invite a response. In that it discourages dialogue, it is not communicative. The message it offers is, in fact, a warning—an apotropaic statement that is explicitly antisocial. It says "hands off" in an unambiguous way, but it does so through its own expressive ambiguity.

In understanding how this sensory image is realized, it is instructive to examine the brow, not only as a predominant feature in the expression of rage and fear, delight and surprise, but also as an extension of the eye itself. That the eyebrows are connected with various emotional states is widely recognized, but that there is a common language of eyebrow movement is a much-debated issue. Eibl-Eibesfeldt has commented on the exaggerated eyebrows of certain Japanese masks as an expression of anger or rage, and has also called attention to the raised-brow motion of certain Old World monkeys whose superciliary gestures may be inter- preted as either positive or as threatening signals (1972, 301–2). Ekman (1979) has developed a system of facial coding that purports to describe all configurations of the human brow; the relationship between this sys- tem, however, and expressive meaning remains open to cultural variation. Two considerations that argue against a coding more specific than— I will maintain—the horrific archetype permits must be attended to. The first is of the emotive and sensory role of the superciliary vibrissae:

> Experiments of Ahrens (1953) and Fantz (1967) with babies, and of Hess (1965) and Coss (1969) with adults, demonstrate that we react strongly to two horizontally presented dark spots [Pl. 94] and even more strongly when a central dark spot is surrounded by a brighter iris-like circle. (Eibl-Eibesfeldt 1972, 306)

Might we here not have the basis for the element of surprise that was conjectured, in conjunction with the Gorgon and forehead marks, as de- riving from some aggressive/apotropaic decorative sign? It is an interest- ing possibility and one not without its parallel in the animal world. Gaze, whether it be in the widely recognized concept of the evil eye, or as a threat or predatory signal, seems to be an important analogue to the

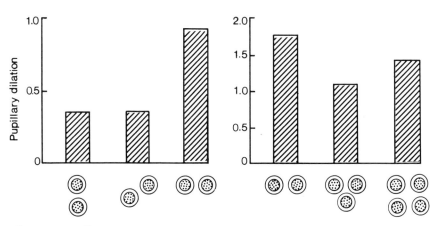

Plate 94. Pupillary reactions to eyespot patterns. Experimenters have discov- ered that subjects have the strongest emotional response to two spots or "eyes" set horizontally. Significantly, they react yet more strongly to a central circum- scribed spot. Drawing by Mary Ryder, after Coss 1970.

fixating forehead mark and the power of such marks, while a natural concomitant of the nucleated eye, according to Argyle, "may simply be due
to their being strong stimuli with good black and white contrast" (Argyle
1975, 245). Gaze can either be threatening or inviting—a point we shall
come to shortly—but the significant conclusion about round, bulging
eyes, or a single eye, and superciliary marks is that they are arrestive:

> Human infants, in the first hour of life, will follow a moving object with
> their eyes; by three or four weeks they respond particularly to a pair of
> eyes, or to masks including this design. (Argyle 1975, 245–46)

Infants, in fact, will respond to a simple surface with two dots. In a quite
anthropomorphic way, some ethologists have identified the spots by
means of which certain birds and fish repel predators as "fake eyes." In
this interpretation, animals evolve the capacity to protect themselves
through mimicking what look like eyes; when such spots are removed
from the wings of certain butterflies, for example, predatory birds will
suddenly move in to eat the insects (ibid., 245). But as Argyle points out,
one ought not to infer from this phenomenon that eyes are involved,
rather only that the dots or their absence act as a stimulus.

Pocock, in studying facial vibrissae (1914), offered the interesting hypothesis that the facial vibrissae originally grew in tufts for tactile purposes and that their eventual evolutionary failure has its correlate in primates in the gradual perfection in the use and sensitivity of the hands.
This is an especially important association since, iconographically, hands
and eyes appear together in various apotropaic configurations (pls. 90
and 95).[7] As the lion is not only the apotropaic animal *par excellence*, but
also an apotropaic animal with very prominent superciliary vibrissae, it
seems that the ancients, despite their lack of scientific method, suc-
cessfully isolated the forehead marks both as the symbolic manifestation
of the senses and as an apotropaic, attention-arresting device.

But what transformational role do the superciliary marks play in the
leonine expression that is so much a part of the apotropaic face? If
Schaller is correct in accepting the assumption that primates are almost
identical to lions in their facial expressions (1972, 98), then a thesis on
transformation would seem tenable whereby eyes or superciliary marks
arrest *because* of the ambivalence between the expression of fear through
withdrawal and the opposite expression of attack and aggression. It
is this ambivalence, in turn, that constitutes the second consideration arguing against a specific meaning for all coded facial expressions. Of
monkeys, for example, Bolwig remarks:

> If no antagonistic drive, such as a drive to flee, interferes, the eyebrows
> become lowered and probably drawn somewhat together into a frown.

Plate 95. a, Balinese *kāla songsang* (i.e., upside down). Courtesy H. W. J. Bosch. *b, karang bhoma.* Ramseyer 1977, Fig. 1. In these two Balinese figures is seen the explicit iconographical association between the hands and the horrific face.

. . . Whenever the drive to flee interferes with the drive to attack threat postures appear. . . . How threat has developed in each case is not clear, but it is possible that all threat postures, facial and otherwise, show elements of submission, as for example laying back the ears, lifting the eyebrows, ducking and readiness to flee. (Bolwig 1963–64, 186)

With lions, according to Schaller, the problem of interpretation is much the same, though the facial expression itself is unmistakable:

At a high intensity the mouth is open, exposing all teeth, and the expression is reinforced with lunges, bites, and slaps if the other animal persists with the contact.

> . . . [U]sually, however, vocalizations are so much a part of the
> functional unit that the effect of the expression in itself is difficult to
> measure.
> . . . On the other hand, lions attack man with bared teeth. The ex-
> posed teeth represent a defensive reaction . . . in other words, they
> contain an element of fear. (Schaller 1972, 97–98)

We see, therefore, that there is very little indication that would enable us to distinguish between a threatened and a threatening pose, though in both cases the ability of the face to arrest would be the same. Indeed, it would seem that the arresting feature of this expression is intimately tied to an awareness that an unpredictable change is imminent, a change marked, as with Gorgons, by a horrific roar.

On the assumption, then, that the elements of surprise and arrest are central to monstrous faces, we may posit that gnashing teeth, protruding tongues, and large noses, ears, and tactile receptors (such as superciliary marks or large hands) all become part of an idealized exaggeration and visual externalization of the senses. But what does this ideally sensitized face tell us about the expression of sensation in human beings, and is there some natural proclivity in human beings for apprehending and representing such a face? Is there, in other words, some direct connection between the iconography of the apotropaic face and the capacity of the human senses? Modern science, in a graphic reconstruction of the somatic sensory cortex for the functions of the parts of the human body, has provided us with just such an illustration. In Plate 96, the various body parts are rendered in proportion to the sensitivity of that part within the right hemisphere of the human brain. We need only rearrange this representation, this "homunculus," so that our view is a frontal one, to see how close the Hindus throughout the world have come to constructing a natural image grounded in the senses. In the frontal view, the tongue is seen within the mouth and both hands are visible. Even given the effects of centuries of stylization, the representation of the sensory proportions is quite remarkable (cf. pls. 90 and 95).[8]

The likelihood of considering the leonine face as a natural image grounded in the senses rests in the fact not merely that the homunculus is descriptive of the capacities of the sensory cortex, but that the apprehension of facial expression appears to be hemispherically oriented:

> Campbell . . . used chimeric face stimuli (composites of two half-faces
> showing different individuals or facial expressions or mirror-reversed
> expressions) to study lateralization effects in the production and per-
> ception of facial expression. Her findings reveal that—in right-handed
> adults—the perception of facial expression is dominated by the left vi-
> sual field (i.e. by the viewer's right hemisphere), corresponding to the

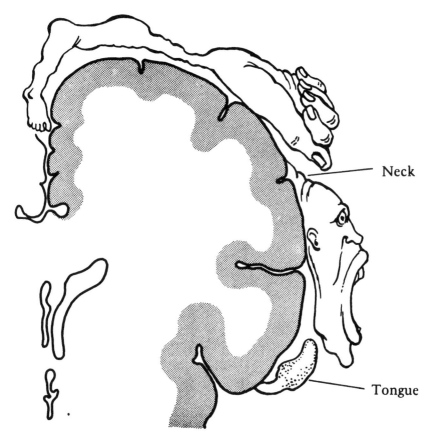

Plate 96. The *homunculus.* In this graphic reconstruction of the somatic sensory cortex for the right hemisphere of the brain, a huge face, tongue, and hands are evidence that the facial expressions of Greek and Hindu monsters are grounded in the senses. Drawing by Mary Ryder, after T. J. Teyler.

right side of the face stimuli. At the same time, emotion actually may be expressed more strongly by the left side of the face, controlled by the producer's right hemisphere. Lesion studies . . . provide further evidence of right-hemisphere superiority for emotional expression. (Ekman and Oster 1979, 548)

Thus not only is the horrific apotropaic face a decidedly "left" one, but studies confirming the emotional supe.iority of the right hemisphere would seem to demonstrate adequately that the expression of arrest is grounded in an iconography derived from the dominant locus of human sensory control. Several emotional and nervous disorders give rise to spontaneous faces that also confirm the unity of the expression of arrest as a high-order complex. Examples of its emotional manifestation are hysteria and birth trauma; physiologically, it may be seen in such disorders as epilepsy—the "sacred" disease, in which the tongue may be bitten or swallowed—and tetany, the violent contraction of the voluntary muscles, where the hands are frequently thrown up and back. Moreover, that this face must be considered a total complex or archetype, rather than a series of isolated signs, is a conclusion that also has a degree of experimental support:

> Several converging lines of evidence (brain lesion studies, research on commisurotomized patients, recognition and reaction time experiments with normal subjects) point to a right hemisphere advantage in recognizing faces. This advantage is especially pronounced when the task requires processing in terms of the higher-order, configurational properties of the face, rather than isolated features. . . . (Ekman and Oster 1979, 548)

If, then, demonic faces may be said to be grounded in an autonomous archetypal image representing the manifestation of the predominant sensory capacities of the brain, what may be said about the use of these faces by the Balinese? In that masks are the medium in Bali through which gods manifest themselves, it is appropriate at this juncture to discuss Balinese masks specifically.

Rangda and Barong: Displaying Archetypes

It is difficult, without a lengthy and detailed study, to determine what, if any, culturally defined display rules govern horrific mask types employed in Balinese drama. It is also difficult to determine how the rules governing the use of masks might be transposed into a commentary on cultural attitudes toward physical gestures and facial expressions in general. As is obvious, for example, from the studies of Balinese child-rearing practices pioneered by Bateson and Mead (1942), while we may recognize the significance of behavioral rules, we enter into uncertain territory when we attempt to impute as the rules of others analytical categories employed in the course of research. Not only must we be able to demonstrate in such cases that covert categories are, indeed, at work, but we must also be able, in the case of facial iconography, to address the far more difficult question of whether or not such display rules have a recognized significance in the culture in question. What is the relationship, in other words, between the horrific faces of Balinese art and the expressions the people of Bali themselves recognize in their interactions with the world around them? As if this problem were not difficult enough, we must also contend with the fact that an apotropaic iconography, as we have just seen, may be deliberately ambivalent and ambiguous. It may, in other words, deliberately undermine our ability to perceive what rules are at work in the masked display.

Fortunately, in Bali we do not have to resort to considering what covert categories might govern mask iconography and performance. For the Balinese, it is not just chance that covert categories are unnecessary. This fact may be partially attributed to native genius; more relevant perhaps is the overwhelming necessity in Balinese culture that the microcosmic reflect the macrocosmic and vice versa. Such an aesthetic principle demands that things become greater or smaller in proportion to all other things that are contextually related. The kind of linear logic in which a single line of reasoning may become tangential and explainable only by recourse to covert categories is not only undesirable but unaesthetic. *Rasa*, feeling, is the essence of everything, the embryo of the waters that is also the source of individual sensation. As the great permeator of all things, *rasa* is not only the vital sap of plants, semen, *madhu*, and so on; its essential character is so powerful that all important symbolic complexes in one way or another relate to it.

In East Java, the *kīrttimukha*, or Face of Glory, that hovers protectively over temple gates is called *banaspati* in deference to his role as Lord of the Forest. In Bali, the mask of the holy Barong, the most famous of protective images, occurs in many forms, but the most popular is also called Lord of the Forest (*banaspati raja*), and the generic *bhoma* figures that are placed above temple gates always grasp in their thumbs the foliage that connects them to the forest and to the vital sap stored within plants (Pl. 97). Likewise, the temple gate itself is an exercise in negative imagery. It is an empty space that is also a column and Cosmic Tree,[9] that signifies a point of transformation. Just as Narasiṃha burst from a column, the most sacred of Balinese masks emerges from the temple gate to bring to life the static image of the Lord of the Forest, the face of all *rasa*, the visual image that displays the natural capacities of the cerebral cortex.

That *rasa* is all feeling is clear from the extent to which the face of *banaspati* cannot be wholly read outside of the context within which it occurs, or at least it is only within a specific context that the face can be said to have only one meaning. This is not because the iconography is unrefined; quite the contrary. It is rather a face exaggerated, often into pure abstraction, as when the mouth of the monster opens to become the gate itself, its tongue and lower jaw disappearing entirely (Pl. 92), or when this same space is recognized as a column or tree. The Face of

Plate 97. Protective *bhoma* head. Closeup of temple gate, illustrating the horrific monster grasping the foliage that signifies his role as Lord of the Forest. Pura Dalem Nataran. Sanur, Bali. (Photo: author.)

Glory must incorporate all possibility, all contradiction since, as in India, every kind of *rasa* is combined in ambivalent deities such as the Goddess or Śiva (O'Flaherty 1969, 276). For the Balinese, the *bhoma* head is pure, total sensation, and its opposite in terms of radical categories is the brave-serene expression so common of heroes of the quasi-historical masked performance called *topéng* and of the *wayang kulit*, the ancient shadow theater. "Such is the content of the smile," begins the prologue of one such shadow play, "which reveals not the heart; at the moment serenity may conceal a troubled mood. Still undetermined, he cares not to make clear his thoughts. His intentions he will not quickly tell" (McPhee 1970, 196). Strange, it seems to us, that such an ideal should prevail in a society filled with Barongs and *banaspati* monsters. But, in fact, both the brave-serene expression and its *banaspati*-like opposite are equally ambivalent faces. The first gives very little information; the second, which expresses everything, gives all too much. It gives so much, in fact, that, depending on context, the Balinese find it horrific or humorous, terrifying or ridiculous. The power, as elsewhere in Bali, rests in understanding how radical categories define every level at which *rasa* is manifested, from the microcosmic to the macrocosmic.

Thus, on the one hand, we have the microcosmic *rasa*, the sap of plants, understood as the embryonic basis for the whole world, while on the other, this *rasa* is refined into an archetype: the Cosmic Tree that is not only a column and a temple gate, but ultimately the Sacred Mountain, the *axis mundi*. The face above the temple gate is, therefore, *rasa* manifested, just as the mask of Barong, Rangda, or any other *bhoma*-like image is *rasa* realized. *Rasa* is given an active character through masks, and masks in turn have, as we shall see, specific referents for each of the above images. At each level, too, *rasa* has, by definition, a radical opposite; the Lord of the Forest is an inversion of brave serenity, complementary opposition being required for expressing the scope of *rasa* and, thus, a necessary feature of all symbols based upon it. The extent to which the face of *banaspati* is itself a microcosm of *rasa* is readily seen by the way in which sacred masks in Bali relate to the macrocosmic juxtaposition between the Great Mountain (*Gunung Agung*), abode of the ancestral gods, and the sea, home of everything demonic. This geographic opposition is a cosmic one that affects—as it did in Greece and India, and as it does in Indonesia—everything in the lives of people. In Bali, masks are no exception. The *pura dalem*, the so-called temple of the dead,

> is situated at the end of the village farthest removed from the Mountain, the Goenoeng Agoeng, where the ancestors live and towards which every village is orientated; at the opposite end from the *poera poeseh*, the

temple *par excellence* of the ancestors, which is the first one comes to in approaching the village from the Mountain. In south Bali *kadja* means north, in north Bali south. In both cases it is the region of the Mountain, of which the sea is the polar opposite. The sea is the region of impurity, and for this reason leper colonies are always planted there. It is from the sea that demons come, bringing disease and pestilence. (de Zoete and Spies [1938] 1973, 88–89)

That this radical opposition between mountain and sea is fundamental to even the most basic understanding of the Barong is a truism. Brahma, the god of the *kelod* direction—that is, the south—is, as is the Barong, known as *banaspati raja*. Barong masks may be of many colors, but as *banaspati raja* they are most often red, the color of Brahma and the south. The Barong costume is four-legged; worn by two people, it symbolizes the fact that *banaspati raja* is the god of everything four-legged and beastly—a fear of which extends in Bali to the way humans define themselves. Infants, for example, are carried so as not to crawl on all fours and thereby appear beastly; witches, similarly, are often depicted as crawling, and their black magic is supposed to be most powerful when carried out by the sea or in the *kelod* direction. Similarly, when the Balinese seek out the most sacred of woods for a powerful Barong mask, they resort to an enormously complex classificatory system for identifying sacred and spiritually powerful trees; and when they take the wood to be used for such a mask they will take it, preferably, from a tree standing at the *kelod* (i.e., more demonic) side of the graveyard or a similarly known locus of demonic power (Pl. 98). They will even go so far as to take the wood out of the *kelod* or *kelod kauh* side of the tree, *kelod kauh*, or southwest, also being a demonic direction (Arsana 1977, 15–18).

Of the trees used for making sacred masks, the most important of sacred woods is *kayu pulé*. *Pulé* (*Alstonia scholaris*) is a tree that grows mostly in the graveyard, in the place to which the sacred masks periodically return in recognition of their place of origin, the place where they go for *paśupati*, a word the Balinese use not only to describe Siwa (Śiva) as Lord of the Animals but one that is used generally to refer to the acquisition of magic power, a magic charge such as is given by the *brahmana* priest's magic arrow. *Pulé* is one of the sacred trees that, because of its milky sap, has extraordinary *rasa*; it possesses so much of this powerful life force that it may, as may other milky trees in both Bali and India, become the residence of a demonic spirit. For this reason, the Balinese traditionally cut down such trees before they reach the size where a spirit might take up residence within them. Otherwise, the spirit therein must be placated with offerings. A quick look across the horizon in Bali to the

Plate 98. Pulé tree (*Alstonia scholaris*). Giant tree shows old scars from the removal of wood for making sacred masks. Near Petang, Bali. (Photo: author.)

places where tall trees are found always tells one immediately where are the spiritually powerful places such as temples and cemeteries—places where such trees may grow undisturbed, where the spirits that reside in them conduct their life-threatening machinations and where humans go to placate them. Among the sacred plants listed in the *Lontar Taru Premana*—that is, the palm leaf manuscript dealing with sacred trees—are others, such as *datura* and *brumangsia*,[10] that contain a milky sap and have, as does *pule*, known medicinal properties.

There is a famous passage in the *Ādiparva*, the first book of the *Mahābhārata*, where the gods, after making the sacred mountain into a churning-staff, and using the snake Vāsuki for a twirling-rope, commence to churn the ocean in order to make the Elixir of Immortality. As they churned, the *Mahābhārata* tells us,

> a mighty roar rose from [the ocean] like rumbling thunder in the clouds. All kinds of creatures that inhabit the deep were crushed asunder by the big mountain and by the hundreds went to their perdition in the salty ocean. . . . [L]arge trees crashed into one another and tumbled down from the peak with their nestling birds. The friction of the trees started fire after fire, covering the mountain with flames like a black monsoon cloud with lightning streaks. . . . Then Indra the Lord of the Immortals flooded the fire that was raging everywhere with rain pouring from the clouds. The many juices of herbs and the manifold resins of the trees flowed into the water of the ocean. And with the milk of these juices that had the power of the Elixir . . . the Gods attained immortality.
> (*Mahābhārata* I, 5, 16)

This passage provides an interesting answer to the question of what *madhu* has to do with the Elixir of Immortality; more important for iconography, it indicates how it is that trees, and especially sacred trees, are envisaged as the archetypes for the Cosmic Mountain, temple column and gate, ecstasy, Barong face, and so on. A yet closer analysis of the mask itself reveals even more microcosmic manifestations of *rasa*. Of the mask's details, the most important are, first, the seven openings that correspond to the dwelling places of divine power for the "Seven Divisions of the Sacred Sound OM" (Soebadio 1971, 137ff.), as described in the *Doctrine of Siddhānta*. These seven openings take the form of flames: two above the eyes, two in front of the ears, two next to the nose, and the flaming mouth that, in Barong masks not possessing a working jaw and in almost all masks of the witch Rangda, takes the form of an elaborately decorated flame made of leather (Pl. 99). These seven flames, combined with the flaming *sesimping*, the fiery leather decoration that surrounds the head (Pl. 100), provide us with the image of the disembodied flaming head that becomes the basis for the Balinese Barong mask—an image

Plate 99. Devi Krishna, as Rangda, bursts through the temple gate. The famous Balinese trance dance, in which kris dancers turn against themselves, is caused by the powers of the witch Rangda. De Zoete and Spies [1938] 1973, Pl. 58.

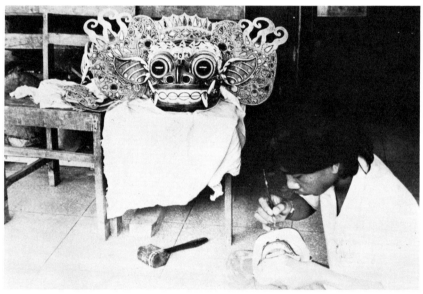

Plate 100. a, Barong *ket.* One of several varieties of Barong masks, the Barong *ket* represents Barong in his capacity as *banaspati raja,* or Lord of the Forest. De Zoete and Spies [1938] 1973, Pl. 34. *b,* Maskmaker's apprentice and Barong mask with leather *sesimping* by Cokorda Tublen. Singapadu, Bali. (Photo: author.)

Plate 101. Barong mask by Cokorda Tublen. Singapadu, Bali. (Photo: author.)

that has its origin in the ancient Brahmanical idea of the flaming head

Of the other important iconographic details, three remain: *bajra,* *cuṇḍang,* and *semut sadulur.* Bajra is the tridentate forehead mark (Pl. 101); it means, literally, "the hard one"; it is the thunderbolt and Siwa's trident, the priest's five-pointed scepter that is three-pointed when shown two-dimensionally. As in India, it stands for the Hindu trinity, for three in one, and is explained by several sectarian legends, such as the myth whereby Śiva strikes Viṣṇu on the forehead with his trident, or in the worship of the Ganges, where it is the sacred water of the River that issues forth in the form of the Elixir of Immortality. As with *bajra, cuṇḍang* is also an elaboration of the iconography of the forehead; it is the central forehead mark (Pl. 101) that has its basis in the notion of the third eye. The important distinction between *bajra* and *cuṇḍang* is that the latter, like the Lotus of Command (*ājñā-cakra*), signifies more specifically an inner light that is also an outward force. *Cuṇḍang* is a term applied to a defeated cock, a conceding of defeat that is also part of a temple sacrifice. As such, the sacrifice is an external manifestation of inner self-denial and sacrifice. When Śiva distinguished himself from the self-consuming *kīrttimukha,* his pleasure derived also from recognizing in the manifestation a pleasing self-interpretation. It is worthwhile remembering here that the *kīrttimukha* that is the *kāla* (Time) monster adorning the tops of temple gates in Indonesia is also known in East Java as *banaspati raja*, the same name by which the most popular form of Barong is known in Bali. The last important iconographic detail that needs to be considered is the magic writing on the lips of the Barong mask (Pl. 101). These magic marks are known collectively as *semut sadulur*. *Semut* means "ant" and *sadulur* "together," "having brothers." *Semut sadulur* refers to calendric burial restrictions, but here specifically denotes the fact that the magic marks, like ant tracks, are drawn in a line or row. It is a kind of writing that is inscribed upon the lips of the mask to give it the power of divine speech. In a general sense, the *semut sadulur* is part of the mask's ability to speak in the interest of the community, as the term also refers to rules that concern restricted days—rules, in other words, that enable the community to function as a whole, to function collectively.

To try, however, to understand the meaning of any specific set of marks is another matter, for they are secret (Bagus 1980), and to disclose their meaning would be to risk the loss of power for the mask. What can be known about the *semut sadulur* is something about the graphic tradition of which it is an outgrowth. The Balinese say that it is, like the *padma*, or lotus, a place of residence for the god. More specifically, the *semut sadulur* is, like the *ongkara*, or Word of Words, a sign that is at least as old as the philosophy of Brahmanism—one that came to Indochina from Bengal by the seventh century A.D. at the very latest, and to Java and Bali during the Hindu-Balinese period starting in the eighth century. Like the *ongkara*, the *semut sadulur* is a sign that in its own right is a source of power—power that may be called up by the proper *mantra* or *mantras*. Like the Siwa-Siddhānta *ongkara*, which begins with the waking of Brahma the Creator at the navel and ends with the supreme Brahma at the fontanelle, the *semut sadulur* emphasizes enclosure—that there is a beginning and an end, that the marks are different and yet the same, and that in order to be efficacious, they must be utilized in the proper sequence. These *maṅgala* symbols are, therefore, not only auspicious signs, but signs that "promote the preservation of the contents" (Boeles 1947, 43) of the magic they effect. The use of them, moreover, "is quite in accordance with the old Brahmanic principle that it is necessary to pronounce OM" (ibid., 42) at the beginning and end of a lesson in the Vedas in order to preserve the holy script (*Law of Manu* [II, 74]). Like the flames that emanate from the Barong head, they are signs of power; in fact, certain Buddhist statues in India and Indonesia emit flames in the very shape of the magic sign OM, as do the Nava Durgā masks of Nepal (Teilhet 1978). In Bali, various forms of the *ongkara* are also inscribed on the inside of the mask at its consecration, and a magic cloth called a *kuḍung* is often covered with a special magic drawing composed of secret arrangements of *ongkara*s. This cloth may, at times, also be made of the *kain poléng*, the checkered cloth found in Balinese art for at least the last thousand years, symbol of the complementarity of black and white magic, of the radical categories that are both part of the mask's power, of *rasa*, a potential force unmanifested. The *kuḍung* protects the mask from harmful forces when not in use and increases the intrinsic power of the mask once removed.

That these magic signs enclose a specific magical sequence and that they are secret are no accident; implicit in this is the awareness that to know that secret is to confiscate its power and thereby to have the power of destroying it. Implicit, also, is the understanding that to invert or reverse the sequence is to undo its force, or even to reverse its power. Black magic (*pengiwa*) is effected by taking the magic of the white (*penengen*) and reversing it. As in all Hindu literature, the most evil people are *paṇḍita*s gone awry—people who know all the sacred formulas and recite them backwards, people who belong to a religious sect or ascribe to a set of principles that appears to be the inverse of one's own. Masks, especially sacred demonic masks, are explicitly related to the left, since the demons who are personified by them are the functionaries of *pengiwa*, which is also left-handed (Covarrubias 1937, 341). In the tale of the witch Calonarang, the quasi-historical manifestation of Rangda, it is said that Calonarang's power was derived from a book of magic *lontar*s whose "teaching was good, but [she] turned it all to evil by doing everything to the left instead of right" (de Zoete and Spies [1938] 1973, 117). Similarly, chapter 25 of the *Rāmāyaṇa* lists all of the sacrificial rituals performed by the Rākṣasa demons—but in the interest of black magic—that is, backwards.

The idea of inverting convention is extremely important for understanding the ritual conflict between the protective Barong and the witch Rangda (Pl. 102). Though there may, for example, be several Rangdas in any one performance (Pl. 103), the general plot of the sacred play is quite simple. The story concerns the battle between the Barong, who is the protective demon of the village, and the witch Rangda, the purveyor of disease and destruction. In the course of their famous battle, the so-called kris dancers come to the aid of Barong against Rangda. The battle is enacted over and over again but no one ever wins:

> What happens is that dozens of villagers, aroused by the excitement held incarnate in these two figures and by the stylized interplay between them, go into trance, go through patterned behavior in a somnambulistic state, attack the witch with their krisses, are revived by the

Plate 102. Rangda and Barong. Their conflict is one between the personification of wickedness and destruction and the protector of the village order. (Photo: Urs Ramseyer, Museum of Ethnography, Basel.)

> Barong, attack their own chests with their krisses, and preferably work themselves to a climax, a true convulsive seizure of hysterical order. After such a performance everyone goes home feeling perfectly great and at peace with the world. (Belo [1949] 1966, 12)

Though the performance may have many variations,[11] the plot remains essentially the same. This apparent simplicity, however, is in contrast to the complexity of the personae involved—that is, the figures of Barong, Rangda, and the kris dancers.

While Belo, as I said, identifies the Barong as "a holy masked figure of a lion or tiger" (ibid., 11), de Zoete and Spies maintain that "as to its name we can get no further than that it probably means some kind of wild beast, or rather, wild beast generalized" ([1938] 1973, 90). According to Covarrubias, "Barong" is simply a generic name for a type of monster, since he is also addressed by several other names.[12] And though the Barong, as a protective figure, is generally associated with kadja (toward the mountain) and the right, and Rangda, conversely, with kelod and the left, this distinction is in no way absolute. The Barong may also have evil traits, and in one mystical Tantric interpretation is even described as an actual emanation of Rangda, "won over by offerings to take the part of the village against her" (de Zoete and Spies [1938] 1973, 97). What matters here is the fact that the village as an organized social entity is being challenged by a purveyor of chaos, and to this end the Barong is more protective than destructive. Whereas Rangda has the fiery scorching tongue of Agni that destroys everything in its path, the Barong frequently dons a beard of human hair (Pl. 104)—hair that becomes the locus of the Barong's power to bring men out of trance, part of a man used to return a man to a socialized condition. Conversely, Rangda represents all that is chaotic. Her name, de Zoete and Spies tell us,

> is the Balinese word for widow; but to the idea of widow is attached a certain awe, even a degree of fear or horror. For a widow is the wife of a spirit and ought really to have given up her bodily form when her husband died, and to have followed him to the underworld. (de Zoete and Spies [1938] 1973, 95)

Plate 103. Rangdas in Barong performance. Because the villagers are forbidden to kill Rangda, they turn their rage on themselves. Her "left-handed" magic— that is, black or evil magic—is balanced by Barong's association with the "right." De Zoete and Spies [1938] 1973, Pl. 35.

Rangda is a true example of matter out of place, of a figure threatening to undermine the natural and supernatural order. Rangda is disorder personified, and the consequences of disorder are nothing less than total destruction. It is because the men of the village are incapable of killing Rangda that each is forced to turn his kris upon himself in the performance of *onying* (self-stabbing). Like so many myths of India, Greece, and the Near East, the story is told of how a god, Siwa (Śiva), lost his seed into a mountain and thereby created monstrous children, children who turn on their parents or grandparents because of the chaotic situation created by an older generation's indiscretion. In Bali, it is in attempting to back the forces of order that men can be sent into trance or even, if they are either unlucky or unprepared, self-destruction—into a chaos that cannot be overcome without divine intervention. Like Perseus, even a Balinese hero cannot win without the aid of a god.

Plate 104. Procession of Barong, the "Big Lord" (Bhatara Gedé). (Photo: Urs Ramseyer, Museum of Ethnography, Basel.)

Epilogue

*the spectacle of the floating masks among the broken reflections
of the volcano was perhaps the strangest moment of all.*
—DE ZOETE AND SPIES

When the Greek hero Perseus conquers the Gorgon Medusa, he does not, in any common sense, come face to face with what he is meant to be in conflict with. How is it, then, that he is a hero? What do we admire in him or what is it that he does that lets us define him in heroic terms? Perhaps, of all things, it is the fact that he permits himself to become involved with, and even volunteers for, the heroic conflict, though it may well be beyond him to conquer. Perseus somehow steps forward and goes about the business that he is, in all apparent respects, unprepared to undertake. As with the hero David in his conflict with Goliath, social role is placed before individuality, and the more ambivalent the nature of the demon to be conquered, the more important becomes the awareness of social role. Goodness, in other words, is not an innate property that may be stored and measured in the vacuum of individuality; it is something so easily spoiled that for good truly to conquer evil, for order truly to win out over chaos, it must do so in complete harmony with the social contexts that give rise to it and to the rituals that humans construct to revivify the cosmic order created by the heroic act. At least partially this is why ambivalence is so fundamental to certain sorts of belief. Ambivalence, in other words, emphasizes how easily what is good may become what is bad. Calonarang, the widow (Rangda) who ought to have followed her husband through the cycle of reincarnation, does indeed resort to witchcraft, but she does so unknowingly. This most horrible of monsters, who makes garlands of her victims' entrails, in the end thanks the holy man, Bharada, for destroying her and thereby releasing her from the dreadful role she had assumed. That her accidentally doing things to the left rather than the right was an accident is no matter. In becoming a widow she lost her ability to perform a conventional social role and in so doing lost her ability to affect positively any kind of performance, be it ritual, social, or dramatic; for each of these forms of performance cannot be completely separated from any other. Their interrelationships are totally in keeping with the character of Hinduism in the most general sense. Acting, as the *Nāṭyaśāstra* would indicate in about the second century A.D., is an entirely sensory experience. On the level of ritual drama, the four styles of dramatic representation (*vṛtti*s) became known to the universe as the result of Viṣṇu's conflict with the demons Madhu and Kaiṭabha, an episode in the *Rāmāyaṇa* that, itself, is in essence about the uses and abuses of ritual. Whether or not it is accidental that Madhu's name is the same as the spirituous liquor that affects sensory experience, it is clear that the origins of acting are in a heroic act elevated into a commentary on ritual performance.

It is not for the current study to judge whether those who function in worlds motivated by ambivalent forces actually think that good and evil are as close in their unsocialized state as mythology seems to suggest. They may be pushed together as a means of emphasizing the essential character of communal activities properly performed, so much so that it may be the contradiction of good and evil—that good and evil are radical categories but competers for the same power, which is knowledge—that Hinduism offers as its message. When a Balinese *pedanda (brahmana* priest) makes a demonic mask, it is not because he has forsaken his defense of white magic to participate in the black; it is because of his total understanding of the white, right-hand, path. More so, it is because the defender of the white must remember how quickly an expression of withdrawal and submission can become one of aggression and assault, and how two things having an identical form can have opposite meanings if the sequence, the context, is reversed.

Though to the Western mind—or for that matter the mind of any monotheist—this kind of thinking can promote extreme psychological instability, it also, more positively, shows how being aware of ambivalence involves recognizing how good can become evil through ignorance if not intent, how the power of the good, if not cared for, if not understood in relative social terms, can quickly become an evil force, and how the maintenance of good can only be certified by constantly putting that goodness to the social test, by social acts or by ritual performance. Individuals, likewise, having also ambivalent forces working within them, must constantly test out social roles in ritual contexts. For monotheists, the refinement of the individual character out of visual—social and ritual—manifestations can result in split or multiple personalities rather than personalities struggling to control an ambivalence that is fundamental, and it is this latter struggle that makes performance so essential for character development in the Hindu view.

In Balinese drama, gentle or noble characters are frequently presented unmasked, but acting the role of a demon may also require no mask if the demon appears in the performance in a refined or noble role. Everything here inveighs against the idea of the incorruptibility of the good. Harsh as this view may appear, it does help prevent the assumption that the good can do no wrong. Coping with ambivalence requires special skills and dramatic conceits, and some particularly powerful de-monic parts are too dangerous to play without masks. In such cases, the mask object is not only a vehicle for the demon to become manifest but also some assurance that the actors can divest themselves of person-alities that they might otherwise have had to live with. This great atten-tion in polytheism to the *idea* of appearances—to masks that may or may not be incarnations, to humans who may be masked in their natural physical state, able or unable to divest themselves of a role—is both the great intellectual invention of polytheism as well as its enormous emo-tional burden. To make this system work requires not only considerable social skill, but a complex understanding of the transformation of emo-tions manifested in the face of *rasa*.

In attempting to understand what makes such systems work, my study has centered on three major concerns: first, the role of visual ap-pearances and the incarnation of deities lacking omniscience; second, the phenomenon of impersonation and the problems posed by the stage for defining notions of the person; and third, the consequences of am-bivalence for the actual iconography of masks that embody forces both natural and supernatural. It has been my intention, in light of these con-siderations, to study the nature and meaning of masks and to suggest through specific examples how a simple metaphysical supposition, such as that of divine ambivalence, may result in attitudes that greatly affect our interpretation of the visible world, our perceptions of ourselves and others, our ability to accept Aristotle's remarkable thesis that what makes the world one will also be what makes a man.

Notes

1 · Masks, Transformation, and Paradox

1. *Webster's New International Dictionary of the English Language*, s.v. "identity."

2. See, e.g., Lloyd's lengthy discussion of the origins of atomic theory and especially his remarks on the various classical arguments following upon Zeno's considerations about the discreteness of entities (Lloyd 1979, 73ff.).

3. Garton notes that there is disagreement about these figures in his sources and points out that his figures are conservative.

4. Compare R. F. Gombrich's discussion of the "accretive" nature of Sri Lankan religion (1971, 46–50), wherein he mentions the slogan, recorded by Copleston in 1892, that read, God bless our Lord Buddha!

5. Harnack 1958, 3:85ff. A discussion of the various Church Councils and Trinitarian controversies is well beyond the scope of this inquiry. (For an overview of the major terminological debates relevant to this discussion, see Rougier 1917.) The tension created by Sabellius is, however, for the present purposes demonstrated in the general problem posed by the negative descriptive tendencies of Neoplatonic metaphysics on the one hand (see, e.g., Strong 1902) and the unavoidably theatrical sense of the words *persona* and *prosōpon*. (See M. Marshall 1950.) For a general consideration of the etymological complexities the ancient terms entail, see Bloch 1959a.

6. For additional source material on the evolution into medieval times of the problem of personality and substance, see M. Marshall 1950, 479 n. 11.

7. Taking a different tack, we might view this objectification as clarifying rather than complicating categories. Paul Henry, for example, credits Augustine with establishing the notion of personality. According to Henry, the Greeks had, in fact, no word for "person," at least in the sense that we now know it. This interpretation has special merit for scholars of Plotinus who, like Father Henry, must contend with the problem of the individuality of souls and with what came to be seen through Augustine as "the triumph of neo-platonic psychology over neo-platonic metaphysics" (Strong 1902, 39). See Henry 1960.

8. To suggest the extent of this *persona/prosōpon* transformation and how much the theater must have displeased the Church Fathers, we may recall Butcher

on Aristotle: "A work of art reproduces its original, not as it is in itself, but as it appears to the senses." See Butcher 1951, 127.

9. This passage from *Metaphysics* 1.980ᵇ26f. is especially important in light of the sensory role of repetitive theatrical experience.

10. Note how Aristotle, according to Clark, attempts to resolve this tension:

> Nothing can affect itself . . . , nor therefore know itself where this implies touching and being touched . . . , unless it has parts. The mouth can gnaw itself only in the sense that the teeth can gnaw the lips. What has no parts cannot turn upon itself. The highest state of all can be described as "a knowing without touching things: that is, without making things into objects in one's consciousness." . . . In this state the gap between subject and object is bridged, for when one knows everything all together in a single, perfect whole . . . there is nothing else against which this Whole can be seen, and hence no awareness of separate selfhood. . . . The knowledge of God is the same as God's knowledge. (Clark 1975, 179)

11. In particular, see Vygotsky's discussion of thinking in complexes and of the classificatory role of what he terms pseudo-concepts ([1934] 1964, 52ff., especially 66ff.).

12. A. P. Rossiter dates the introduction of semi-dramatic elements into established Christian ritual between the ninth and twelfth centuries (1950, 42).

13. Needless to say, given the political role of the Church and its sacred character *per se*, comparing social customs with medieval religious belief may be ill conceived, except of course where an intrusion of custom is recognized as such by the Church itself. If this institution, in other words, has a socio-political prerogative and at the same time is sacred in essence, then it is hard to say what part of society does not also partake of this essence. That this presupposition is fundamental to Catholicism is evidenced by Augustine's wisely advising Christians not to "reject a good thing merely because it was pagan" (Rossiter 1950, 36) while arguing at the same time for the sacrosanct nature of the Church as an institution. R. Bernheimer would seem to support this view: "It was through the acceptance by ecclesiastic authorities of the popular notion that . . . demons could incarnate themselves in human beings . . . that the fear arose of their presence within human society itself, and with it the need of combating them" (1952, 36). Perhaps this is in part why we may discern a greater similarity between certain folk customs and the Christian attitude toward masks than between the popular roles of masks in Christian and classical societies.

14. Given the exegetic problems outlined in my note 13, we should not make too little of such criticism, which comes from the Church itself. More pervasively, we note the predominance of words such as *larva* to refer to the disfigurements of masking and to testimonies such as Gervais de Tilbury's *lamias . . . vulgo mascas* (cited by both Bernheimer and Chastel) to disclaim their use.

15. From the Stoics, for example, we have inherited the logical paradigm called the *larvatus*, the "masked man." According to this paradigm, I do not know the identity of a certain masked man; I know well the identity of my father; the masked man, therefore, is not my father.

16. On the consequences of this dilemma for modern psychology, see Hillman 1975.

17. See, especially, Needham 1975 and Vygotsky [1934] 1964, 61–69. Webster (1954, 19) calls a genealogy "the commonest way of relating personifications."

18. There is just such a comparison made by R. Hooykaas (1959).

19. If the Sacraments were in themselves holy, then in theory it became possible for a sinner, for example, to perform a legitimate Baptism. In the same way, the indelible character of the Holy Orders meant that priesthood was irrevocable and that even heretics could baptize in the name of the Trinity.

20. This problem appears to have attracted considerable recent attention among historians of the philosophy of science. See, especially, Feyerabend 1965 and 1975.

21. On the problem of providing an empirically compatible visual impression of the quantum world, see Hooker 1972.

22. See, for example, Mayr's discussion of Aristotle, and his idea of *teleonomics* in particular (1976).

23. That this is so is not only clear from what has already been said about Christian psychology and the changing notion of the term *persona*; it may also be seen in the frequent contention that Augustine was our first autobiographer.

24. Compare the Christian notion of the purity of the soul regardless of the condition of the body with the common Hindu beliefs that ugliness is often the punishment for wickedness and that physical appearance can reflect one's spiritual condition.

25. Optatus in Hastings 1912, 4:844–45. See also Harnack 1958, 5:38ff.

26. This is a point that philosophers of science have perhaps done more than anthropologists to disseminate.

27. A possible case of such transition in meaning may be noted in the medieval transformation (hypothesized by Basford, after Hahnloser) of the meaning of the foliated visage (*Tête de Feuilles* and *Masque Feuillu*). Corroborating what has herein been said about the evolution of the persona concept, Basford remarks that the *Tête de Feuilles* is "more closely related to the antique leaf *mask*, while the *Masque Feuillu* is more obviously developed from the 'leaf-demons' with branches growing from the mouth, nose, and ears" (Basford 1977, 115 [my emphasis]).

28. I am indebted to Basford for this latter allusion. Of course, the idea of the wild man is by no means restricted to the Middle Ages; it has been almost universally recorded and is a convenient label in "us/them" cultural distinctions.

29. Hooykaas, for example, leaves unanalyzed only one of the four metaphysical positions he outlines. The blending of "miracle" and "nature," according to him, "especially belongs to polytheistic religions, which regard trees, springs and rivers as inhabited by spirits, deities or demons. It goes without saying that this view makes science practically impossible" (R. Hooykaas 1959, 171). It also goes without saying that for this very reason polytheism becomes important in the study of paradox and apparent change. Furthermore, it is also the reason that science and polytheism cannot—except, perhaps, in an Aristotelian way—be readily compared. See also Lloyd (1979, 27) for the point—recognized in anthropology since the first studies of animism—that "the divine is in no sense *super*natural." Rose (1935) explores the role of language as a controlling factor in this phenomenon.

All analysis is inherently determined by the discriminable continuity of sensible experience. In contemporary interpretations of pre-Euclidean Greek science, there is, interestingly, a puzzlement about why the Greeks emphasized final causes rather than an analytic heuristic (see Lakatos 1978a, 70ff.). Hooykaas would seem to suggest, as anthropologists frequently have, that scientific analysis is thwarted by the complexity of polytheistic experience. Conversely, it is also thwarted when appearance comes to be viewed as inessential, or subordinate to other considerations—as, for example, in the Royal Society's pre-Newtonian preference for argument over experimentation. "Blessed are those who have not seen and yet believe" (John 20.29).

30. "It was, in fact, the least 'honest' elements of Roman entertainment which were best fitted to survive in a theatreless world. Whereas a tragedian requires a tragedy and some at least of the refined resources of illusion, a tumbler needs no more than a mat to fall back on. . . .

". . . almost everywhere the reformers and repressors cry out against masks (*larvae* and *personae*) and 'monstrous' or 'hideous' disguises.

"Too much should not be made of the famous letter issued by the Dean of the Faculty of Theology at Paris in 1445, for it is an *ex parte* statement aimed at getting the whole game [Feast of Fools, *theatrales ludi*] suppressed. But as a collection of evidences of an utter inversion of Christian order and decency, and of deliberate parody and profanation, it has its value:

> Who, I ask you, with any Christian feelings, will not condemn when priests and clerks are seen wearing masks and monstrous visages at the hours of Office: dancing in the Choir, dressed as women, panders, or minstrels (*histrionum*), singing lewd songs (*cantilenas inhonestas*)? They eat black-pudding at the horn of the altar next the celebrant, play at dice there, censing with foul smoke from the soles of old shoes, and running and leaping about the whole church in unblushing shameless iniquity; and then, finally, they are seen driving about the town and its theatres in carts and deplorable carriages (*vehiculis sordidis*) to make an infamous spectacle for the laughter of bystanders and participants, with indecent gestures of the body and language most unchaste and scurrilous." (Rossiter 1950, 35, 59)

31. Panofsky 1962, 223. Panofsky is, in fact, describing the later case, the use of abstract personifications in the Renaissance. The dangers of transubstantiation are nowhere more strikingly perceived than in the roles of the *incubus* and *succubus* in medieval thought. See Cohn 1975.

32. The quality of human thought is an essential aspect of the fact of experience; "the recognition of our existence is," as Whitehead observes, "more than a succession of bare facts" (1926, 80).

33. "Indeed," writes Huxley, "we have always thought that Mr. Darwin has unnecessarily hampered himself by adhering so strictly to his favourite 'Natura non facit saltum.'" Darwin's position applies, of course, not only to evolutionary theory but also to such notions as instinct and natural selection. For an enlightening historical discussion of the inherent epistemological problems presented by these terms, see Richards 1979.

34. Cf. Sir Thomas Browne's "Locusts . . . being ordained for saltation, their hinder legs do far exceed the other" (Browne 1968, 308).

35. See especially Lakatos's discussion of *hidden* lemmas (1978a, 96ff.).

36. As the term "saltation" refers to leaping in the sense of dancing as well as in the sense of sudden change, it is interesting to note that Tertullian, in inveighing against the Roman spectacles, promises that his unpopular view of entertainment will bring the patient Christian rewards on the Last Day: "*then* will be the time to hear the tragedians, made truly poignant by their unfeigned agonies, and *then* the hour to admire the antics of the quick comedians, made nimbler than ever by the sting of unquenchable fire!" (Rossiter 1950, 32).

37. For additional material on *phersu*, see Bloch 1959a, 79-81. Bloch discusses *phersu* elsewhere (e.g., 1960, 116-17). Both Croon and Bloch provide sources for readers interested in further research (e.g., Croon 1955, 15-16; Bloch 1960, 159). See also Dumézil 1970a, 2:574-75.

38. See, for example, Lévi-Strauss 1975.

39. Despite the occasional use of masks since medieval times to represent good as well as evil, I do not think this an unjust conclusion, especially as any mask of God was—as in the case of Christian icons—singled out as particular, inflexible, and incomparable with any other representation. See Anderson 1963, 164ff.

40. Malcolm maintained that "Wittgenstein once said that a serious and good philosophic work could be written that would consist entirely of jokes (without being facetious)" (1958, 29).

41. Vygotsky wrote of the difficulty of identifying pseudo-concepts by reference to appearance. "The outward similarity between the pseudo-concept and the real concept, which makes it very difficult to 'unmask' this kind of complex, is a major obstacle in the genetic analysis of thought" (Vygotsky [1934] 1964, 68). Again, one solution is to institutionalize visual paradox—as, for example, Bohr does by legitimizing apparent incommensurability through his notion of complementarity. Bohr's position bears an uncanny resemblance to theological positions normally attributed to priests, shamans, and other "mediators" insofar as he is advocating a modulation (of the subject/object differentiation employed in phenomenal descriptions) that proceeds from a doctrine attempting to discount our normal apprehensions about sensible experience. "While, in the mechanical conception of nature, the subject-object distinction was fixed, room is provided for a wider description through the recognition that the consequent use of our concepts requires different placings of such a separation" (Bohr 1958, 91-92). Notice, also, with reference to masks, his use of light-partitions and the almost complete absence of any other visual analogy in his argument.

42. Though widely misrepresented as propounding an incommensurability thesis, B. L. Whorf pointed to the comparative disjunction between our own "time" and the Hopi sense of "duration" (1956, 158). By recognizing, for example, the role of Newtonian or Euclidean space as an intellectual tool for Western thought, Whorf could have made an equally strong case for the uniqueness of Hopi categories by describing in detail the mechanics of the Hopi pantheon. Horton (1964; 1967), conversely, focuses on the methodological similarity existing between science in practice and the observational acuteness of many African descriptions of the environment. On the level of theorizing about our apprehensions of the objective world, however, Horton calls attention to the effect of a pantheon of spirits that "are directly associated with most of the happenings in people's immediate environment" (1964, 95). Horton's analogy between traditional African modes of thought and modern scientific ones is also mitigated by his argument that the traditional modes do not have our Thomist distinction between essence and existence.

43. Isaiah Berlin has pointed to the meaninglessness of statements that are metaphysical in a bad sense, i.e., to those that are meaningless because "they purport, in the language which resembles that which we normally use to describe situations which we regard as capable of being empirically experienced, to

describe something which is alleged to transcend such experience, and to be incommunicable by any kind of analogy with it" (1968, 34).

44. "The Egyptian no more asked whether the sun god Ra was shining as he should than the modern astronomer asks whether sunlight travels at a proper speed. . . . Conditions might not be all the heart would wish, but what impressed the polytheist was that they might be a great deal worse. For if the powers of nature reside in many gods—in Mesopotamia their number was in the thousands—there was always the danger that these gods might fall out among themselves and universal chaos result" (H. Smith 1958, 238).

45. Bernheimer remarks upon the role of even Aquinas and Bonaventura in this codification; it is, thus, all the more interesting that both should draw upon Boethius's discussion of *persona* while discounting his knowledge of its classical theatrical sense. See M. Marshall 1950, 478.

46. Clark is here referring to G. G. Simpson's *Major Features of Evolution* (New York, 1953).

47. Walter Cannon's famous study (1942) of death by suggestion and its inverted role as a destructive form of catharsis especially comes to mind. But it is also worthwhile to take notice of the concept making that becomes indispensible when scientists refer to interactions occurring within a living organism. The visceral brain hypothesis (see, among others, Papez 1937 and MacLean 1949) and the more recent research on split-brain interactions are two interesting examples that work away at the sense of categorical integrity to which we cling in our descriptions of human morphology. Along the general lines of Cannon's research, it is today especially interesting to observe the scientific utilization of identity terms—as (metaphorically?), for example, when certain cells are said to have failed properly to have "identified" other cells in allergic reactions.

48. Huxley is referring to Lys's discovery that an independently hypnotized individual can sometimes bring about a patient's cure by miming while under hypnosis. See F. Huxley 1977, especially 32–33.

49. The use of kachinas as a mode of instruction among the Pueblo Indians is one excellent example.

2 · Masks and the Beginnings of Greek Drama

1. Even though it has been argued since the time of Kant that there is no necessary connection between reason and knowledge (the synthesis of sensory experience being the function of reason, and unity of consciousness the basis of knowledge), it is clear that an experience of the supernatural or of common make-believe is held to be both unreasonable and unknowable, despite what may or may not be its structural unity. The particular and subjective, in other words, is radically opposed to the universal except when the particular conforms to the transcendental character of consciousness.

2. This distinction is clearly a simplification into radical categories of an infinitely complicated problem. If, for example, our descriptive categories are organized under "types of drama," we might be speaking not only in terms of secu-

lar versus profane drama, but also of cases where drama involves a ritual story performed, or of cases of ritualized secular activities.

3. There is a parallel feature of Western thought that appeared at the same time as a proper theater, and that is the general attack on the reliability of the senses beginning with Parmenides and Melissus, his fifth-century follower. According to Lloyd, Parmenides "is the first thinker to set up a fundamental opposition between the senses and abstract argument or reason" (1979, 71; see especially 17ff., 70ff., 76ff.).

4. The most famous examples are Frazer's vegetation spirit and Murray's year-spirit, or *Eniautos-Daimōn*, theory—what Ridgeway referred to as the Dieterich-Harrison-Cornford-Murray theory (Ridgeway 1915, 58).

5. Vickers is quite correct, it seems to me, in criticizing the idea that there is any necessary evolutionary connection between ritual and drama, but I do not see why they should be necessarily antithetical. For example, it is easy to see how similar an ecstatic religious practice is to a dynamic performance. In fact, anthropologists continually encounter situations wherein transitions between these categories occur in the context of a single event, as well as cases wherein certain testimonies about a single performance characterize it as efficacious in some supernatural sense while others see it as an affective imitation.

6. On the problem of participation, see, e.g., Lévy-Bruhl [1949] 1975. For Lévy-Bruhl, participation is seen as the only viable answer to old vocabularies that cause misunderstanding and to new ones that both distract from accepted meanings and place excessive demands upon the reader (ibid., 64–65).

7. See, for example, Black 1972, E. Gombrich 1972, Hochberg 1972, and Brilliant 1971.

8. That attempt did not stop Aristophanes from using the persona of Dicaeopolis to lampoon the policies of Cleon in the *Acharnians* (see Garton 1972, 30).

9. There are many examples of ritual practices or events becoming part of an actual performance. For example, during the sorrows of Electra,

> Polus, acting the Sophoclean Electra, when at the lowest pitch of desolation she mourns over the supposed ashes of her brother, took into his arms no property urn of the theatre but that containing the ashes of his recently deceased son. (Garton 1972, 37)

Pickard-Cambridge points out, in speaking of masks, that mourning personages were frequently presented as shorn; he suggests that "the locks might be cut off during the play" (1953, 184) and also notes Webster's idea that specific hair styles may have been developed to distinguish the members of certain clans (ibid., 211). See also Else 1965, 29.

10. "Authors" in the first sentence of this excerpt should read "leaders" (*exarchontes*).

11. For an interesting discussion of the complexities of this development, see Else 1965, especially 20ff. Else argues that Aristotle's pro-Dorian bias might have been an ethnocentric force in his rendition of the origins of drama. On the Dorian problem and Aristotle, see, among others, Burkert 1966, 95. For purposes of comparison, see my discussion in chapters 5 and 6 of the manipulation of aetiological myths in the interest of caste ideology in India and Bali.

12. It would be injudicious to argue that a functionalist perspective could give an exhaustive account of ritual; efficacy, however, need not imply a definable causal relationship. In some cases, as in art, efficacy may involve only a more agreeable, creative, or simply more interesting approach to a commonly followed rule.

13. Other kinds of subterranean passages had their own mythological analogues. Volcanos, for example, originated at the forge of Hephaestus, who crafted the shields of Achilles and Heracles—shields that were themselves, as discs surrounded by the river Oceanus, microcosmic symbols of the world.

14. Though this boat-car with phallus is an imaginative reconstruction, there are known examples of boat-cars carrying Dionysus and Satyrs as well as figures of Dionysus that are regularly referred to as ithyphallic. Also cf. the Roman *carrus navalis*.

3 · Satyr, Centaur, Theriomorphic Healer

1. Examples of variation in facial types are to be found throughout the Old Comedy. Aristophanes in the *Acharnians* is said to have employed a mask consisting of nothing but "a huge eye and a Persian beard" (Pickard-Cambridge 1953, 198), and, furthermore, Pickard-Cambridge points out that

> the double derivation of Attic comedy, from animal-masqueraders in Attica and from such impersonations of coarsely padded and phallic beings as are depicted on early Corinthian vases, is reflected in the appearance of the Athenian performers in the fifth century. There were many animal choruses in the comedies, and these doubtless wore appropriate masks; and when the choruses were not strictly animal, but at the same time not human, as in Aristophanes' *Clouds*, grotesque masks were invented to suit the poet's fancy. Thus the "Clouds" were like women, only half disguised. (Pickard-Cambridge 1953, 194–95)

His list goes on (Pickard-Cambridge 1927, 244–53) and includes among other personae the Bees of Diocles, the Swine of Cephisodorus, choruses of Riders on Dolphins and Ostriches, and more (Pickard-Cambridge 1953, 195 n. 1).

2. For the manipulation of personae in the interest of slander, see Chapter 2.

3. Cf. Jevons's remark about *imagines* in Chapter 1.

4. For a convenient list of references on the masks of Artemis and Demeter at Sparta and Lycosura, see Bieber 1961, 276 n. 16.

5. One is, of course, frequently unsure as to whether the picture illustrates someone in costume or is an attempt at representing the mythical beast.

6. Note, for example, how appropriately the Satyr face was adapted even to Etruscan underworld spirits (e.g., Bieber 1961, 146).

7. See my discussion of Agdistis and Cybele in Chapter 4.

8. This legend is similar to many popular tales involving the capture of a daimon who can convey secret information. In Greek mythology the case of Silenus is closely paralleled by that of Proteus, who is polymorphous and therefore difficult to catch, but who, when caught, discloses his very special secret knowledge.

9. The decipherment of Linear B has since 1953 influenced the interpretation of the early evidence for Dionysus by proving the existence of his name in Mycenaean times (ca. thirteenth century B.C.). As Lesky points out, however, even though the worship of Dionysus may be older than was previously thought, "this teaches us little about the history of his cult, for we know nothing about this early Dionysus and ideas connected with him as well as his cult may have undergone profound changes in the course of time" (Lesky [1964] 1978, 41). Whether the Mycenaean Dionysus is the same as the Archaic one is perhaps unanswerable; it is necessary, however, to call attention to the scholarly view that the ecstatic cult of Dionysus was not born on the soil of central Greece, a view that the *Oxford Classical Dictionary* calls well founded. On the transformation of early figures by newer influences, compare, e.g., the Argolid transformation of Perseus into an ancestor of the Persians (Jeffery 1976, 139–40 and notes).

10. His ritual role is also emphasized by the fact that he is the patron of beekeepers. Honey frequently had a special ritual significance for fertility figures, such as Demeter, as well as for the Mithraic cults, and bees are often shown as displaying a superior intelligence. See, e.g., Burkert (1979, 123ff.) on the theme of the bee that finds the hiding god, and see my discussion of *madhu* and *soma* in following chapters.

11. It is either the knowledge or the ugliness of Socrates that is emphasized by the frequent similarity of their portraits.

12. The worship and impersonation of bulls, for example, extend back to the very earliest of Mediterranean cultures—that is, at least to the sixth millennium B.C. See, e.g., Mellaart 1967, 101–30; Gimbutas 1974, especially 89–93, 224–26.

13. This ambiguity seems to be something that the ancients were quite willing to accept. Compare, also, the Scythian horse that wore the horned mask of a deer or elk. See, for example, Gryaznov 1969, pls. 114, 122–24.

14. On masks and sensation, see Chapter 6.

15. Note also Plate 22, the Thracian slaying of the semi-human Centaur (Medusa?) by Perseus.

16. Graves (1957, 209) compares the fate of Ixion—who, for his deed, is ceaselessly rolled through the sky in the form of a fire wheel—to the European seasonal custom of rolling burning wheels downhill at the midsummer solar zenith. Though Ixion seems to have been depicted spread-eagled on a fire wheel in an Etruscan example (for representations of Ixion, see Simon 1975, 177ff.), very little indeed is known of Ixion's mythology.

17. To what extent these excesses were, in India, due to the imbibing of psychoactive substances is much debated. The role of hallucinogenic or alcoholic substances in Indo-European ritual is well known. In Greek mythology, not only are the Satyrs central to the preparation of wine and the bacchanal itself, but mushrooms appear in illustrations of both Ixion, the sire of the Centaurs, and Perseus, who, as we have seen, slays a Centaur rather than a Gorgon in the early illustration from Boeotia (Pl. 22). It is worth noting that both Perseus and Ixion fly by means of an external, magical contrivance.

18. One might compare structurally Ridgeway's unsubstantiated assertion that a human may have been sacrificed during the Dionysia with the fact that a human could have been substituted for the *aśvamedha* horse.

19. Because of their often subtle iconography, it is difficult to assign an exact date to the Satyrs and Centaurs, though the Centaurs have Late Mycenaean correlates, as Nilsson points out (1972, 158).

20. This transformation calls to mind the theme of the divine victim (see, e.g., Sauvé 1970, 177ff.), the notion that a sacrifice may involve a victim who is also a god.

21. As a rule, Dumézil contrasts their roles—one contractual, the other ambivalent. For an alternate view, see Gonda 1972, 102ff.

22. E.g., Heracles kills the tri-bodied Geryon, who is the grandson of Medusa and the nephew of the horse Pegasus, who, like Chiron, is the offspring of a sea god. Pegasus, the messenger of the gods, who is both immortal and sterile, is the offspring of the sea god Poseidon and the mortal Medusa. Achilles, who is also instructed by Chiron (who is his great-grandfather) is known through many iconographic examples for the Gorgon head on his battleshield—even though Homer attributes the Gorgon shield to Agamemnon rather than to Achilles. Athena, who like Zeus has the Medusa head, which she receives from Perseus, as her aegis, befriends Heracles in her capacity as the goddess of warfare, and so on.

23. See note 13 above.

24. The acting-out of dreams was an important aspect of much of Greek cathartic curing. See note 29 below.

25. "For if it were not for Dionysus that they were holding processions and singing the hymn to the phalli, it would be a most shameless act" (Heraclitus, fr. 15). See Lloyd 1979, 12ff. for discussion.

26. Competition in sport, or between one chorus and another, became not only a means of distinguishing a particular group, but a great unifying force, a perfect context for a tyrant like Pisistratus both to unite the people of Athens and to gain for himself enormous prestige by giving public status, for the first time, to tragic drama. Consider, also, the rising political power of the actors themselves and the serious nature their play could assume. The political intrigues of the Ionian guild of the Artists of Dionysus became legendary, as when, much later (ca. 88 B.C.), the Armenian ruler Mithridates VI tried twice to have himself crowned "our new Dionysus" (Garton 1972, 39).

27. Cf. Lloyd's detailed consideration of the ancient treatise *On the Sacred Disease* (1979, 15ff.).

28. This most famous center of the healing arts was not built until the fourth century B.C.—the Asclepieion at Athens was founded in the fifth century—and its fame was not at its height until the second century A.D.

29. Asclepius's celebrated ability to heal through dream analysis depended entirely on environmental symbolism that reiterated mythic structure. Such architectural symbols included subterranean chambers—as in the sanctuary of Asclepius at Epidaurus; tunnels—architectural symbols for *rites de passage*—that connected the patients' sleeping quarters to the treatment centers; and sacred springs around which the curing centers were built and that may originally have been associated with the worship of underworld daimons and with the arriving at cathartic cures through contact with the underworld.

30. See my note 17 above and discussion of *madhu/soma* in Chapter 5. By contrast, see Diderot's *The Paradox of Acting* (1883) for the classic description of a good actor's calculated, detached behavior.

31. Likewise, in the case of the diseases themselves, "the idea that certain diseases are cured by what causes them, or by their opposites, is," as Lloyd points out, "a common one in Greek medical writings" (1979, 22).

4 · Perseus and the Gorgon Head

1. Nilsson calls the Perseus-Gorgon tale "the best instance of a folk-tale received into Greek heroic mythology" (1932, 40). For discussion of Nilsson's belief that the Perseus-Gorgon story was known in pre-Homeric times see Hopkins 1934, 342ff.; Howe 1954, 218ff.

2. For a good summary of the various primary sources for the story of Perseus, see Woodward 1937.

3. For a discussion, see Karo 1948, 35.

4. An analogous case is that of Adonis, who is such a beautiful child that he is hidden in a coffin by Aphrodite and given to Persephone, who back in the underworld refuses to return him. As with so many figures who make that journey, he must thenceforth spend part of each year there.

5. As with Acrisius and his twin, the idea of brothers vying for a single throne is reiterated here.

6. According to Hesiod, the immortal sisters were Stheno, "the mighty," and Euryale, "the wide-leaping."

7. The gray old women are another important Spartan mask type. Note how their grotesque iconography resembles the masks of the Gorgons (cf. pls. 9–12 and 34).

8. I am grateful to Nicholas Richardson for calling my attention to this passage as well as to *Iliad* 17.133–36, discussed below (p. 115).

9. This derivation, though widely accepted in the past, is now the subject of some debate.

10. Cf. Latin *garrio*.

11. See Monier-Williams [1899] 1970, 349 for comprehensive definitions of *garj* and related terms, and Howe 1954, 210–11 for an etymological analysis of the word "Gorgon."

12. See Persson 1942, 90, 109–12, and Burkert 1979, 104-5, 110–11, 119–21 on the idea of the Great Goddess and priestly eunuchs or *galloi*.

13. One thinks here of the Phoenician *moloch* tradition and of the demons of birth as both givers and takers of life—hence the paradox whereby what is sacrificed is often precisely what is requested in return for the sacrifice.

14. This element would seem to connect the Gorgon to the hermaphroditic or self-fecundating monsters of Asia Minor.

15. See Hopkins 1934, 344 for a more extensive list of theories.

16. Though specific foreign place names (such as the Syrtes) are mentioned in conjunction with the Perseus-Gorgon legend, their role in its mythology or iconography is not clear enough to suggest any foreign influence.

17. The importance of this Greek and Scythian similarity has led to a certain controversy regarding the precise dating of the Ziwiyeh treasure. On these bicorporate similarities, see Hoffmann 1972, 38–39 and notes. A Gorgon bicorporate also appears on the interior of a black-figure cup in Copenhagen. On the signifi-

cance of Assyrian influences for Cretan and Corinthian leonine representations, see Rodenwaldt 1939, 2:143–45, 150–51, 189–90.

18. For a discussion of the stylistic peculiarities of lions in various Near Eastern cultures and their influences on the lions of Greek art of the Orientalizing period, see Akurgal 1968, 162ff.

19. According to Detienne (1979, 37ff.), the Greeks gradually evolved a mythology about feline creatures whereby the panther, for example, came to be equated with both hunting and sexuality, "attracting" its prey. The lion was thought to have an uncertain, if not nonexistent, sex life, a notion eminently suited to wrathful androgynes and Gorgon-like creatures.

20. One can, of course, never be absolute about such cases, and exceptions to this general rule may occur. Moreover, there are other icons that may be thus represented when shown two-dimensionally; goat horns, for example, might conceivably be depicted by two marks, or the oddly exaggerated superciliary protuberances of some representations of griffins. One such representation (Mylonas 1957, Pl. 15, γ) bears three marks between its eyes, and the so-called Poppy Goddess of Gazi sprouts three poppies from her forehead. This last case seems, already in the Late Bronze Age, to indicate a connection between the forehead and sensation.

21. Barnett also feels that the Phoenicians are responsible for the masks of Artemis Orthia and that these masks are directly influenced by depictions of the face of Humbaba (1960, 145–46).

22. Rodenwaldt (1939, 2:149) uses the term *Löwenpanther* because the difference is not always apparent.

23. Note that in the divinatory plaque, the monsters are accompanied by priests wearing lion masks.

24. The question here is whether that meaning involved the representation of some locus of sensation. Parrot, interestingly, describes the victim as strangely "lost in ecstasy despite his grim predicament" (1961, 152).

25. Note, also, that the "seven" furious Babylonian demons of destruction were said to be incapable of reproduction. As for the Persians, "it may be noted that the Zoroastrians considered it an error to attribute sex to the gods, according to Diogenes Laertius (1.7)" (L. Campbell 1968, 156 n. 87). No doubt this notion of asexuality is as old as those of divine ambivalence and androgyny.

26. For a survey of what is known about the names of these figures, see Eisler 1909, S. Smith 1924, Hopkins 1934, Barnett 1956a, Goldman 1961, and references therein.

27. Pettazzoni (1946) remarks the connection between gods, e.g., the Russian Perun and the Lithuanian Perkūnas, which "passed into the language of the Finnic populations of Karelia ([as] *piru, peruni*) and of Estonia ([as] *porgel*) with the meaning of 'Devil'" (ibid., 150; see also Littleton 1973, 182–83). In discussing the setting up of the idol of Perun, Pettazzoni (1956, 249) talks of the custom of taking the head of the deceased and plating it in gold—a practice Herodotus attributes to the Issedones. On the horse god Perwas, Perseus, and the relationship of the horse to the chthonian Medusa, see also Palmer 1958, 15, 34–35.

28. On Humbaba and the *kumbha* as womb, see Goldman 1961, 18; on concepts related to the word *kumbha*, see Monier-Williams [1899] 1970, 293.

29. While Kassite bears no resemblance to Aryan or Indo-European, among

the documents of the Kassites' Babylonian dynasty (ca. 1750–1170 B.C.) can be found the names of deities having a Sanskrit origin (see Burrow 1973, 28–29). The Kassites, in other words, were well aware of, and even adopted, the names of certain Sanskrit deities.

30. According to L. Campbell (1968, 299), placing the flame to the forehead of the Mithraic initiates "was symbolic of an engendering of the *pneuma* or *asthma* in the reborn *mystes* . . . just as the flame of fire appeared on the head of Mithra while being engendered in the Petra genetrix."

31. According to Zaehner (1961, 163), the position of the Magi "would seem to correspond to that of the Levites among the Jews or, even more closely, to that of the Brāhmans in India: they were a hereditary caste entrusted with the supervision of the national religion, whatever form it might take and in whatever part of the Empire it might be practised. . . . It is quite clear that the Magi were in fact a sacerdotal *caste* whose ethnic origin is never again so much as mentioned. We hear of Magi not only in Persis, Parthia, Bactria, Chorasmia, Aria, Media, and among the Sakas, but also in non-Iranian lands like Arabia, Ethiopia, and Egypt. Their influence was also widespread throughout Asia Minor." "Aristotle, in a fragment from his treatise *On Philosophy*, reproduced the teaching of the magi on the good and evil spirit (Zeus and Oromasdes and Hades or Areimanios)" (Benveniste 1929, 17).

32. Cf. the Greek idea of the Gorgon head guarding Hades. On the possible relationship between dogs and felines, Detienne points to the fact that the Egyptians regarded the cheetah as a dog (1979, 36). Hades, "the Invisible," was said to have worn a dog's cap (see Chap. 5 n. 34). Cf. the cap of invisibility given to Perseus.

33. Benveniste calls attention to the fact that Herodotus makes an important corpses to the dogs and birds (Benveniste 1929, 32).

34. In discussing the role of the dog as a guardian of Varuna's house, Kramrisch states:

> The star Sirius is the dog, the Guardian of the House (Vāstoṣpati). In the annual course of the sun, the dog guards the two gates of the house. The one gate marks the sun's entrance from the nether world, the region of Yama (death), the world of the Fathers, into the Devayāna, the path that the gods take (B. G. Tilak, *The Orion*, p. 26, 108). Sirius rose before the sun at the vernal equinox of a remote age and disappeared shortly, as the sun rose in the sky. It is the same star, Sirius, the Dog Star of the night and the Boar (star) who rises before sunrise. At the rising of Sirius, darkness prevailed and the teeth of the dog glittered. Then, in the dawn, just before sunrise, the star was the ruddy boar who pushed up the sun from the waters of darkness—and disappeared into the sun's light. Sirius, the dog who awakened the ṛbhus at the beginning of the year, is the same star in his capacity as dog, who as a ruddy boar pushed the sun up on the sky in the morning of the spring equinox of a remote aeon. (Kramrisch 1981, 47 n. 36)

35. See the discussion of *madhu* in the following chapter; compare, in particular, the *madhura*, or temporary sacred enclosure.

5 · The Third Eye

1. Aśoka was the first king publicly to acknowledge his patronage of Buddhism.

2. See also Banerjea 1956, 276 and above citations in text.

3. The traditional date of the birth of Gautama is 563 B.C. The suggested date of the founding of Zoroastrianism is 592 B.C. (Finegan 1952, 81). On the origin of the Buddha, see also Bosch 1960, 197ff.

4. The *ūrṇā* and the *uṣṇīṣa*, the bump on the Buddha's head that is the seat of divine knowledge, combine with his pierced, distended earlobes to form the *lakṣaṇā*.

5. "The Buddha's birth is likened to the rising of another sun; on his Enlightenment, like the sacrificial fire of Agni, the Buddha mounts transfigured to the highest heavens of the gods" (Rowland 1977, 54).

6. For further discussion of this problem see Zimmer 1955, 1:61. Other references are in Rowland 1977, 488–89.

7. The three upper castes of Indian society are the Brahmans, or priests, the Kṣatriyas, or warriors (including the kings and tribal leaders), and the Vaiśyas, i.e., merchants, farmers. It has long ago been said that the figure of Gautama represents the revolt launched in his day against the orthodoxy of the cult of Brahmanism, and the *uṣṇīṣa* has been interpreted as a variation of the cropped hair worn by warriors (van Lohuizen-de Leeuw 1949, 163ff.).

8. The hymns describe Indra's near-addiction to *soma* (*RV* 1.104.9). "So essential is Soma to Indra that his mother gave it to him or he drank it on the very day of his birth (3, $48^{2.3}$; $32^{9.10}$; 6, 40^2; 7, 98^3). For the slaughter of Vṛta he drank three lakes of Soma (5, 29^7 cp. 6, 17^{11})" (Macdonell 1897, 56).

9. Some of the most famous discoveries from Mohenjodaro suggest a solar significance. In this regard, of special note are the fillets or medallions placed in the middle of the forehead (Zimmer 1955, 1:29).

10. Pointing to the fact that the cult of Indra was supreme in the Vedic age, Zimmer remarks that the image of Indra as "the conquering and reigning Kṣatriya prince and king" shows him as the archetypal warrior and the predecessor of Viṣṇu and Śiva (Zimmer 1955, 1:40).

11. Narasiṃha is one of the three main iconographic manifestations of Viṣṇu's ten *avatāras*. Three relate to the militancy of the conflict between Brahmans and Kṣatriyas (Banerjea 1956, 419); two are the Boar and Bali dwarf/giant from the *Śatapatha Brāhmaṇa* (ibid., 412ff.).

12. Again we see the transposition of themes, since Hiraṇyakaśipu oddly achieves his power through solemn devotion—presumably to the *wrong* power: that is, to the god no longer in vogue. Compare the idea, discussed in Chapter 1, of the Sacraments being holy in themselves regardless of who happens to perform them, or how Zoroaster defines a liar as one who "performs the sacrificial rites correctly, but thinks slightly of the Wise Lord . . . in his heart" (Zaehner 1961, 136–37).

13. The extent of this ambivalence is, according to Banerjea, also evident in yogic images of Narasiṃha (1956, 417).

14. Again we see the aforementioned adoption of the form of a story about

Viṣṇu by the worshipers of Śiva and the transposing—or, as Banerjea puts it, the "re-naming"—of the characters to suit Śaivite ends.

15. The lunar role of Viṣṇu is also assured. The so-called Narasiṃha festival is held on the eve of the new moon in *Vayasi*, the month of May.

16. Rāhu has a special relationship with the Elixir of Immortality since it is Rāhu's thirst for it that causes eclipses. The head of Rāhu itself causes the lunar phenomenon since, as Rāhu had been decapitated by Viṣṇu for imbibing the drink, the moon merely passes through and is reborn.

17. The word *śakti* refers to the idea of power in general as well as to the power of Śiva personified through his consort, Śakti.

18. Jalandhara's brazen attempt to win Pārvatī recalls Ixion's liking for Hera and his attempt, once granted the favor of Zeus, to seduce her. In Greek mythology, Ixion, as noted in Chapter 3, must roll eternally through the heavens on a fire wheel. In the Indian version, it is the Face of Glory itself that decorates, Gorgon-like, the *umbo* of Viṣṇu's fire wheel. The *cakra* is a disc, a weapon, much like the disc thrown by Perseus.

19. Cf. the ancient idea of the dual aspect of Siva (Banerjea 1956, 477ff.). Many of the names indicate their terrific nature (ibid., 482).

20. This etymology again recalls the Sanskrit *garj*, the roar that is the origin of the Gorgon's name.

21. "The word *Cala*, or *Kala*, signifying *black*, means also, from its root, *Kal*, *devouring*: whence it is applied to Time, and, in both senses in the feminine, to the goddess in her destructive capacity" (Moor 1810, 155).

22. The Avesta, it will be remembered, contain several direct parallels with the Vedic hymns.

23. The most comprehensive study of *soma* is Wasson 1968. Wasson argues that while the term later came to identify various intoxicating or hallucinogenic plants, including those of the family Asclepiadaceae (see, e.g., Gupta 1971, 27–31), the original drug was made from fly-agaric.

24. See O'Flaherty 1969 for variations in the Purāṇas on the theme of the covering of Śiva's eyes and for a discussion of the relationship between the forehead mark (*tilaka*) and the third eye.

25. A Kauśikan hymn (79.10) describes the use of *madugha* as a matrimonial aphrodisiac. See Shende 1952, 53.

26. On Soma the phytomorphic deity see Wasson 1968.

27. According to Russell ([1916] 1969), the *mahua* is still sacred to several forest tribes, including the Gonds, Bhuiya, Bagdi—who, as in the *Atharva Veda*, still tie it around their wrists—Kharwār, Kurmis, Munda, and Santāls. Crooke (1925) cites several cases of the modern-day use of the tree in both women's rites and marriage. He gives not only examples of part of the tree's being worn, but also instances of couples' being married to the tree or even of the tree's representing one of the spouses. It would also not be surprising to find that the tree was of ritual significance outside of northern and central India, since it is well known not only in India but also in Indochina, Malaysia, and Australia (Willis 1966, 685).

As for the connection between the tree and worship of the Goddess in her terrifying aspect, Pott notes that the imbibing of "the delicious wine of the *madhūka*-flower" ([1946] 1966, 15) by both gods and men is an important part of the left-hand path—the "demonic and often repellent mode of behaviour which to an outsider must seem strange and senseless but which nonetheless has a deeper meaning for the practitioner himself" (ibid., 25).

28. This is a characteristic also of the *bodhi* (*Ficus religiosa*).

29. The relationship between the Ganges and sacred trees is certified in the legend of the Ganges' having at its origin a sacred tree from which its waters flowed.

30. According to the *Mahābhārata*, the Ganges makes holy the three spheres; see Darian 1978, 75.

31. As with Kālī, Viṣṇu's symbolic color is black; his monstrous creations, such as Hiraṇyakaśipu, are black; his leonine *avatāra*, Narasiṃha, emanates from his left side, i.e., the side that is more feminine and black. When demons are derived from Viṣṇu, they emerge from his left side, as when the Goddess created Madhu from the substance of his left ear, left being traditionally associated with black magic as well as with the feminine, the earth, and the underworld. On Indo-European aspects of the *vajra* and its ambivalent character, see Nagy 1974, 124.

32. According to Marshall, we find in the Indus Valley civilization nearly all of the non-Aryan elements in Indian religion that are fundamental to Hinduism. Among them are "the cults of Śiva and the Mother Goddess, of the Nāgas and Tree deities, of animal, tree, and stone worship, of phallism and the practice of *yoga*" (J. Marshall 1931, 1:78).

33. In acupuncture, a woman undergoing a uterine operation may be anesthetized by needles implanted in the area of the forehead where, in Tantric *yoga*, the *ājñā-cakra*, or Lotus of Command, is traditionally located. This ancient relationship is both symbolic and based upon a physiological correspondence: as ephedrine (*ma-huang*) is known to affect the activity of the human uterus (Goodman and Gilman 1955, 506), so similar alkaloidal substances, often placed on the forehead and in areas where they can readily penetrate the bloodstream, were responsible for the orgiastic flights of witches in medieval Europe (Harner 1973, 125–50). Recently, the pineal gland—the only part of the brain that is not bilaterally symmetrical—has been shown to function in certain animals as a vestigial, light-sensitive, third eye and, by affecting hormonal production, to influence menstruation, fear and horror, and sexuality in humans (Bleibtreu 1968, 64ff.). Melatonin, the hormone produced by the pineal gland, is, according to Bleibtreu, created by altering serotonin molecules, which are also found in some fruits and in *Ficus religiosa*, India's most sacred tree—and one producing milky sap. Serotonin content may, moreover, be connected to certain mental disorders, such as schizophrenia; the hallucinogen LSD produces its effects "by depriving the brain of its serotonin content" (ibid., 75).

34. It is again worth noting that Hades' cap of invisibility was thought to be a dog's cap, especially since, as we have seen, dogs (and "four-eyed dogs") were thought to be underworld guardians. "In Greek religion the dog was a companion of Artemis and the threefold Hecate as chthonic divinities of fertility and the underworld. A goddess of triform type, whether Hecate or some other chthonic divinity, appears more than once in Mithraic inscriptions and iconography" (L. Campbell 1968, 13).

35. The Cyclopes are also often described as a trinity, one of the very few male trinities in Greek mythology.

36. Argos had proclaimed itself neutral during the Persian War—preferring an alliance with the Medes to one with the Spartans and, conveniently, making Perseus the ancestor of the Persians. (See Jeffery 1976, 139–40.)

37. In the Greek case, Scheinberg states,

> The honey-induced prophetic frenzy of the bee maidens in the *Hymn to Hermes*
> . . . belongs to a tradition in which divination depended upon the ritual drinking of a sacred, perhaps intoxicating liquid, which opened the human psyche to messages from the divine world by bringing the god within the seer. Corollary to this is a still more obscure tradition, nearly forgotten by Greek mythographers and by the Greek language, according to which the men and gods of earlier times drank honey, mixed with wine or fermented with mead. (Scheinberg 1979, 19)

38. This point is also referred to by Palmer (1958, 15): "Is it an accident that Medusa means 'the Ruler (feminine)'? Have we here yet another translation of the now well-known oriental cult title 'The Queen'?" For the sake of comparison, note within the Christian tradition the transformation from the -τός verbal adjective form of χρίω, "anoint," and "Christ," and the translation or borrowing of the Hebrew *masiah*, "anointed," and our "Messiah."

39. See Fontenrose 1959, 285–86 for a list of primary sources.

6 · Balinese Faces and Indian Prototypes

1. At the start, I should point out that this chapter is in no way an attempt to provide a survey of Balinese sacred masks or a thesis about Balinese culture. Sacred masks provide the focus for a separate study; here, I will concern myself *only* with the expression of arrest as an example of ambivalent iconography.

2. The fact that Bali served as a refuge for the Majapahit hierarchy—princes, priests, scholars, skilled artists and artisans who were fleeing from the tide of Islam—may perhaps account for the freshness and clarity of the tradition from Hindu-Javanese times (Belo [1949] 1966, 21). On the dating of the earliest contacts between India and Indonesia, see, for example, Coedès 1968, 14–19, and Gonda 1973, 65–73.

3. To Upaniṣadic thinkers the idea of a sacrifice quite explicitly involved yet further elaborations on this divisive symbolism (de Bary et al., 1966, 27–28). According to the *Bṛhad Āraṇyaka Upaniṣad*,

> Dawn verily is the head of the sacrificial horse. The sun is his eye; the wind, his breath; the universal sacrificial fire (*agni-vaiśvānara*), his open mouth; the year is the body (*ātman*) of the sacrificial horse. The sky is his back; the atmosphere, his belly; the earth, his underbelly [?]; the directions, his flanks; the intermediate directions, his ribs; the seasons, his limbs; the months and half-months, his joints; days and nights, his feet; the stars, his bones; the clouds, his flesh. Sand is the food in his stomach; rivers, his entrails; mountains, his liver and lungs; plants and trees, his hair; the rising sun, his forepart; the setting sun, his hindpart. When he yawns, then it lightnings; when he shakes himself, then it thunders; when he urinates, then it rains. Speech (*vāc*) is actually his neighing (*vāc*). (1.1.1)

4. According to Eibl-Eibesfeldt (1972, 306–12), there appears to be some correlation between phallic display and a protective guardian pose. This idea corre-

sponds very well with the phallic character of the temple pillar or Cosmic Tree and the apotropaic character of both the protruding *kāla* eyes and the extended tongue of Agni.

5. According to Deonna,

> Si nous rappelons ici ces corrélations que l'on a relevées entre l'oeil et d'autres organes du corps, c'est qu'elles permettent de mieux comprendre, non seulement certaines expressions du langage métaphorique, mais certaines croyances, et certaines représentations figurées, qui associent des visages ou des yeux à diverses parties du corps, les ouvrent sur elles, unissant leur fonction particulière à celle de la vue, aux yeux qui les animent, les vivifient, en intensifient l'action. Ce procédé est une des formes de la "répétition d'intensité," qui multiplie le même objet, le même être, ou un seul de ses organes. (Deonna 1965, 55)

6. In an experiment with subjects from various cultures, Ekman found that some cultures, such as the Japanese, display a social mask—in their case in the form of a smile—when watching a stressful film in a group.

7. See, e.g., Rands 1957; Schuster 1951.

8. Notice also the similar positioning of the diminutive bodies in both Plate 95*a* and Plate 96.

9. The Cosmic Tree, which springs from the ocean primeval, connects the underworld with the path of the sun; this tree is synonymous with the Sacred Mountain that touches the sun at its zenith, the latter being equated with the lion-headed manifestation of Agni's fire (Bosch 1960, 140ff.). The connection between Cosmic Column, Cosmic Tree, and monster face, is, moreover, an ancient one; the Lord of the Forest (*vanaspati*) being an epithet not only for the beast but for tree and column as well (e.g., *RV* 3.8).

10. *Datura* is held responsible in Europe for the supposed flights of witches, their exaggerated facial expressions, orgiastic activities, emission of flames, and fiery glow in the night sky. See Chapter 5 n. 33 and discussion in text. It is also worth noting that in India *datura* is sacred to Śiva, that it was singled out as sacred at least as early as the Purāṇas, and that, especially in South India, it occurs decoratively as a common architectural motif.

11. For the most comprehensive study, see Bandem and deBoer 1981.

12. "The Barong would seem undoubtedly to belong to the class of 'protective animals.' The protective lion of Buddhism, which in Buddhist pictures of Indian origin is not shown as a realistic lion but as something much more like the Balinese Barong, is perhaps derived from a pre-Buddhist protective animal, 'friend of the ancestor.' Probably the lions in such paintings are not representations of real lions but of people dressed up as lions in an exorcistic lion-dance" (de Zoete and Spies [1938] 1973, 95). There are enough such lion and tiger dances throughout India and Indianized Southeast Asia to suggest that this hypothesis is correct. As for the origins of the word *barong*, Goris's idea that it derives ultimately from Sanskrit via the word for the Malay wood bear (*beruang*) has been given attention by Bandem (e.g., 1975/76, 26). Also worth noting is the similarity between *barong* and *bérang* (Balinese *wirang*), meaning "furious." This last idea is, of course, totally in keeping with the iconography of the beast.

Bibliography

The bibliography consists of all works cited in the text plus several additional relevant sources. It cannot, given the scope of the topic, be comprehensive; nor does it provide bibliographical information for primary sources except
when a translation has been quoted at length or when additional information
from, for example, an introduction or an appendix is cited. In these cases,
sources are listed by translator and credits thus given in the text.

Ahrens, R.
1954   Beitrag zur Entwicklung des Physiognomie- und Mimikerkennens. *Zeit-
        schrift für experimentelle und angewandte Psychologie* 2: 412–54, 599–633.
Akurgal, Ekrem
1962   *The art of the Hittites.* Trans. Constance McNab. London.
1968   *The art of Greece: Its origins in the Mediterranean and Near East.* Trans.
        Wayne Dynes. New York.
1969   *Ancient civilisations and ruins of Turkey, from prehistoric times until the end of
        the Roman Empire.* Trans. John Whybrow and Mollie Emre. Istanbul.
Altheim, Franz
1929   Persona. *Archiv für Religionswissenschaft* 27: 35–52.
1930   *Griechische Götter im alten Rom.* Giessen.
1931   *Terra Mater: Untersuchungen zur altitalischen Religionsgeschichte.* Giessen.
1938   *A history of Roman religion.* Trans. Harold Mattingly. London.
1950   *Der Ursprung der Etrusker.* Baden-Baden.
Anderson, M.D.
1963   *Drama and imagery in English medieval churches.* Cambridge.
Argyle, Michael
1972   Non-verbal communication in human social interaction. In *Non-verbal
        communication,* ed. R. A. Hinde, 243–69. Cambridge.
1975   *Bodily communication.* London.
Aristotle
1908–62   *The works of Aristotle.* 12 vols. Translated under the editorship of
           W. D. Ross. Oxford.

Arsana, I Gusti Ketut Gde.
1977   Kayu pule dalam konteks kepercayaan orang Bali sebuah studi kasus di desa Kesiman. *Lembaran Pengkajian Budaya* 2: 7–27.
Artamonov, M. I.
1969   *The splendor of Scythian art: Treasures from Scythian tombs*. Trans. V. R. Kupriyanova. New York.
Avalon, Arthur [Sir John Woodroffe]
1958   *The serpent power*. 6th ed. Madras.
1959   *Śakti and Śākta: Essays and addresses*. 5th ed. Madras.
Bachofen, J. J.
1967   *Myth, religion, and mother right: Selected writings of J. J. Bachofen*. Trans. Ralph Manheim. London.
Bagus, I Gusti Ngurah
1980   *Aksara dalam kebudayaan Bali: suata kajian antropologi*. Denpasar, Bali.
[Bandem, I. Madé]
1975/76   *Barong di Bali*. Denpasar, Bali.
Bandem, I. Madé, and Fredrik Eugene deBoer
1981   *Kaja and kelod: Balinese dance in transition*. Kuala Lumpur.
Banerjea, J. N.
1956   *The development of Hindu iconography*. 2d ed. Calcutta.
Banerjee, N. R.
1965   *The Iron Age in India*. Delhi.
Banerjee, P.
1973   *Early Indian religions*. Delhi.
Barb, A. A.
1953   Diva matrix. *Journal of the Warburg and Courtauld Institutes* 16: 193–238.
Barnes, R. H.
1974   *Kédang: A study of the collective thought of an eastern Indonesian people*. Oxford.
1977   *Mata in Austronesia*. Oceania 47: 300–319.
Barnett, R. D.
1944   The epic of Kumarbi and the Theogony of Hesiod. *The Journal of Hellenic Studies* 64: 100–101.
1956a   Ancient Oriental influences on archaic Greece. In *The Aegean and the Near East: Studies presented to Hetty Goldman*, ed. Saul S. Weinberg, 212–38. New York.
1956b   The treasure of Ziwiye. *Iraq* 18: 111–16.
1960   Some contacts between Greek and Oriental religions. In *Éléments orientaux dans la religion grecque ancienne. Colloque de Strasbourg, 22–24 mai 1958*, 143–53. Paris.
1975   A Mithraic figure from Beirut. In *Mithraic studies: Proceedings of the First International Congress of Mithraic Studies*, ed. John R. Hinnells, 2: 466–69. Manchester.
Barthoux, Jules
1930–33   *Les fouilles de Haḍḍa: Figures et figurines*. Paris.
Basford, K. H.
1977   Quest for the green man. In *Symbols of power*, ed. H. R. Ellis Davidson, 101–20. Cambridge.

Bastian, Adolf
1883 Masken und Maskereien. *Zeitschrift für Völkerpsychologie und Sprachwissenschaft* 14: 335–58.
Bateson, Gregory, and Margaret Mead
1942 *Balinese character: A photographic analysis.* New York.
Beare, W.
1939 Masks on the Roman stage. *The Classical Quarterly* 33: 139–46.
1968 *The Roman stage: A short history of Latin drama in the time of the republic.* 3d rev. ed. London.
Beazley, J. D.
1951 *The development of Attic black-figure.* Berkeley and Los Angeles.
1956 *Attic black-figure vase-painters.* Oxford.
1963 *Attic red-figure vase-painters.* 2d ed. 3 vols. Oxford.
Bédouin, Jean-Louis
1961 *Les masques.* Paris.
Begley, W. E.
1973 *Viṣṇu's flaming wheel: The iconography of the Sudarśana-cakra.* New York.
Belo, Jane
[1949] 1966 *Bali: Rangda and Barong.* Seattle.
1960 *Trance in Bali.* New York.
ed. 1970 *Traditional Balinese culture.* New York.
Benthall, Jonathan, and Ted Polhemus, eds.
1975 *The body as a medium of expression.* London.
Benveniste, Émile
1929 *The Persian religion according to the chief Greek texts.* Paris.
1945 La doctrine médicale des indo-européens. *Revue de l'histoire des religions* 130: 5–12.
1962 *Hittite et indo-européen: études comparatives.* Paris.
Berlin, Isaiah
1968 Verification. In *The theory of meaning,* ed. G. H. R. Parkinson, 15–34. London.
Bernet Kempers, A. J.
1959 *Ancient Indonesian art.* Cambridge, Mass.
Bernheimer, Richard
1952 *Wild men in the Middle Ages: A study in art, sentiment, and demonology.* Cambridge, Mass.
Besig, Hans
1937 Gorgo und Gorgoneion in der archaischen griechischen Kunst. Diss., Friedrich-Wilhelms-Universität zu Berlin. Berlin.
Bhattacharji, Sukumari
1970 *The Indian theogony: A comparative study of Indian mythology from the Vedas to the Purāṇas.* Cambridge.
Bieber, M.
1930 Maske. In *Paulys Real-Encyclopädie der classischen Altertumswissenschaft,* ed. Wilhelm Kroll, 14 (2): 2070–2120. Stuttgart.
1961 *The history of the Greek and Roman theater.* Princeton.
Bivar, A. D. H.
1975 Mithra and Mesopotamia. In *Mithraic studies: Proceedings of the First In-*

ternational Congress of Mithraic Studies, ed. John R. Hinnells, 2: 275–89.
Manchester.

Black, Max
1972   How do pictures represent? In Art, perception, and reality, ed. Maurice
       Mandelbaum, 95–130. Baltimore.

Bleibtreu, John N.
1968   Parable of the beast. New York.

Blest, A. D.
1957   The function of eyespot patterns in the Lepidoptera. Behaviour 11:
       209–56.

Bloch, Raymond
1959a Étrurie, Rome et monde romain. In Le masque, 79–86. Paris.
1959b Etruscan art. London.
1960   The origins of Rome. New York.

Bloomfield, Maurice, trans.
1897   Hymns of the Atharva Veda. Oxford.

Boardman, John
1963   Artemis Orthia and chronology. The Annual of the British School at Athens
       58: 1–7.
1967   Pre-classical: From Crete to archaic Greece. Harmondsworth, Middlesex.
1968   Archaic Greek gems: Schools and artists in the sixth and early fifth centuries
       B.C. London.
1974   Athenian black figure vases. New York.
1976   A curious eye cup. Archäologischer Anzeiger 3: 281–90.
1978   Greek art. London.

Bodrogi, Tibor
1972   Art of Indonesia. Trans. Eva Rácz. New York.

Boeles, J. J.
1947   The migration of the magic syllable Oṃ. In India Antiqua: A volume of
       Oriental studies presented by his friends and pupils to Jean Philippe Vogel,
       40–56. Leiden.

Bohr, Niels
1958   Atomic physics and human knowledge. New York.

Bolwig, Niels
1963–64 Facial expression in primates with remarks on a parallel develop-
         ment in certain carnivores. Behaviour 22: 167–92.

Boon, James A.
1977   The anthropological romance of Bali 1597–1972: Dynamic perspectives in mar-
       riage and caste, politics and religion. Cambridge.

Bor, N. L.
1953   Manual of Indian forest botany. Bombay.

Bosanquet, R. C.
1905–6 Laconia. II.—Excavations at Sparta, 1906. §7.—The cult of Orthia as
        illustrated by the finds. The Annual of the British School at Athens 12:
        331–43.

Bosch, F. D. K.
1960   The golden germ: An introduction to Indian symbolism. The Hague.

Boyce, Mary
1975   A history of Zoroastrianism. Vol. 1, The early period. Leiden.

1979   Zoroastrians: Their religious beliefs and practices. London.
Brendel, Otto J.
1978   Etruscan art. Harmondsworth, Middlesex.
Brilliant, Richard
1971   On portraits. Zeitschrift für Ästhetik und allgemeine Kunstwissenschaft 16: 11–26.
Brough, John
1971   Soma and Amanita muscaria. Bulletin of the School of Oriental and African Studies 34: 331–62.
Brown, W. Llewellyn
1960   The Etruscan lion. Oxford.
Browne, Sir Thomas
1968   Selected writings. Ed. Sir Geoffrey Keynes. Chicago.
Buck, C. D.
1949   A dictionary of selected synonyms in the principal Indo-European languages: A contribution to the history of ideas. Chicago.
Buitenen, J. A. B. van, ed. and trans.
1973   The Mahābhārata: I. The book of the beginning. Chicago.
Buraud, Georges
1948   Les masques: essai. Paris.
Burkert, Walter
1966   Greek tragedy and sacrificial ritual. Greek, Roman and Byzantine Studies 7: 87–121.
1972   Homo necans: Interpretation altgriechischer Opferriten und Mythen. Berlin.
1977   Griechische Religion der archaischen und klassischen Epoche. Stuttgart.
1979   Structure and history in Greek mythology and ritual. Berkeley and Los Angeles.
Burn, A. R.
1970   Greece and Rome 750 B.C./A.D. 565. Glenview, Illinois.
Burney, Charles
1977   The ancient Near East. Ithaca.
Burrow, T.
1973   The Sanskrit language. Rev. ed. London.
Butcher, S. H.
1951   Aristotle's theory of poetry and fine art. 4th ed. London.
Campbell, Joseph
1975   The hero with a thousand faces. London.
Campbell, Leroy A.
1968   Mithraic iconography and ideology. Leiden.
Canetti, Elias
1978   Crowds and power. Trans. Carol Stewart. New York.
Cannon, Walter B.
1942   "Voodoo" death. American Anthropologist 44: 169–81.
[1932] 1963   The wisdom of the body. New York.
Cassirer, Ernst
1953–57   The philosophy of symbolic forms. Trans. R. Manheim. 3 vols. New Haven.
Chambers, E. K.
1903   The mediaeval stage. 2 vols. London.

Chanda, Ramaprasad
1927   *The beginnings of art in eastern India with special reference to sculptures in the Indian Museum, Calcutta.* Calcutta.
Chandra, Moti
1940   Cosmetics and coiffure in ancient India. *Journal of the Indian Society of Oriental Art* 8: 62–145.
Charbonneaux, J.
1932   Les masques rituels ou scéniques et l'expression dans la sculpture grecque. In *Mélanges Gustave Glotz* 1: 203–13.
Chastel, André
1959   Les temps modernes: masque, mascarade, mascaron. In *Le masque,* 87–93. Paris.
Chopra, R. N., et al.
1958   *Chopra's indigenous drugs of India.* 2d rev. ed. Calcutta.
Cintas, Pierre
1946   *Amulettes puniques.* Publication de l'Institut des Hautes Études de Tunis, I. Tunis.
Clark, Stephen R. L.
1975   *Aristotle's man: Speculations upon Aristotelian anthropology.* Oxford.
Coedès, G.
1968   *The indianized states of Southeast Asia.* Trans. Susan B. Cowing. Honolulu.
Cohn, Norman Rufus Colin
1975   *Europe's inner demons: An enquiry inspired by the great witch-hunt.* London.
Colodny, Robert G., ed.
1965   *Beyond the edge of certainty: Essays in contemporary science and philosophy.* Englewood Cliffs, New Jersey.
1972   *Paradigms and paradoxes: The philosophical challenge of the quantum domain.* Pittsburgh.
Conteneau, Georges
1938   *La médecine en Assyrie et en Babylonie.* Paris.
1940   *La divination chez les Assyriens et les Babyloniens.* Paris.
1947   *La magie chez les Assyriens et les Babyloniens.* Paris.
1954   *Everyday life in Babylon and Assyria.* Trans. K. R. Maxwell-Hyslop and A. R. Maxwell-Hyslop. London.
Cook, Arthur Bernard
1914–40   *Zeus: A study in ancient religion.* 3 vols. Cambridge.
Coomaraswamy, Ananda K.
1908   *Mediaeval Sinhalese art.* Broad Campden.
1918   *The dance of Śiva: Fourteen Indian essays.* New York.
1927a   *History of Indian and Indonesian art.* London.
1927b   The origin of the Buddha image. *The Art Bulletin* 9: 286–329.
[1928–31] 1971   *Yakṣas.* New Delhi.
1930   Origin of the lotus- (so-called bell-) capital. *The Indian Historical Quarterly* 6: 373–75.
1933   *A new approach to the Vedas: An essay in translation and exegesis.* London.
Coral-Rémusat, Gilberte de
1936   Animaux fantastiques de l'Indochine, de l'Insulinde et de la Chine. *Bulletin de l'École française d'Extrême-Orient* 36: 427–35.

Cornford, F. M.
1912 *From religion to philosophy: A study in the origins of western speculation.* London.
[1934] 1968 *The origin of Attic comedy.* Gloucester, Mass.
Coss, R. G.
1970 The perceptual aspects of eye-spot patterns and their relevance to gaze behaviour. In *Behaviour studies in psychiatry,* ed. S. J. Hutt and Corinne Hutt, 121–47. Oxford.
Covarrubias, Miguel
1937 *Island of Bali.* London.
Crooke, William
1925 *Religion and folklore of northern India.* New Delhi.
Croon, J. H.
1955 The mask of the underworld daemon—Some remarks on the Perseus-Gorgon story. *The Journal of Hellenic Studies* 75: 9–16.
Culican, William
1965 *The Medes and Persians.* London.
Cumont, Franz
[1903] 1956 *The mysteries of Mithra.* Trans. T. J. McCormack. New York.
Dalton, Edward Tuite
[1872] 1960 *Descriptive ethnology of Bengal.* Calcutta.
Daniélou, Alain
1964 *Hindu polytheism.* London.
Darian, Steven G.
1978 *The Ganges in myth and history.* Honolulu.
Darwin, Charles
[1872] 1955 *The expression of the emotions in man and animals.* New York.
de Bary, T., S. Hays, R. Weiler, and A. Yarrow, comps.
1966 *Sources of Indian tradition.* New York.
Deonna, W.
1915 Essai sur la génèse des monstres dans l'art. *Revue des études grecques* 28: 288–349.
1965 *Le symbolisme de l'oeil.* Paris.
Detienne, Marcel
1963 *De la pensée religieuse à la pensée philosophique: la notion de daïmôn dans le pythagorisme ancien.* Paris.
1972 *Les jardins d'Adonis.* Paris.
1979 *Dionysos slain.* Trans. Mireille Muellner and Leonard Muellner. Baltimore.
Detienne, Marcel, and Jean-Pierre Vernant
1978 *Cunning intelligence in Greek culture and society.* Trans. Janet Lloyd. Hassocks, Sussex.
de Zoete, Beryl
1957 *Dance and magic drama in Ceylon.* London.
de Zoete, Beryl, and Walter Spies
[1938] 1973 *Dance and drama in Bali.* London.
Dickins, G.
1929 Terracotta masks. In *The sanctuary of Artemis Orthia at Sparta,* ed. R. M. Dawkins, 163–86. London.

Diderot, Denis
1883   *The paradox of acting*. Trans. Walter Herries Pollock. London.
Dodds, E. R.
1951   *The Greeks and the irrational*. Berkeley and Los Angeles.
ed. 1960   *Euripides, "Bacchae."* Rev. ed. Oxford.
Dover, K. J.
1972   *Aristophanic comedy*. London.
Duchesne-Guillemin, Jacques
1966   *Symbols and values in Zoroastrianism: Their survival and renewal*. New York.
1973   *Religion of ancient Iran*. Bombay.
Dugas, Charles
1956   Observations sur la légende de Persée. *Revue des études grecques* 69: 1-15.
Dumézil, Georges
1924   *Le festin d'immortalité: étude de mythologie comparée indo-européenne*. Paris.
1929   *Le problème des centaures: étude de mythologie comparée indo-européenne*. Paris.
1934   *Ouranós-Váruna: étude de mythologie comparée indo-européenne*. Paris.
1947   *Tarpeia: essais de philologie comparative indo-européenne*. Paris.
1948   *Mitra-Varuna: essai sur deux représentations indo-européennes de la souveraineté*. Paris.
1949   *L'héritage indo-européen à Rome*. Paris.
1954   *Rituels indo-européens à Rome*. Paris.
1968–73   *Mythe et épopée*. 3 vols. Paris.
1970a   *Archaic Roman religion*. Trans. Philip Krapp. 2 vols. Chicago.
1970b   *The destiny of the warrior*. Trans. Alf Hiltebeitel. Chicago.
1977   *Les dieux souverains des indo-européens*. Paris.
Dumont, Louis
1970   *Homo hierarchicus: The caste system and its implications*. Trans. Mark Sainsbury. London.
Dumont, P. E.
1927   *L'aśvamedha: description du sacrifice solennel du cheval dans le culte védique d'après les textes du Yajurveda blanc*. Paris.
1948   The horse-sacrifice in the Taittirīya-Brāhmaṇa: The eighth and ninth Prapāṭhakas of the third Kāṇḍa of the Taittirīya-Brāhmaṇa with translation. *Proceedings of the American Philosophical Society* 92: 447–503.
Dunbabin, T. J.
1957   *The Greeks and their eastern neighbors: Studies in the relations between Greece and the countries of the Near East in the eighth and seventh centuries B.C.* London.
Durkheim, Émile, and Marcel Mauss
1963   *Primitive classification*. Ed. and trans. Rodney Needham. London.
Dussaud, René
1950   Le dieu mithriaque léontocéphale. *Syria* 27: 253–60.
Edelstein, Emma J., and Ludwig Edelstein
1945   *Asclepius: A collection and interpretation of the testimonies*. 2 vols. Baltimore.
Eibl-Eibesfeldt, I.
1972   Similarities and differences between cultures in expressive movements. In *Non-verbal communication*, ed. R. A. Hinde, 297–314. Cambridge.

Eisler, Robert
1909   Kuba-Kybele. *Philologus* 68: 118–51, 161–209.
Ekman, Paul
1977   Biological and cultural contributions to body and facial movement. In *The anthropology of the body*, ed. John Blacking, 39–84. London.
1979   About brows: Emotional and conversational signals. In *Human ethology: Claims and limits of a new discipline*, ed. M. von Cranach, K. Foppa, W. Lepenies, and D. Ploog, 169–202. Cambridge.
Ekman, Paul, and Wallace V. Friesen
1975   *Unmasking the face: A guide to recognizing emotions from facial clues.* Englewood Cliffs, New Jersey.
Ekman, Paul, Wallace V. Friesen, and Phoebe Ellsworth
1972   *Emotion in the human face: Guidelines for research and an integration of findings.* New York.
Ekman, Paul, and Harriet Oster
1979   Facial expressions of emotion. *Annual Review of Psychology* 30: 527–54.
Eliade, Mircea
1954   *The myth of the eternal return: or, Cosmos and history.* Trans. Willard R. Trask. Princeton.
1962   Marginalien zum Wesen der Maske. *Antaios* 4: 396–404.
1964   *Shamanism: Archaic techniques of ecstasy.* Trans. Willard R. Trask. Rev. ed. New York.
Else, Gerald F.
1963   *Aristotle's Poetics: The argument.* Cambridge, Mass.
1965   *The origin and early form of Greek tragedy.* Cambridge, Mass.
Elwin, Verrier
1951   *The tribal art of middle India: A personal record.* Bombay.
Endo, Shusaku
1969   *Silence.* Trans. William Johnston. Rutland, Vt.
Evans, Arthur J.
1901   Mycenaean tree and pillar cult and its Mediterranean relations. *The Journal of Hellenic Studies* 21: 99–204.
Evans, Elizabeth C.
1969   Physiognomics in the ancient world. *Transactions of the American Philosophical Society*, n.s., 59, part 5: 1–101.
Ewer, R. F.
1973   *The carnivores.* Ithaca.
Fabri, C. L.
1932   Mesopotamian and early Indian art: Comparisons. In *Études d'orientalisme. Publiées par le Musée Guimet à la mémoire de Raymonde Linossier*, 1: 203–53. Paris.
Fales, De Coursey, Jr.
1966   An unpublished fragment of Kleitias. *Greek, Roman and Byzantine Studies* 7: 23–25.
Fantz, Robert L.
1967   Visual perception and experience in early infancy: A look at the hidden side of behavior development. In *Early behaviour: Comparative and developmental approaches*, ed. Harold W. Stevenson, Eckhard H. Hess, and Harriet L. Rheingold, 181–224. New York.

Farnell, L. R.
1896–1909   *The cults of the Greek states.* 5 vols. Oxford.
1921   *Greek hero cults and ideas of immortality.* Oxford.
Festugière, André-Jean
1944–54   *La révélation d'Hermès Trismégiste.* 4 vols. Paris.
1951   Les cinq sceaux de l'aiôn alexandrin. *Revue d'égyptologie* 8: 63–70.
1954   *Personal religion among the Greeks.* Berkeley and Los Angeles.
Feyerabend, Paul K.
1965   Problems of empiricism. In *Beyond the edge of certainty: Essays in contemporary science and philosophy,* ed. Robert G. Colodny, 145–260. Englewood Cliffs, New Jersey.
1970   Problems of empiricism, part II. In *The nature and function of scientific theories,* ed. Robert G. Colodny, 275–353. Pittsburgh.
1975   *Against method: Outline of an anarchistic theory of knowledge.* London.
Filliozat, Jean
1943   *Magie et médecine.* Paris.
1964   *The classical doctrine of Indian medicine: Its origins and its Greek parallels.* Trans. Dev Raj Chanana. Delhi.
Finegan, Jack
1952   *The archaeology of world religions: The background of Primitivism, Zoroastrianism, Hinduism, Jainism, Buddhism, Confucianism, Taoism, Shinto, Islam, and Sikhism.* Princeton.
Finley, M. I.
1970   *Early Greece: The Bronze and Archaic Ages.* London.
1975   *The ancient Greeks.* Harmondsworth, Middlesex.
Fitzhardinge, L. F.
1980   *The Spartans.* London.
Flattery, David Stophlet
1978   Haoma. Ph.D. diss., University of California, Berkeley.
Floren, Josef
1977   *Studien zur Typologie des Gorgoneion.* Münster Westfalen.
Fontein, Jan, R. Soekmono, and Satyawati Suleiman
1971   *Ancient Indonesian art of the central and eastern Javanese periods.* New York.
Fontenrose, Joseph
1959   *Python: A study of Delphic myth and its origins.* Berkeley and Los Angeles.
1978   *The Delphic oracle.* Berkeley and Los Angeles.
Francis, E. D.
1980   Greeks and Persians: The art of hazard and triumph. In *Ancient Persia: The art of an empire,* ed. Denise Schmandt-Besserat, 53–86. Malibu, California.
Freyer-Schauenberg, Brigitte
1970   Gorgoneion-Skyphoi. *Jahrbuch des Deutschen archäologischen Instituts* 85: 1–27.
Frothingham, A. L.
1911   Medusa, Apollo, and the Great Mother. *American Journal of Archaeology,* 2d series, 15: 349–77.
Furtwängler, Adolf, and Karl Reichhold
1900–1932   *Griechische Vasenmalerei.* 3 vols. Munich.

Gajjar, Irene N.
1971   *Ancient Indian art and the West: A study of parallels, continuity, and symbolism from proto-historic to early Buddhist times.* Bombay.
Garton, Charles
1972   *Personal aspects of the Roman theatre.* Toronto.
Gaster, T. H.
1950   *Thespis: Ritual, myth and drama in the ancient Near East.* New York.
Geertz, Clifford
1960   *The religion of Java.* Glencoe, Illinois.
1973   *The interpretation of cultures.* New York.
Gennep, Arnold van
1909   *Les rites de passage.* Paris.
Gershevitch, Ilya
1974   An Iranianist's view of the Soma controversy. In *Mémorial Jean de Menasce*, ed. Ph. Gignoux and A. Tafazzoli, 45–75. Louvain.
Ghiron-Bistagne, Paulette
1976   *Recherches sur les acteurs dans la Grèce antique.* Paris.
Ghirshman, Roman
1954   *Iran: From the earliest times to the Islamic conquest.* Harmondsworth, Middlesex.
1964   *Persia: From the origins to Alexander the Great.* Trans. Stuart Gilbert and James Emmons. London.
Giglioli, Giulio Quirino
1935   *L'arte etrusca.* Milan.
Gimbutas, Marija
1974   *The gods and goddesses of old Europe, 7000 to 3500 B.C.: Myths, legends and cult images.* Berkeley and Los Angeles.
Glotz, Samuël, ed.
1975   *Le masque dans la tradition européenne.* [Catalogue of an exhibition 13 June–6 October. Musée international du carnaval et du masque, Binche, Belgium.]
Goldman, Bernard
1961   The Asiatic ancestry of the Greek Gorgon. *Berytus* 14: 1–23.
Gombrich, E. H.
1972   The mask and the face: The perception of physiognomic likeness in life and in art. In *Art, perception and reality*, ed. Maurice Mandelbaum, 1–46. Baltimore.
Gombrich, Richard F.
1971   *Precept and practice: Traditional Buddhism in the rural highlands of Ceylon.* Oxford.
Gonda, J.
1954   *Aspects of early Viṣṇuism.* Utrecht.
1966   *Ancient Indian kingship from the religious point of view.* Leiden.
1969   *Eye and gaze in the Veda.* Amsterdam.
1970   *Viṣṇuism and Śivaism: A comparison.* London.
1972   *The Vedic god Mitra.* Leiden.
1973   *Sanskrit in Indonesia.* 2d ed. New Delhi.
1980   *Vedic ritual: The non-solemn rites.* Leiden.

Goodman, L. S., and A. Gilman
1955 *The pharmacological basis of therapeutics.* 2d ed. New York.
Goonatilleka, M. H.
1978 *Masks and mask systems of Sri Lanka.* Colombo.
Gopinatha Rao, T. A.
1914–16 *Elements of Hindu iconography.* 2 vols. Madras.
Goris, R.
1960 The temple system. In *Bali: Studies in life, thought, and ritual,* ed. W. F. Wertheim et al., 103–11. Brussels.
Graves, Robert
1957 *The Greek myths.* New York.
Grünwedel, Albert
1901 *Buddhist art in India.* Trans. Agnes C. Gibson; rev. James Burgess. London.
Gryaznov, Mikhail
1969 *The ancient civilization of southern Siberia.* Trans. James Hogarth. New York.
Guiart, Jean
1966 *Mythologie du masque en Nouvelle-Calédonie.* Paris.
Gupta, Shakti M.
1971 *Plant myths and traditions in India.* Leiden.
Haigh, A. E.
1898 *The Attic theatre: A description of the stage and theatre of the Athenians, and of the dramatic performances at Athens.* 2d rev. ed. Oxford.
Hallade, Madeleine
1968 *The Gandhara style and the evolution of Buddhist art.* Trans. Diana Imber. London.
Halliday, W. R.
1913 *Greek divination: A study of its methods and principles.* New York.
Harden, Donald
1962 *The Phoenicians.* New York.
Hardison, O. B., Jr.
1965 *Christian rite and Christian drama in the Middle Ages: Essays in the origin and early history of modern drama.* Baltimore.
Harnack, Adolph von
1958 *History of dogma.* Trans. Neil Buchanan et al. 7 vols. New York.
Harner, Michael J., ed.
1973 *Hallucinogens and shamanism.* London.
Harrison, Jane Ellen
[1885] 1902 *Introductory studies in Greek art.* 5th ed. London.
1905 *The religion of ancient Greece.* London.
1908 *Prolegomena to the study of Greek religion.* 2d ed. Cambridge.
[1912] 1977 *Themis: A study of the social origins of Greek religion.* London.
Hartland, E. Sidney
1894–96 *The legend of Perseus.* London.
Hastings, James, ed.
1912 *Encyclopedia of religion and ethics.* 13 vols. New York.

Henry, Paul, S.J.
1960   *Saint Augustine on personality.* New York.
Hepding, Hugo
1903   *Attis, seine Mythen und sein Kult.* Giessen.
Herm, Gerhard
1975   *The Phoenicians: The purple empire of the ancient world.* Trans. Caroline Hillier. New York.
Hermann, Werner
1963   Gorgo und Acheloos. *Mitteilungen des Deutschen archäologischen Instituts, Römische Abteilung* 1: 1–3.
Herzfeld, E. E.
1947   Early historical contacts between the Old-Iranian Empire and India. In *India antiqua: A volume of Oriental studies presented by his friends and pupils to Jean Philippe Vogel*, 180–84. Leiden.
1968   *The Persian Empire: Studies in geography and ethnography of the ancient Near East.* Ed. Gerold Walser. Wiesbaden.
Hess, Eckhard H.
1965   Attitude and pupil size. *Scientific American* 212 (April): 46–54.
Hillman, James
1975   *Re-visioning psychology.* New York.
Hinde, R. A., ed.
1972   *Non-verbal communication.* Cambridge.
Hinnells, John R.
1973   *Persian mythology.* London.
ed. 1975   *Mithraic studies: Proceedings of the First International Congress of Mithraic Studies.* 2 vols. Manchester.
Hocart, A. M.
1928   Many-armed gods. *Acta Orientalia* 7: 91–96.
[1950] 1969   *The life-giving myth and other essays.* Ed. Rodney Needham. London.
Hochberg, Julian
1972   The representation of things and people. In *Art, perception, and reality*, ed. Maurice Mandelbaum, 47–94. Baltimore.
Hoffmann, Herbert
1972   *Early Cretan armorers.* Cambridge, Mass.
Hood, Sinclair
1978   *The arts in prehistoric Greece.* Harmondsworth, Middlesex.
Hooker, Clifford A.
1972   The nature of quantum mechanical reality: Einstein versus Bohr. In *Paradigms and paradoxes: The philosophical challenge of the quantum domain*, ed. Robert G. Colodny, 67–302. Pittsburgh.
Hooykaas, C.
1973   *Religion in Bali.* Leiden.
1974   *Cosmogony and creation in Balinese tradition.* The Hague.
1980   *Drawings of Balinese sorcery.* Leiden.
Hooykaas, R.
1959   *Natural law and Divine miracle: A historical-critical study of the principle of uniformity in geology, biology and theology.* Leiden.

Hopkins, Clark
1934   Assyrian elements in the Perseus-Gorgon story. *American Journal of Archaeology* 38: 341–58.
1961   The sunny side of the Greek Gorgon. *Berytus* 14: 25–35.
Horton, Robin
1964   Ritual man in Africa. *Africa* 34: 85–104.
1967   African traditional thought and western science. *Africa* 37: 50–71, 155–87.
Howe, Thalia Phillies
1952   An interpretation of the Perseus-Gorgon myth in Greek literature and monuments through the classical period. Ph.D. diss., Columbia University.
1954   The origin and function of the Gorgon-head. *American Journal of Archaeology* 58: 209–21.
Hume, David
[1739–40] 1888   *A treatise of human nature.* Ed. L. A. Selby-Bigge. 3 vols. Oxford.
Huxley, Francis
1959   The miraculous Virgin of Guadalupe. *International Journal of Parapsychology* 1: 19–31.
1966   The ritual of voodoo and the symbolism of the body. *Philosophical Transactions of the Royal Society of London*, series B, 251: 423–27.
1976   *The way of the sacred.* New York.
1977   The body and the play within the play. In *The anthropology of the body*, ed. John Blacking, 29–38. London.
1979   *The dragon: Nature of spirit, spirit of nature.* London.
Huxley, T. H.
1874   *Lay sermons, addresses and reviews.* New York.
Irwin, John
1976   "Aśokan" pillars: A reassessment of the evidence—IV: Symbolism. *The Burlington Magazine* 118 (November): 734–53.
Iyer, K. Bharatha
1977   *Animals in Indian sculpture.* Bombay.
1980   *Dance dramas of India and the East.* Bombay.
Jackson, D. A.
1976   *East Greek influence on Attic vases.* London.
James, E. O.
1957   *Prehistoric religion: A study in prehistoric archaeology.* London.
Jarvie, I. C.
1964   *The revolution in anthropology.* London.
Jastrow, Morris, Jr.
1915   *The civilization of Babylonia and Assyria: Its remains, language, history, religion, commerce, law, art, and literature.* Philadelphia.
[1911] 1971   *Aspects of religious belief and practice in Babylonia and Assyria.* New York.
Jeffery, L. H.
1976   *Archaic Greece: The city states, c. 700–500 B.C.* New York.
Jevons, Frank Byron
1902   *An introduction to the history of religion.* 2d rev. ed. London.

1913   *Comparative religion.* Cambridge.
1916a   *Masks and acting.* Cambridge.
1916b   Masks and the origin of the Greek drama. *Folk-lore* 27: 171–92.
Jones, John
1971   *On Aristotle and Greek tragedy.* London.
Jouveau-Dubreuil, G.
1937   *Iconography of southern India.* Trans. A. C. Martin. Paris.
Kahn, Charles H.
1966   Sensation and consciousness in Aristotle's psychology. *Archiv für Geschichte der Philosophie* 48: 43–81.
Kantor, Helene J.
1962   A bronze plaque with relief decoration from Tell Tainat. *Journal of Near Eastern Studies* 21: 93–117.
Karageorghis, Vassos
1971   Notes on some Cypriot priests wearing bull-masks. *Harvard Theological Review* 64: 261–70.
Karo, Georg
1934   *Führer durch Tiryns.* Athens.
1948   *Greek personality in archaic sculpture.* Cambridge.
Keith, Arthur Berriedale
1925   *The religion and philosophy of the Veda and Upanishads.* 2 vols. Cambridge, Mass.
Kerényi, C.
1948   Mensch und Maske. *Eranos-Jahrbuch* 16: 183–208.
1959   *Asklepios: Archetypal image of the physician's existence.* Trans. Ralph Manheim. London.
1976   *Dionysos: Archetypal image of the indestructible life.* Trans. Ralph Manheim. London.
Keuls, Eva
1974   *The water carriers in Hades: A study of catharsis through toil in classical antiquity.* Amsterdam.
Kirk, G. S.
1970   *Myth: Its meaning and functions in ancient and other cultures.* Cambridge.
1974   *The nature of Greek myths.* Harmondsworth, Middlesex.
Kirk, G.S., and J. E. Raven
1957   *The Presocratic philosophers.* Cambridge.
Kirkwood, G. M.
1958   *A study of Sophoclean drama.* New York.
Kramrisch, Stella
1981   *The presence of Śiva.* Princeton.
Kuhn, Thomas S.
1970   *The structure of scientific revolutions.* 2d ed., enl. Chicago.
Kunze, Emil
1963   Zum Giebel des Artemistempels in Korfu. *Mitteilungen des Deutschen archäologischen Instituts, Athenische Abteilung* 78: 74–89.
Laín Entralgo, Pedro
1970   *The therapy of the word in classical antiquity.* Ed. and trans. L. J. Rather and John M. Sharp. New Haven.

Lakatos, Imre
1978a   *Mathematics, science and epistemology.* Ed. John Worrall and Gregory Currie. Cambridge. [*Philosophical papers*, volume 2.]
1978b   *The methodology of scientific research programmes.* Ed. John Worrall and Gregory Currie. Cambridge. [*Philosophical papers*, volume 1.]
Laroche, Emmanuel
1960   Koubaba, déesse anatolienne, et le problème des origines de Cybèle. In *Éléments orientaux dans la religion grecque ancienne. Colloque de Strasbourg, 22–24 mai 1958,* 143–53. Paris.
Larson, Gerald James, ed.
1974   *Myth in Indo-European antiquity.* Berkeley and Los Angeles.
Lawson, J. C.
1910   *Modern Greek folklore and ancient Greek religion: A study in survivals.* Cambridge.
Leach, Edmund R.
1954   A Trobriand Medusa? *Man* 54: 103–5.
1961   Time and false noses. In *Rethinking anthropology,* 132–36. London.
1964   Anthropological aspects of language: Animal categories and verbal abuse. In *New directions in the study of language,* ed. Eric H. Lenneberg: 23–63. Cambridge, Mass.
ed. 1967   *The structural study of myth and totemism.* London.
Leenhardt, Maurice
1970   *La structure de la personne en Mélanésie.* Milan.
1979   *Do kamo: Person and myth in the Melanesian world.* Trans. Basia Miller Gulati. Chicago.
Lesky, Albin
1966   *A history of Greek literature.* Trans. James Willis and Cornelis de Heer. London.
[1964] 1978   *Greek tragedy.* Trans. H. A. Frankfort. London.
Lévi, Sylvain
1923   Pré-aryen et pré-dravidien dans l'Inde. *Journal asiatique* 203: 1–57.
1926   *L'Inde et le monde.* Paris.
Lévi-Strauss, Claude
1975   *La voie des masques.* 2 vols. Geneva.
1977   Les dessous d'un masque. *L'homme* 17: 5–27.
Lévy-Bruhl, Lucien
1935   *Primitives and the supernatural.* Trans. Lilian A. Clare. New York.
[1949] 1975   *The notebooks on primitive mentality.* Trans. Peter Rivière. Oxford. [Originally published as *Les carnets.* Paris.]
Lindner, Paul
1933   Das Geheimnis um Soma, das Getränk der alten Inder und Perser. *Forschungen und Fortschritte* 9, no. 5: 65–66.
Littleton, C. Scott
1970   The "kingship in heaven" theme. In *Myth and law among the Indo-Europeans: Studies in Indo-European comparative mythology,* ed. Jaan Puhvel, 83–121. Berkeley and Los Angeles.
1973   *The new comparative mythology: An anthropological assessment of the theories of Georges Dumézil.* Rev. ed. Berkeley and Los Angeles.

Lloyd, G. E. R.
1966   *Polarity and analogy: Two types of argumentation in early Greek thought.*
       Cambridge.
1979   *Magic, reason and experience: Studies in the origin and development of Greek
       science.* Cambridge.
Löhrer, P. Robert
1927   *Mienenspiel und Maske in der griechischen Tragödie.* Paderborn.
Lucas, Heinz
1973   *Java-Masken: Der Tanz auf einem Bein.* Kassel.
Macdonell, A. A.
1897   *Vedic mythology.* Strasbourg.
1921   Vedic religion. In *Encyclopaedia of religion and ethics,* ed. James Hastings,
       12: 601–18. Edinburgh.
1924   *A practical Sanskrit dictionary, with transliteration, accentuation, and ety-
       mological analysis throughout.* London.
Macdonell, A. A., and A. B. Keith
1912   *Vedic index of names and subjects.* London.
Mackay, Ernest
1937   *Further excavations at Mohenjo-Daro.* 2 vols. Delhi.
1948   *Early Indus civilizations.* 2d ed., rev. and enl. Dorothy Mackay. London.
MacLean, Paul D.
1949   Psychosomatic disease and the "visceral brain": Recent developments
       bearing on the Papez theory of emotion. *Psychosomatic Medicine* 11:
       338–53.
McPhee, Colin
1970   The Balinese *Wayang Kulit* and its music. In *Traditional Balinese culture,*
       ed. Jane Belo, 146–97. New York.
Malcolm, Norman
1958   *Ludwig Wittgenstein: A memoir.* London.
Mallowan, M. E. L.
1956   *Twenty-five years of Mesopotamian discovery (1932–1956).* London.
Mannhardt, Wilhelm
1875–77   *Wald- und Feldkulte.* 2 vols. Berlin.
Marchal, H.
1938   The head of the monster in Khmer and Far Eastern decoration. *Journal
       of the Indian Society of Oriental Art* 6: 97–105.
Marshall, Sir John, ed.
1931   *Mohenjo-Daro and the Indus civilization.* 3 vols. London.
Marshall, Sir John, and A. Foucher
1939   *The monuments of Sāñchī.* 3 vols. Calcutta.
Marshall, Mary Hatch
1950   Boethius' definition of *persona* and mediaeval understanding of the Ro-
       man theater. *Speculum* 25: 471–82.
Matt, Leonard von, et al.
1968   *Ancient Crete.* Trans. D. J. S. Thomson. London.
Mauss, Marcel
1935   Les techniques du corps. *Journal de psychologie normale et pathologique* 32:
       271–93. [Reprinted in Marcel Mauss, *Sociologie et anthropologie,* 4th ed.,
       364–86. Paris, 1968.]

1938   Une catégorie de l'esprit humain: la notion de personne, celle de "moi."
        Huxley Memorial Lecture. *Journal of the Royal Anthropological Institute* 68:
        263–81.

Mayr, Ernst
1976   Teleological and teleonomic: A new analysis. In *Evolution and the diver-
        sity of life: Selected essays,* 383–404. Cambridge, Mass.

Mehren, Günther
1969   Sinn und Gestalt der Maske. Über den Umgang mit Göttern und Dä-
        monen. *Antaios* 11: 136–53.

Mellaart, James
1967   *Çatal Hüyük: A neolithic town in Anatolia.* London.

Meuli, Karl
1935   Scythica. *Hermes* 70: 121–76.
1975   *Gesammelte Schriften.* Ed. Thomas Gelzer. 2 vols. Basel.

Meyer, Eduard
1914   *Reich und Kultur der Chetiter.* Berlin.

Minns, Ellis H.
1913   *Scythians and Greeks: A survey of ancient history and archaeology on the north
        coast of the Euxine from the Danube to the Caucasus.* New York.

Modi, J. J.
1937   *The religious ceremonies and customs of the Parsees.* 2d ed. Bombay.

Monier-Williams, Sir Monier
1891   *Brāhmanism and Hindūism: or, Religious thought and life in India, as based on
        the Veda and other sacred books of the Hindūs.* 4th ed. New York.
[1899] 1970   *A Sanskrit-English dictionary, Etymologically and philologically ar-
        ranged with special reference to cognate Indo-European languages.* Rev. and
        enl. ed. Oxford.

Moor, Edward
1810   *The Hindu pantheon.* London.

Murray, Gilbert
1935   *Five stages of Greek religion.* 2d ed. London.

Mylonas, George E.
1957   Ὁ πρωτοαττικὸς ἀμφορεὺς τῆς Ἐλευσῖνος. Βιβλιοθήκη τῆς ἐν Ἀθήναις
        Ἀρχαιολογικῆς ἑταιρείας. no. 39. Athens.

Nagy, Gregory
1974   Perkunas and Perunu. In *Gedenkschrift Hermann Güntert,* ed. M. Mayr-
        hofer et al., 113–31. Innsbruck.

Narain, A. K.
1962   *The Indo-Greek.* Oxford.

Needham, Rodney
1964   Blood, thunder, and mockery of animals. *Sociologus* 14: 136–49.
1967   Percussion and transition. *Man,* n.s., 2: 606–14.
1972   *Belief, language, and experience.* Chicago.
1975   Polythetic classification: Convergence and consequences. *Man,* n.s., 10:
        349–69.
1976   Skulls and causality. *Man,* n.s., 11: 71-88.
1978   *Primordial characters.* Charlottesville.
1979   *Symbolic classification.* Santa Monica, California.

1980   *Reconnaissances.* Toronto.
ed. 1973   *Right and left: Essays on dual symbolic classification.* Chicago.
Nilsson, M. P.
1925   *A history of Greek religion.* Trans. F. J. Fielden. Oxford.
1932   *The Mycenaean origin of Greek mythology.* Cambridge.
1940   *Greek popular religion.* New York.
[1927] 1950   *The Minoan-Mycenaean religion and its survival in Greek religion.* 2d rev. ed. Lund.
1972   *The Mycenaean origin of Greek mythology.* Rev. ed. Berkeley and Los Angeles.
Oates, Joan
1979   *Babylon.* London.
Obeyesekere, Gananath
1966   The Buddhist pantheon in Ceylon and its extensions. In Manning Nash et al., *Anthropological studies in Theravada Buddhism,* 1–26. New Haven.
O'Brien, Michael J.
1964   Orestes and the Gorgon: Euripides' *Electra. American Journal of Philology* 85: 13–39.
O'Flaherty, Wendy Doniger
1969   The symbolism of the third eye of Śiva in the Purāṇas. *Purāṇa* 11: 273–84.
1971   The submarine mare in the mythology of Śiva. *Journal of the Royal Asiatic Society* 1: 9–27.
1973   *Asceticism and eroticism in the mythology of Śiva.* London.
1975   *Hindu myths.* Harmondsworth, Middlesex.
1976   *The origins of evil in Hindu mythology.* Berkeley and Los Angeles.
1979   Sacred cows and profane mares in Indian mythology. *History of Religions* 19: 1–26.
1980a   Dionysus and Śiva: Parallel patterns in two pairs of myths. *History of Religions* 20: 81–111.
1980b   *Women, androgynes, and other mythical beasts.* Chicago.
Onians, Richard Broxton
1951   *The origins of European thought about the body, the mind, the soul, the world, time, and fate.* Cambridge.
Onions, C. T.
1966   *The Oxford dictionary of English etymology.* Oxford.
Oppenheim, A. Leo
1977   *Ancient Mesopotamia: Portrait of a dead civilization.* Rev. ed. Chicago.
Östör, Ákos
1980   *The play of the gods: Locality, ideology, structure, and time in the festivals of a Bengali town.* Chicago.
Pallotino, Massimo
1952   *Etruscan painting.* Trans. M. E. Stanley and Stuart Gilbert. Geneva.
1968   *Etruscologia.* Milan.
[1942] 1978   *The Etruscans.* Trans. J. Cremona. Harmondsworth, Middlesex.
Palmer, L. R.
1958   New religious texts from Pylos (1955). *Transactions of the Philological Society:* 1–35.

Panofsky, Erwin
1962 *Studies in iconology: Humanistic themes in the art of the Renaissance*. New York.

Papez, James W.
1937 A proposed mechanism of emotion. *Archives of Neurology and Psychiatry* 38: 725–44.

Parrot, André
1961 *Nineveh and Babylon*. Trans. Stuart Gilbert and James Emmons. London.
1969 De la Méditerranée à l'Iran: masques énigmatiques. *Ugaritica* 6: 409–18.

Partridge, Eric
1966 *Origins: A short etymological dictionary of modern English*. London.

Payne, Humfry
1931 *Necrocorinthia: A study of Corinthian art in the archaic period*. Oxford.

Persson, Axel W.
1942 *The religion of Greece in prehistoric times*. Berkeley and Los Angeles.

Pettazzoni, Raffaele
1922 Le origini della testa di Medusa. *Bollettino d'arte*, 2d series, 1: 491–510.
1946 The pagan origins of the three-headed representation of the Christian Trinity. *Journal of the Warburg and Courtauld Institutes* 9: 135–51.
1956 *The all-knowing God: Researches into early religion and culture*. Trans. H. J. Rose. London.

Picard, Gilbert
1964 *Carthage*. Trans. Miriam Kochan and Lionel Kochan. London.

Picard, Gilbert, and Colette Picard
1968 *The life and death of Carthage: A survey of Punic history and culture from its birth to the final tragedy*. Trans. Dominique Collon. London.

Pickard-Cambridge, Sir Arthur
1927 *Dithyramb, tragedy and comedy*. Oxford.
1953 *The dramatic festivals of Athens*. Oxford.
[1946] 1956 *The theatre of Dionysus in Athens*. Oxford.
1962 *Dithyramb, tragedy and comedy*. 2d ed. rev. T. B. L. Webster. Oxford.
1968 *The dramatic festivals of Athens*. 2d ed. rev. John Gould and D. M. Lewis. Oxford.

Piggott, Stuart
1950 *Prehistoric India to 1000 B.C.* Harmondsworth, Middlesex.

Pocock, R. I.
1914 On the facial vibrissae of mammalia. *Proceedings of the Zoological Society of London*: 889–912.

Pollitt, J. J.
1972 *Art and experience in classical Greece*. Cambridge.

Popper, Karl R.
1959 *The logic of scientific discovery*. Trans. J. Freed and L. Freed. London.
1972 *Objective knowledge: An evolutionary approach*. Oxford.

Pott, P. H.
[1946] 1966 *Yoga and yantra: Their interrelation and significance for Indian archaeology*. Trans. Rodney Needham. The Hague.

Prestige, G. L.
[1936] 1964 *God in patristic thought*. London.

Pritchard, James B.
1958 *Archaeology and the Old Testament*. Princeton.
1969 *The ancient Near East in pictures relating to the Old Testament*. 2d ed. with supplement. Princeton.

Puhvel, Jaan
1970 Aspects of equine functionality. In *Myth and law among the Indo-Europeans: Studies in Indo-European comparative mythology*, ed. Jaan Puhvel, 159–72. Berkeley and Los Angeles.

Quasten, Johannes
1950–60 *Patrology*. 3 vols. Utrecht.

Quincy, J. H.
1963 The beacon-sites in the *Agamemnon*. *The Journal of Hellenic Studies* 83: 118–32.

Quine, W. V.
1960 *Word and object*. Cambridge, Mass.
1976 *The ways of paradox and other essays*. Rev. ed. Cambridge, Mass.

Ramsey, Ian T., ed.
1965 *Biology and personality: Frontier problems in science, philosophy and religion*. Oxford.

Ramseyer, Urs
1977 *The art and culture of Bali*. Oxford.

Rands, Robert L.
1957 Comparative notes on the hand-eye and related motifs. *American Antiquity* 22: 247–57.

Rawlinson, H. G.
1926 *Intercourse between India and the western world from the earliest times to the fall of Rome*. 2d ed. Cambridge.

Riccioni, Giuliana
1960 Origine e sviluppo del gorgoneion e del mito della gorgone-medusa nell'arte greca. *Rivista dell'Instituto nazionale d'archeologia e storia dell'arte*, n.s., 9: 127 206.

Rice, Tamara Talbot
1965 *Ancient arts of central Asia*. London.

Richards, Robert J.
1979 Influence of sensationalist tradition on early theories of evolution and behavior. *Journal of the History of Ideas* 40: 85–105.

Richter, Gisela M. A.
1949 *Archaic Greek art against its historical background*. New York.
1980 *A handbook of Greek art: A survey of the visual arts of ancient Greece*. New York.

Ridgeway, William
1901–31 *The early age of Greece*. 2 vols. Cambridge.
1910 *The origin of tragedy with special reference to the Greek tragedians*. Cambridge.
1915 *The dramas and dramatic dances of non-European races in special reference to the origin of Greek tragedy with an appendix on the origin of Greek comedy*. Cambridge.

Ringgren, Helmer
1973 *Religions of the ancient Near East*. Trans. John Sturdy. London.

Robbins, Robin, ed.
[1672] 1981   Sir Thomas Browne's "Pseudoxia Epidemica." 2 vols. Oxford.
Robertson, Martin
1975   A history of Greek art. 2 vols. Cambridge.
Rodenwaldt, Gerhart, ed.
1939   Korkyra: archaische Bauten und Bildwerke. 2 vols. Berlin.
Rose, H. J.
1928   A handbook of Greek mythology. London.
1935   Numen inest: "Animism" in Greek and Roman religion. Harvard Theological Review 28: 237–57.
Rossiter, A. P.
1950   English drama from early times to the Elizabethans: Its background, origins and development. London.
Rougier, Louis
1917   Le sens des termes Οὐσία, Ὑπόστασις et Πρόσωπον dans les controverses trinitaires post-nicéenes. Revue de l'histoire des religions 74: 48–63, 133–89.
Rouse, W. H. D.
1902   Greek votive offerings: An essay in the history of Greek religion. Cambridge.
Rowland, Benjamin
1977   The art and architecture of India: Buddhist, Hindu, Jain. Rev. J. C. Harle. Harmondsworth, Middlesex.
Russell, R. V.
[1916] 1969   The tribes and castes of the central provinces of India. 4 vols. Oosterhout, The Netherlands.
Ryle, Gilbert
[1949] 1963   The concept of mind. Harmondsworth, Middlesex.
Sakar, Himansu Bhusan
1970   Some contributions of India to the ancient civilization of Indonesia and Malaysia. Calcutta.
Sankalia, H. D.
1978   Pre-historic art in India. New Delhi.
Sauvé, James L.
1970   The divine victim: Aspects of human sacrifice in Viking Scandinavia and Vedic India. In Myth and law among the Indo-Europeans: Studies in Indo-European comparative mythology, ed. Jaan Puhvel, 173–91. Berkeley and Los Angeles.
Schaller, George B.
1972   The Serengeti lion: A study of predator-prey relations. Chicago.
Schauenburg, Konrad
1960   Perseus in der Kunst des Altertums. Bonn.
Schefold, Karl
1966   Myth and legend in early Greek art. Trans. Audrey Hicks. New York.
1967   The art of classical Greece. London.
Scheinberg, Susan
1979   The bee maidens of the Homeric Hymn to Hermes. Harvard Studies in Classical Philology 83: 1–28.

Schuster, Carl
1951   Joint-marks: A possible index of cultural contact between America, Oceania and the Far East. *Koninklijk instituut voor de tropen, Mededeling no. 94, Afdeling culturele en physische anthropologie no. 39* (Amsterdam): 3–52.
Sedlar, Jean W.
1980   *India and the Greek world: A study in the transmission of culture.* Totowa, New Jersey.
Seligmann, C. G., and Brenda Z. Seligmann
1911   *The Veddas.* Cambridge.
Shastri, Hari Prasad, trans.
1959   *The Ramayana of Valmiki.* Vol. 3. London.
Shende, N. J.
1952   *The religion and philosophy of the Atharvaveda.* Poona.
Shulman, David Dean
1980   *Tamil temple myths: Sacrifice and divine marriage in the South Indian Śaiva tradition.* Princeton.
Sifakis, G. M.
1967   *Studies in the history of Hellenistic drama.* London.
Simon, Erika
1975   Kratos und Bia. *Würzburger Jahrbücher*, n.s., 1: 177–86.
1976   *Die griechischen Vasen.* Munich.
Sinha, Binod Chandra
1979   *Tree worship in ancient India.* New Delhi.
Skeat, Walter W.
[1879–82] 1974   *An etymological dictionary of the English language.* Oxford.
Smith, Huston
1958   *The religions of man.* New York.
1976   *Forgotten truth: The primordial tradition.* New York.
Smith, Sidney
1924   The face of Humbaba. *Annals of Archaeology and Anthropology* 11: 107–14.
1926   The face of Humbaba. *Journal of the Royal Asiatic Society* 26: 440–42.
Soebadio, Haryati, ed. and trans.
1971   *Jñānasiddhânta.* The Hague.
Sperber, Dan
1975   *Rethinking symbolism.* Trans. Alice L. Morton. Cambridge.
Stein, Aurel
1931   On the Ephedra, the Hūm plant, and the Soma. *Bulletin of the London School of Oriental Studies* 6: 501–14.
Stern, E.
1976   Phoenician masks and pendants. *Palestine Exploration Quarterly* 108: 109–18.
Strong, T. B.
1901   The history of the theological term "Substance": Part I. *The Journal of Theological Studies* 2: 224–35.
1902   The history of the theological term "Substance": Part II. *The Journal of Theological Studies* 3: 22–40.

Sturtevant, Edgar H.
1947   *An introduction to linguistic science.* New Haven.
Stutterheim, Willem F.
1925   *Rāma-Legenden und Rāma-Reliefs in Indonesien.* 2 vols. Munich.
1929   The meaning of the kāla-makara ornament. *Indian Art and Letters,* n.s., 3: 27–52.
1935   *Indian influences in old-Balinese art.* London.
1956   *Studies in Indonesian archaeology.* The Hague.
Sykes, Sir Percy
1930   *A history of Persia.* 2 vols. London.
Taddei, Maurizio
1970   *India.* Trans. James Hogarth. London.
Tambiah, S. J.
1968   The magical power of words. *Man,* n.s., 3: 175–208.
1976   *World conqueror and world renouncer: A study of Buddhism and polity in Thailand against a historical background.* Cambridge.
Teilhet, Jehanne H.
1978   The tradition of the Nava Durga in Bhaktapur, Nepal. *Kailash* 6: 81–98.
Thieme, P.
1957   *Mitra and Aryaman.* New Haven.
Thomas, P.
1960   *Hindu religion, customs and manners.* 4th rev. ed. Bombay.
Thureau-Dangin, F.
1925   Humbaba. *Revue d'assyriologie et d'archéologie orientale* 22: 23–26.
Trendelenburg, Adolf
1910   A contribution to the history of the word "person": A posthumous treatise. Trans. Carl H. Haessler. *The Monist* 20: 336–63.
Tucci, Guiseppe
1963   Oriental notes. *East and West* 14: 133–82.
Vallois, R.
1922   L'"agalma" des Dionysies de Délos. *Bulletin de correspondance hellénique* 46: 94–112.
van Kooij, K. R., ed.
1972   *Worship of the goddess according to the Kālikāpurāna.* Leiden.
van Lohuizen-de Leeuw, J. E.
1949   *The "Scythian" period: An approach to the history, art, epigraphy and palaeography of North India from the 1st century B.C. to the 3rd century A.D.* Leiden.
Vermaseren, Maarten J.
1956–60   *Corpus inscriptionum et monumentorum religionis Mithriacae.* 2 vols. The Hague.
1963   *Mithras, the secret god.* London.
1966   *The legend of Attis in Greek and Roman art.* Leiden.
1977   *Cybele and Attis: The myth and the cult.* Trans. A. M. H. Lemmers. London.
Vernant, Jean-Pierre
1969   *Mythe et pensée chez les Grecs: études de psychologie historique.* 2d ed. Paris.
Vickers, Brian
1979   *Towards Greek tragedy: Drama, myth, society.* London.

Vygotsky, Lev Semenovich
[1934] 1964   *Thought and language*. Ed. and trans. Eugenia Hanfmann and Gertrude Vakar. Cambridge, Mass.
Walcot, P.
1966   *Hesiod and the Near East*. Cardiff.
Waley, Arthur
1938   *The analects of Confucius*. London.
Ward, William Hayes
1910   *The seal cylinders of western Asia*. Washington, D.C.
Wasson, R. Gordon
1968   *Soma: Divine mushroom of immortality*. The Hague.
Watson, William
1971   *Cultural frontiers in ancient East Asia*. Edinburgh.
Webster, T. B. L.
1939a   *Greek art and literature 530–400 B.C.* Oxford.
1939b   Greek theories of art and literature down to 400 B.C. *The Classical Quarterly* 33: 166–79.
1949   The masks of Greek comedy. *Bulletin of the John Rylands Library* 32: 97–133.
1951   Masks on Gnathia vases. *The Journal of Hellenic Studies* 71: 222–32.
1952   Notes on Pollux' list of tragic masks. In *Festschrift Andreas Rumpf*, ed. Tobias Dohrn, 141–50. Krefeld.
1954   Personification as a mode of Greek thought. *Journal of the Warburg and Courtauld Institutes* 17: 10–21.
1956   Scenic notes. *Wiener Studien: Zeitschrift für klassische Philologie* 69 [*Festschrift Albin Lesky*]: 107–15.
1957   Some psychological terms in Greek tragedy. *The Journal of Hellenic Studies* 77: 149–54.
1958   Some thoughts on the pre-history of Greek drama. *Bulletin of the Institute of Classical Studies of the University of London* 5: 43–48.
1959   *Greek art and literature 700–530 B.C.: The beginnings of modern civilization*. Dunedin.
1964   *From Mycenae to Homer*. 2d ed. London.
1965   The poet and the mask. In *Classical drama and its influence: Essays presented to H. D. F. Kitto*, ed. M. J. Anderson, 5–13. London.
1970a   *The Greek chorus*. London.
1970b   *Greek theatre production*. 2d ed. London.
Weill, Raymond
1940   *Phoenicia and western Asia to the Macedonian conquest*. Trans. Ernest F. Row. London.
West, M. L.
1971   *Early Greek philosophy and the Orient*. Oxford.
Whitehead, Alfred North
1926   *Religion in the making*. New York.
1927   *Symbolism: Its meaning and effect*. Cambridge.
1929   *The function of reason*. Princeton.
Whorf, Benjamin Lee
1956   *Language, thought, and reality*. Ed. John B. Carroll. Cambridge, Mass.

Wilamowitz-Moellendorff, Ulrich von
1959   *Der Glaube der Hellenen*. 3d ed. Darmstadt.
Will, E.
1947   La décollation de Méduse. *Revue archéologique* 6: 60–76.
Willis, J. C.
1966   *A dictionary of the flowering plants and ferns*. 7th ed., rev. H. K. Airy Shaw. Cambridge.
Wirz, Paul
1928   *Der Totenkult auf Bali*. Stuttgart.
1954   *Exorcism and the art of healing in Ceylon*. Leiden.
Wittgenstein, Ludwig
1971   Remarks on Frazer's *Golden Bough*. *The Human World* 3 (May): 18–41.
Woods, James Haughton
1927   *The yoga-system of Patañjali: or, The ancient Hindu doctrine of concentration of mind*. Cambridge, Mass.
Woodward, Jocelyn M.
1937   *Perseus: A study in Greek art and legend*. Cambridge.
Wundt, Wilhelm Max
1908   *Völkerpsychologie. Eine Untersuchung der Entwicklungsgesetze von Sprache, Mythus und Sitte*. 2d ed. Vol. 3, *Mythus und Religion*. Leipzig.
Yalman, Nur
1964   The structure of Sinhalese healing rituals. *Journal of Asian Studies* 23: 115–50.
Young, Karl
1933   *The drama of the medieval church*. 2 vols. Oxford.
Zaehner, R. C.
1955   *Zurvan: A Zoroastrian dilemma*. Oxford.
[1956] 1975   *The teachings of the magi: A compendium of Zoroastrian beliefs*. London.
1961   *The dawn and twilight of Zoroastrianism*. New York.
1962   *Hinduism*. Oxford.
1966   *Hindu scriptures*. London.
Zafiropulo, Jean
1966   *Mead and wine: A history of the Bronze Age in Greece*. Trans. Peter Green. London.
Zimmer, Heinrich
1955   *The art of Indian Asia: Its mythology and transformations*. Ed. Joseph Campbell. 2 vols. New York.
1971   *The king and the corpse: Tales of the soul's conquest of evil*. Ed. Joseph Campbell. Princeton.
[1946] 1972   *Myths and symbols in Indian art and civilization*. Ed. Joseph Campbell. Princeton.
[1951] 1974   *Philosophies of India*. Ed. Joseph Campbell. Princeton.

Index

Designer: Sandy Drooker
Compositor: G & S Typesetters, Inc.
Text: 10/13 Palatino
Display: Palatino
Printer: Braun-Brumfield, Inc.
Binder: Braun-Brumfield, Inc.